The Outreach and Membership Idea Book

URJ Department of Outreach and Synagogue Community

The Brody-Hassenfeld Outreach Library
URJ Press
New York, New York

"*. . . And you shall walk in God's way.*" (Deuteronomy 28:9)

"*As an explanation of this mitzvah,
our Sages taught the following:
Just as God is called 'Gracious,'
you shall be gracious;
Just as God is called 'Merciful,'
you shall be merciful;
Just as God is called 'Holy,'
you shall be holy . . .*"
Maimonides, *Mishneh Torah, Hilchot De'ot,* 1:6

This book is dedicated to all those in our Reform
congregations who do the work of *keruv*
with graciousness and love,
who bring near those who may be far
and, in doing so, build holy communities.
We are grateful to all who labor to
make each of our synagogues a place of
support, openness, knowledge, and spiritual sustenance.

The work of your hands is represented by the creative
and lovingly crafted program offerings,
generously shared in this volume.

Copyright © 2005 by URJ Press
Manufactured in the United States of America
This book is printed on acid-free paper.
10 9 8 7 6 5 4 3 2 1

2005 URJ-CCAR Commission on Outreach and Synagogue Community

Jane Rips, *Chairperson*
Rabbi Stephen J. Einstein, *Co-Chairperson*
Austin Beutel, *Vice-Chairperson*
Rabbi Howard Jaffe, *Vice-Chairperson*
Judy Berg, *Vice-Chairperson*
Kathryn Kahn, *Director and Executive Editor*
Naomi Gewirtz, *Assistant Director and Editor*
Rabbi Michelle Pearlman, *Program Coordinator*
Emily Wulwick, *Administrative Assistant*

Dr. Marcia Abraham*
Wendy Adamson
Rabbi Aryeh Azriel
Rabbi Larry Bach
Jim Ball
Rabbi Morris Barzilai
Rabbi Marc Berkson
Lisa Bock
Rabbi Eric Bram
Rabbi John Bush
Rabbi Harry Danziger**
Georgia DeYoung
Rabbi Michael Dolgin
Joyce Engel
Justin Felder
Catherine Fischer
Rabbi Steven Foster*
Cantor Jennifer L. Frost
Susanne Geshekter
Shirley Gordon
Barbara Gould
Dr. Dorothy Greenbaum

Rabbi Fred Greene
Marcia Grossfeld
Mike Grunebaum
Janice Grutfreund
Rabbi Debbie Hachen
Frieda Haidt
Rabbi Stephen Hart
Robert Heller**
Diana Herman
Rabbi Robert Jacobs
Rabbi Jerry Kane
Renee Karp
Dawn Kepler
Phoebe Kerness
Rabbi Elliott Kleinman**
Rabbi Judy Lewis
Carole Lieberman
Rabbi Alan Litwak
Rabbi Jill Maderer
Rabbi Rosalin Mandelberg
Rabbi Paul Menitoff**
Melvin Merians*

Rabbi Jonathan Miller
Rabbi Jeremy Morrison
David Oney
Myra Ostroff*
Rabbi Jack Paskoff
Dr. Robert Mike Rankin
Joyce Raskin
Jon Rosen
Marcia Rosenblum
Rabbi Mark Schiftan
Rhea Schindler*
Rabbi Jonathan Singer
Debra Siroka
Sy Sokatch
Rabbi Cy Stanway
David Toomim
Dr. Nancy Wiener
Audrey Wilson
Diane Winer
Rabbi Eric Yoffie**
Jane Young

* Lifetime Member
** Ex-Officio

Outreach and Synagogue Community Regional Staff
Dr. Paula Brody, *Northeast Council*
Arlene Chernow, *Pacific Northwest and Pacific Southwest Council*
Ruth Goldberger, *Mid Atlantic and Pennsylvania Council*
Karen Kushner, *Pacific Central West Council*
Julie Webb, *Great Lakes and Northeast Lakes Council*

Special thanks to the professional staff and Outreach chairs and committees of the congregations who received Belin Outreach Awards and whose work appears here:

BELIN OUTREACH AWARDS

Anshe Chesed–Fairmount Temple—Beachwood, OH
Beth Tikvah Congregation—Hoffman Estates, IL
Congregation Beth Israel—San Diego, CA
Congregation B'nai Israel—Bridgeport, CT
Congregation Emeth—Gilroy, CA
Stephen S. Wise Temple—Los Angeles, CA
Suburban Temple–Kol Ami—Beachwood, OH
Temple Beth Sholom of Orange County—Santa Ana, CA
Temple Chai—Phoenix, AZ
Temple Emanu-El—Cleveland, OH
Temple Isaiah—Lexington, MA
The Temple–Tifereth Israel—Beachwood, OH

§

BELIN OUTREACH AWARDS HONORABLE MENTIONS

Congregation Emanu-El—San Francisco, CA
Congregation Shaarai Zedek—Tampa, FL
Rodeph Sholom—New York, NY
Temple Emanu-El—Tucson, AZ
Temple Israel of Hollywood—Los Angeles, CA
Temple Jeremiah—Northfield, IL
Temple Sharey Tefilo-Israel—South Orange, NJ
University Synagogue—Los Angeles, CA
Washington Hebrew Congregation—Washington, DC

Contents

Foreword — vii

Chapter 1: Lifelong Community: Finding, Engaging, and Retaining Your Members — 1
First-Year Voluntary Dues
New Member Workshops
Chavurah Program and Guide
Achim Men's Group
Faces of Reform Judaism
Membership Retention Phase—Transition Mentoring

Chapter 2: Honoring Our Interfaith Families and Inviting Conversion — 107
Sharing Shabbat: A Program for Jewish Children and Their Non-Jewish Grandparents
Walking the Interfaith Family Through the Jewish Year
Everything You Wanted to Know about Judaism
The Many Voices of Conversion

Chapter 3: Bridging the Membership Gap: Reaching 20s/30s — 165
Young Congregation
20s/30s: A Total Approach
Love Conquers All: The Gift of Dual-Faith Relationships
Young Leadership Initative

Chapter 4: Outreach Programming All Year for All — 217
Taste II: Jewish in America
Entrée to Judaism

Temple Chai Outreach Brochures
Opening Doors to Shabbat

Chapter 5: From Generation to Generation   **279**
Synaplex at B'nai Israel
The Challah Wagon
Babies and Bagels Club

Foreword

The Outreach and Membership Idea Book reflects, in its new title, the evolution of our commission. Three years ago the Commission on Outreach and the Commission on Synagogue Affiliation merged into one. This new, single entity was named the Commission on Outreach and Synagogue Community and embodies the idea that all outreach is inreach—that all the programming our congregations do for the non-Jewish strangers among us can also be valuable for *all* our membership, Jewish or not. The idea of *keruv*, of bringing near those who are far, is an ancient mitzvah that we must continue to practice in our synagogues every day.

And so, as the title suggests, the programming in this book has chapters on both traditional outreach to interfaith couples and those contemplating conversion, *and* chapters on membership recruitment, integration, and retention. The creative ideas collected herein reflect the priorities of our Reform congregations across North America. These programs meet the needs of increasingly diverse constituencies and include a commitment to attracting people in their 20s/30s to our communities. We should point out that two of the chapters reflect Rabbi Eric Yoffie's Biennial Initiatives: **Honoring Our Interfaith Families and Inviting Conversion** contains programs that honor parents who are not Jewish yet are raising children with strong Jewish identities, and programs that invite and support conversion. **Lifelong Community: Finding, Engaging, and Retaining Your Members** offers a programming focus on lifelong membership through engagement in synagogue life.

We invite you to replicate these creative offerings in your own congregations, tailoring and modifying them to suit the needs of your membership. We extend our thanks to every one of those congregations that submitted their programs and to those congregations whose award-winning programs are contained herein, that generously shared their ideas and materials with us and with all of our Reform synagogues.

Yasher koach to every one of our congregations that engages in the sacred work of outreach and membership every day, to the benefit of our Jewish community. On your behalf we particularly thank the commission members of our Belin selection committee, Rabbi John Bush, Renee Karp, and Debra Siroka, ably led by Assistant Director Naomi

Gewirtz, who dedicated many hours to the reading of over fifty entries and the difficult process of selecting the winning programs.

The mitzvah of *keruv* is embedded in our tradition and has brought many blessings to our congregations and our movement. As we read in Pesikta D'Rav Kahana, "And thou shalt rejoice in thy feast, thou, and thy son and thy daughter, and thy maidservant and thy manservant, and the Levite and the stranger, and the fatherless and the widow. . . . All, those in My household and those in your household, will share in the joy of the Temple in Jerusalem. As it is written: 'Even them will I bring to My holy mountain and make them joyful in My house of prayer'" (Piska 10:10, Isaiah 56:7).

Jane Rips Rabbi Stephen J. Einstein
Chair Co-chair
URJ-CCAR Commission on Outreach and Synagogue Community

Chapter One

Lifelong Community: Finding, Engaging, and Retaining Your Members

How do congregations ensure that prospective members know they are welcome? Can congregations create meaningful relationships among members so that they feel engaged, valued, and needed? Retaining members for a lifetime involves creative programming that touches people throughout their lives, in ways that are meaningful enough to maintain their membership. The programs contained in this chapter model successful outreach and inreach efforts focusing on the three primary areas of membership: recruitment, integration, and retention.

First-Year Voluntary Dues is a joint advertising and membership program that invites individuals to experience temple membership by offering first-year voluntary dues to one of four participating congregations. Cost is often a barrier to membership and this program lowers that barrier, inviting prospective members to get to know the congregation and make a financial commitment that is comfortable for them.

Once an individual and/or family makes a commitment of membership to your congregation, you will need to provide programs that begin to integrate them into the congregation. **New Member Workshops** are one successful model of programming that provide an opportunity for new members to meet with clergy, to study Torah with fellow congregants, to learn about congregational culture, and to begin to understand the core values of the congregation. Most importantly, these workshops begin relationships, which are a critical component of the membership process.

Whether small or large, every congregation can strive to create opportunities for people with shared interests or those who are at a similar stage of life to meet through synagogue-related programming. The **Chavurah Program and Guide** offers an in-depth explanation of the process for beginning and maintaining *chavurot* programs that can enhance your members' experience in your congregation. These groups have been found to be effective in both integrating and retaining members by offering connections with groups for young families, empty-nesters, and single parents.

Are you wondering how to involve the men in your congregation? How can they feel more connected to the congregation and to each other? The **Achim Men's Group** is an ongoing gathering for men in the congregation to come together to worship, study, get to know one another better, and discuss issues that are of particular importance to men. This model program will offer the men in your congregation an opportunity to strengthen their relationship with Judaism together and to get involved in the life of the temple.

Is your congregation the face of Reform Judaism? There are many ways to create an environment that recognizes and honors the diversity within your congregation and **Faces of Reform Judaism** is one program for you to replicate. This Shabbat program uses the Outreach and Synagogue Community poster, "The Face of Reform Judaism," to highlight the diversity within the Reform Movement and in your synagogue. This kind of program offers an opportunity to engage your current members while sending a message of welcome to the greater community.

Every congregation has struggled with the issue of retaining its members. **Membership Retention Phase** is a program that attends to the needs of members who might be considering the option of resigning from the congregation. Through conversations with either the rabbi or a lay leader, this program helps members to recognize that their primary purpose for being a part of the congregation can change, and helps the congregants to evaluate additional opportunities they have for engagement with the congregation, other members, and Jewish traditions.

First-Year Voluntary Dues

Congregations:	Anshe Chesed–Fairmount Temple
	Suburban Temple–Kol Ami
	The Temple–Tifereth Israel
	Temple Emanu-El
Address:	Suburban Cleveland, Ohio
Phone Number:	(216) 991-0700 (Suburban Temple–Kol Ami)
Contact's Name and E-mail:	Loree Resnick, lresnik@suburbantemple.org
Number of Member Units:	4,425 units in four congregations
URJ Region:	Northeast Lakes Council
Rabbis:	Howard Ruben, Eric Bram, Richard Block, Steven Denker
Program Directors:	Shea Waldron, Loree Resnick, Jeremy Handler, Renee Higer

Brief Description: This is a program inviting the unaffiliated Jewish population of Cleveland, Ohio, to experience temple membership by offering a first-year voluntary dues program. This is the first effort of a consortium of Reform congregations to come together to address the issue of affiliation.

Program Goal: To open the doors of synagogue life to the unaffiliated Jewish population of Cleveland.

Target Population: Unaffiliated Jews of all genders and age groups living in Greater Cleveland.

Staffing Required: Temple administrators and membership and communications directors where they exist. Otherwise this program could be done by a strong membership chairperson and committee.

Total Cost of Program: See page 4. There was, however, a loss of income in this first year due to the voluntary memberships.

Source of Funding: Individual congregations funded their own portion of this program, either out of operating funds or through special contributions from members.

Fee for Attendees: Each new congregant individually determined what he/she would pay, ranging from zero to full dues level.

Evaluation of Program: As we now are venturing into our second year of this project, we will be able to assess it at the end of fiscal 2005-2006. Certainly, it was very well received by the participants, who indicated they felt warmly welcomed by this program. The executive directors and the boards of the four congregations are monitoring the program and will continue to do so during the next fiscal year.

Follow-up: Each congregation is now working with these new members to determine what their status will be for 2005-2006. Of course, welcoming them in special ways has been a part of the program of each of the four congregations, including special Shabbat celebrations, welcome baskets, High Holy Day baskets, and other individualized projects. While the congregations have worked together in the establishment and promotion of the project, each will handle the follow-up in its own way, according to the *minhag* (customs) of that congregation.

VOLUNTARY DUES PROGRAM
Joint Consortium

	Cost	Date
Ad in *Cleveland Jewish News*	$750.00	2-Apr-04
Ad in *Cleveland Jewish News*	free due to error	9-Apr-04
Front page article in *CJN*	no cost	16-Apr-04
Ad in *Solon/Chagrin Valley Times*	$581.00	27-May-04
Article in *East Side Sun*	no cost	1-Jul-04
Postcard mailing to 8,700 unaffiliated homes	$2,087.00	14-Jul-04
Article in *Solon/Chagrin Valley Times*	no cost	22-Jul-04
Total Cost	$3,418.00	
Cost per congregation	$854.50	

These were the costs, dates, and marketing efforts of the consortium for this campaign.

Reform temples try to gain unaffiliated via voluntary dues

by Douglas J. Guth, staff reporter
Cleveland Jewish News
April 16, 2004

A misconception among Jews is that synagogues care more about money from yearly dues than a member's participation, remarks Edward Weintraub, president of Anshe Chesed Fairmount Temple.

Correcting this misconception is the basis for a new membership program sponsored by Fairmount and three other East Side Reform temples.

The four—Fairmount Temple, Suburban Temple–Kol Ami, Temple Emanu El and The Temple–Tifereth Israel—are now offering first-year voluntary dues to encourage unaffiliated Jews to find a spiritual home. The joint effort kicked off at the beginning of April with two advertisements in the CJN.

"People say how expensive it is to be Jewish," says Renee Higer, Temple Emanu El executive director. "We just want to get them involved."

Participants can pay as much or as little as they want during their first year, says Jeremy Handler, executive director of The Temple–Tifereth Israel. New members could even pay nothing for their initial year, but this does not entitle them to a free membership over the lifetime of their commitment.

"Disassociating dues" payment from the first year of membership takes some of the pressure off the commitment, Handler notes. By year two, congregants can then "determine what value they place on that membership."

The Temple's standard yearly fee is $1,495, with a variety of payment packages available based on age and family composition. After the first year of the voluntary dues program, explains Handler, "the expectation is that (members) fall into the various payment categories that apply to them."

The Temple, with a current membership of 1,500 households, also offers a "dues reduction package" for those unable to pay the recommended fee. Officials from each synagogue involved with the voluntary dues program stress that this option has always been available.

This community effort among local Reform congregations "is meant to open doors and remove barriers," says Rabbi Howard Ruben, spiritual leader of Fairmount Temple. "It encourages those who are not yet affiliated to find the synagogue that fits them best."

Locally, throughout all denominations, synagogue memberships range between $200 (for a bare-bones shul) and $2,000 plus a mandatory building fund contribution and school fees for a full-service synagogue. Synagogues give reduced rates to young adults, newlyweds, and singles. Younger members, who often get a financial break as an incentive to join, are expected to pay full fare when they come of age, but most synagogues will offer financial assistance with demonstrated need.

The voluntary dues program is not based on financial need, "but on the family's or individual's determination of what they wish to pay," says Loree Resnik, executive director of Suburban Temple–Kol Ami.

The four participating synagogues have been planning the program since last fall. Membership-based institutions, particularly in the Midwest, are facing challenges when it comes to attracting new members, The Temple's Handler admits.

Cleveland's Jewish community, with an estimated population of about 80,000, has become stagnant, as "more (Jews) are going out than coming in." Handler estimates that half of Cleveland's Jewish community is unaffiliated.

Statistics back him up: A 1996 Jewish Population Study of Greater Cleveland revealed that about 52% of 33,700 Cleveland area Jewish households were dues-paying members of a synagogue. These numbers are currently being updated by the Jewish Community Federation of Cleveland in conjunction with Cleveland State University's Levin College of Urban Affairs.

Meanwhile, Fairmount Temple and its neighbor synagogues will continue to reach out to the unaffiliated community. Two families, for example, have already expressed interest in Suburban Temple's voluntary dues program.

Officials encourage other congregations to pick up the program. "This is just a starting point," says Fairmount Temple's Ruben. "If others want to join the effort, that would be wonderful."

(with reports by Susan Rzepka)

Belonging to a Temple Community... *Priceless!*

As a community effort among local Reform congregations, we are working together to offer **first-year voluntary dues** to encourage synagogue affiliation. It is our hope that this incentive will allow those who have not affiliated with a Cleveland synagogue during the past year to consider this a perfect time to see how being part of a temple family can enrich your lives, both personally and spiritually.

Sponsored by:

Anshe Chesed Fairmount Temple
23737 Fairmount Boulevard
Beachwood, Ohio 44122
216-464-1330
www.fairmounttemple.org

Suburban Temple - Kol Ami
22401 Chagrin Boulevard
Beachwood, Ohio 44122
216-991-0700
www.suburbantemple.org/welcome

Temple Emanu El
2200 South Green Road
University Heights, Ohio 44121
216-381-6600
www.teecleve.org

The Temple - Tifereth Israel
26000 Shaker Boulevard
Beachwood, Ohio 44122
216-831-3233
www.ttti.org

Make This Your Time To Belong!

Don't Pass-over This Opportunity!

As a community effort among local Reform congregations, we are working together to offer **first-year voluntary dues** to encourage synagogue affiliation. It is our hope that this incentive will allow those who have not affiliated with a Cleveland synagogue during the past year to consider this a perfect time to see how being part of a temple family can enrich your lives, both personally and spiritually.

Sponsored by:

Anshe Chesed Fairmount Temple
23737 Fairmount Boulevard
Beachwood, Ohio 44122
216-464-1330
www.fairmounttemple.org

Suburban Temple - Kol Ami
22401 Chagrin Boulevard
Beachwood, Ohio 44122
216-991-0700
www.suburbantemple.org/welcome

Temple Emanu El
2200 South Green Road
University Heights, Ohio 44121
216-381-6600
www.teecleve.org

The Temple - Tifereth Israel
26000 Shaker Boulevard
Beachwood, Ohio 44122
216-831-3233
www.ttti.org

Make This Your Time To Belong!

Voluntary dues again at four Reform shuls

by Douglas J. Guth, Senior Staff Reporter
Cleveland Jewish News
July 15, 2005

Four local Reform synagogues will continue to offer first-year voluntary dues to attract unaffiliated Cleveland Jews.

The program, a joint effort of Anshe Chesed Fairmount Temple, Suburban Temple–Kol Ami, Temple Emanu El, and The Temple–Tifereth Israel, debuted in April 2004 with two advertisements in the CJN.

Synagogue officials report varying degrees of success with the voluntary dues program, which allows participants to pay as much or as little as they want during their first year of membership. After the first year of the program, "the expectation is that (members) fall into the various payment categories that apply to them," explains Jeremy Handler, executive director of The Temple–Tifereth Israel.

The community effort among local Reform congregations "is meant to open doors and remove barriers," Rabbi Howard Ruben, spiritual leader of Fairmount Temple, told the CJN last year. "It encourages those who are not yet affiliated to find the synagogue that fits them best."

"We've gotten people who said they never thought they could belong to a synagogue," says Renee Higer, executive director of Temple Emanu El. "People say how expensive it is to be Jewish. We just want to get them involved."

The program has not had a major impact on membership at Suburban Temple–Kol Ami, but "we're not looking at this as just a one-year initiative," asserts executive director Loree Resnik.

The synagogue director believes voluntary dues will continue to attract the unaffiliated. Suburban Temple welcomed a 90-year-old member into the congregation this year. "When cost is eliminated as a barrier, it begins a (membership) conversation in a different way," she says.

The Temple has enjoyed a "significant increase" in membership over the past year, Handler notes. This increase, he adds, can be at least partially attributed to the voluntary dues initiative. (The Temple does not interview new members about their reasons for joining the synagogue.)

Much sought-after young congregants accounted for a large part of this increase, Handler notes. Of the 84 new congregants who signed up for the program, 24 of them were singles or couples under age 45.

Locally, throughout all denominations, synagogue memberships range between $200 and $2,000 annually, plus a mandatory building fund contribution and school fees for a full-service synagogue.

Synagogues often give reduced rates to young adults, newlyweds, and singles. Younger members, who often get a financial break as an incentive to join, are expected to pay full fare when they come of age. Most synagogues also will offer financial assistance with demonstrated need.

Officials from each synagogue involved with the voluntary dues program stress that a "dues reduction package" has always been available for those who qualify.

Fairmount Temple says it measures success in outreach rather than numbers. The voluntary dues program has attracted new members from Painesville, Aurora, and Chagrin Falls, remarks executive director Shea Waldron.

These communities are well outside the inner-ring suburbs (Beachwood, University Heights, Shaker Heights) from where the synagogue draws most of its congregants. "Our goal was to get people who would not normally consider affiliating with a synagogue," Waldron explains. "We're thrilled that our outreach has been successful."

That success has not gone unnoticed. The synagogue consortium will be given the [Union for Reform Judaism (URJ)] Belin Outreach Award in November for its efforts in devising and executing Jewish interfaith and outreach programs.

Recruitment is the first hurdle to determine the program's success. The next is retention. The Temple will retain nearly all its members garnered through voluntary dues over the last year, notes executive director Handler.

Cleveland's Jewish community has an estimated population of about 80,000. A demographic profile compiled last year by The Jewish Community Federation of Cleveland and Cleveland State University's (CSU) Maxine Goodman Levin College of Urban Affairs estimates 61.5% of Jewish Clevelanders are members of a synagogue. The national average is 46%.

Handler wonders if year two of the voluntary dues program will bring more unaffiliated Jews into the fold. "Did we saturate the market in year one?" he asks. "That is the big question."

Synagogue officials report varying amounts of success with the voluntary dues program.

New Member Workshops

Congregation:	Congregation Rodeph Sholom
Address:	7 West 83rd Street New York, NY 10024
Phone Number:	(212) 362-8800
Contact's Name and E-mail:	Sandy Abramson, Sandyaaaa@aol.com
Number of Member Units:	1,800
URJ Region:	Greater New York Council of Reform Synagogues
Rabbis:	Robert Levine, Matthew Gewirtz, Lisa Grushkow
Membership Chair:	Sandy Abramson

Program Description: This is a yearly program run by the membership committee with the help of the clergy and temple staff. The purpose is to welcome and to acclimate the new members into temple life through socialization, study, and involvement. The course runs for two sessions and is facilitated by membership committee members. In the first session, a temple administrator or school head gives a brief history of the temple. This is followed by committee members and the clergy telling about their "Jewish journeys." Then the participants are divided into groups where they tell their stories to each other. A few people volunteer to comment on their group's stories, and then the clergy holds a discussion on a Torah portion appropriate for strangers to a community, such as *Lech L'cha*.

The second class includes a guided study of the *Sh'ma* with group reading and questions, with the clergy helping to answer any questions. Then, heads of volunteer committees present a very brief overview of their committees and encourage the new members to join. The class is concluded with another text-based study, if there is time, or a closing story illustrating the usefulness of new members to a synagogue and vice-versa. The participants gather together in a circle to sing a closing song and receive a blessing by the rabbis.

Target Population: Members new to the synagogue, and any other people who feel "new" to the temple: those people who have not been active or in attendance for awhile and want to reconnect.

Number of Participants: Usually thirty to forty.

Number and Length of Sessions: Two or three sessions lasting one and a half to two hours each.

Staffing Required: Maintenance staff to set up the room, office staff to copy letters of invitation and mail to new members, same staff to receive return postcards, administration staff to order refreshments.

Source of Funding: Line item in membership budget.

Fee for Attendees: Free.

Logistics: Name tags, prepared study materials, sign-up attendance lists, announcements of upcoming programs, lists of committee opportunities, refreshments (coffee, tea, water, cookies, crudités, etc.)

Instructions to Facilitators: We've had discussions on the best ways to have the participants meet others while learning about the temple and studying at the same time. The facilitators have always told their Jewish journeys, too. The facilitator has to line up the clergy, temple administrator, president of the temple, and heads of committees, while organizing the order of the class, which changes a bit each time.

Evaluation of Program: The program fills a real need for the new member who knows very few, if any, people in the temple. It is a very welcoming occasion for most of the participants since they want to get to know others who are looking to connect. We continue to explore new ways to make the classes interesting, but from the feedback, people like the guided study sessions, the chance to get to know other new members, and the opportunity to talk about their Jewish upbringing with like-minded people. Even though each person's background is different, patterns emerge about Orthodox upbringings, little knowledge of Torah or Hebrew, conversion, or ways in which Judaism has enriched their lives. We are also discussing ways in which we can make an interfaith family feel more welcome.

Follow-up: Attendees fill out evaluations, which help us improve the next class. We do not do formal follow-ups, but it is an issue that we often talk about. Years later when we meet people who attended the classes, we find that the people appreciated the classes very much and tell us that they made good friends in the classes. They report that the classes helped them to get comfortable in temple and that just meeting a couple of people got them "over the hump."

September 1, 2004
15 Elul 5764

Dear Amanda,

Welcome to Congregation Rodeph Sholom. If you are receiving this letter, that means you have probably joined our congregation sometime during this past year. We are absolutely delighted that you have joined our congregational community and only wish you many years of happiness, good health, and spiritual fulfillment, as you and/or your family becomes part of our community.

Our congregation has a rich and wonderful history. We pride ourselves on juxtaposing our religious tradition with modern ethics and values that continue to help us evolve as a community. As well, we are a community that cares deeply about Jewish literacy and continuously works steadfastly at offering the best education possible in our religious and day schools, as well as in our adult education program. What we care most about, however, is ensuring that our large community feels like a small home. We as clergy, board, and community attempt in every way we know possible to reach out with a warm embrace so that the good times are celebrated to their fullest and the painful ones are weathered with a caring community there to help.

To make your transition into your new community a smooth one, we invite you to attend our "New Member Workshops," a series of two classes co-taught by the synagogue clergy and educators from our day and religious schools. These classes will explore our "Jewish Journeys," the foundations of Judaism with accompanying text and readings, and the Jewish communal experience as expressed at Congregation Rodeph Sholom. The classes will serve not only to familiarize you with our wonderful community, but also to lend you the chance to personally get to know our clergy team and other new members going through this transition.

The dates of the classes are: Thursday, October 28, and Wednesday, November 3, from 7:15 P.M. to 8:45 P.M.

Please return the enclosed postcard reserving your place in the class. So that we may accommodate everyone, we request a reply at your earliest convenience. For more information, please call the synagogue at (212) 362-8800 ext. 8115.

We hope this note finds you productive and well. All of us here at Rodeph Sholom look forward to getting to know you as the months progress.

Warmly,

Robert N. Levine
Senior Rabbi

Sandy Abramson
Chair, Membership Committee

Facilitators' Overview of Curriculum

Orientation
Session 1, Oct. 28, 7:15-8:45
Theme: Jewish Journeys

Goal

To provide a venue for new members to find a "home" in Rodeph and not to feel lost in a large temple.

Confirmed Attendees
- Lead Clergy: Rabbi Matt Gewirtz
- Facilitator: Joanne Hoffer
- Registration: Claire Sauerhoff and Barbara Gerson
- Others: Nancy Solomon
                 Sandy Abramson
                 Cantor Frost

Materials/Logistics
- Sign in list
- Name tags
- Copies of adult education brochure
- Times/dates/temple contact information for new members
- Snacks
- Learning materials

Joanne (7 minutes)
- Quick welcome
- Brief overview of agenda for Oct. 28, Nov. 3
- Introduce staff and clergy
- Personal introduction
  - Why we joined
  - Our Rodeph experience this past year

Group (23 minutes)
- Each member/family introduces themselves
  - The reason we joined Rodeph Sholom this year is because...

Rabbi Matt (60 minutes)
- Learning session 1

Joanne
- Reminder of next week/goodbye

Orientation
Session 2, Nov. 3, 7:15-8:45

Joanne (2 minutes)
- Quick welcome
- Introduce staff and clergy

Clergy and Staff (15 minutes)
- Personal introductions

Rabbi Levine (45 minutes)
- Learning session 2

Sandy Abramson (10 minutes)
- Worship opportunities
- Committees

Joanne (5 minutes)
- Evaluations

Welcome to Our New Members

Congregation Rodeph Sholom
October 9, 2002 - 3 Cheshvan 5763
Rabbi Randy Sheinberg

SHEHECHEYANU

בָּרוּךְ אַתָּה, יְיָ אֱלֹהֵינוּ, מֶלֶךְ הָעוֹלָם,
שֶׁהֶחֱיָנוּ וְקִיְּמָנוּ וְהִגִּיעָנוּ לַזְּמַן הַזֶּה.

Baruch Atah Adonai Eloheinu Melech ha'olam shehecheyanu vekiyemanu vehigianu lazeman hazeh.

We praise You, Eternal God, Sovereign of the universe, for giving us life, for sustaining us, and for enabling us to reach this season.

PRAYER FOR OUR NEW MEMBERS

Rabbi: We welcome our new members to the Rodeph Sholom family. May you find community here, people who share your aspirations and yearnings. May this synagogue help invigorate your commitment to God, Torah and the heritage of Israel.

New Members: *We respond as did our ancestors to the call for renewal: Hineni-- I am here. Here to join the search for holiness, here to work for the improvement of our world in the quest for Tikkun Olam.*

Congregation: May the One who blessed our ancestors bless our community and all who work to secure God's kingdom on earth.

New Members: *Therefore, O God, bless us all, give meaning to our lives and substance to our hopes; help us to understand those about us and fill us with the desire to serve them.*

Together: *Let us remember that we depend on them as they depend on us; quicken our heart and hand to lift them up, and teach us to make our words of prayer fruitful by deeds of lovingkindness.*
Amen.

בָּרוּךְ אַתָּה יְיָ, אֱלֹהֵינוּ מֶלֶךְ הָעוֹלָם, אֲשֶׁר קִדְּשָׁנוּ בְּמִצְוֹתָיו וְצִוָּנוּ לַעֲסוֹק בְּדִבְרֵי תוֹרָה.

Baruh atah adonay eloheynu meleh ha'olam asher kideshanu bemitzvotav vetzivanu l'asok bedivrey torah.

Blessed are you. The One of Sinai, our God, the sovereign of all worlds, who made us your mitzvoth, and commanded us to occupy ourselves with words of Torah

New Member Workshop Series Evaluation

Please respond to the following questions now that you have completed the series:

What were your expectations of the New Member Workshop Series? _____
_____
_____
_____

Were they met? Yes ___   No ___   Comment: _____
_____
_____

Please circle one response for each session:

Expectations	Very Effective	Effective	Not Effective
Theology, foundations	Very Effective	Effective	Not Effective
Jewish communal experience	Very Effective	Effective	Not Effective

Which sessions were the most meaningful? Why? _____
_____
_____
_____

How would you change any of the sessions? _____
_____
_____
_____

How did the sessions affect your views of the meaning of synagogue membership? _____
_____
_____
_____

Any additional comments: _____
_____
_____
_____

New Member Workshop Series

The membership committee, with the help of Rabbis Matthew Gewirtz and Randy Sheinberg, inaugurated a new series of classes designed to help acclimate new members to the temple. Following a syllabus designed by the Outreach Committee of the UAHC-CCAR Commission on Synagogue Affiliation, we adapted a three-class series, which was meant to develop a "convenant" between the individual and the community. These classes hoped to provide an avenue for new members to meet people quickly, solving the problem of feeling lost in a large temple.

The classes were held in the morning as well as evening, beginning on Thursday evening, October 25, and Tuesday morning, October 30, running for three consecutive weeks, each session one and one-half hours long. The classes were taught by Rabbis Matt Gewirtz and Randy Sheinberg, Irwin Shlachter, Kerith Braunfeld, assistant director of the religious school, and facilitated by Sally Kaplan and Sandy Abramson. The membership committee organized registrars to welcome the new members and followed up with return phone calls to ensure attendance. Thirty-six people accepted for the evening class and eleven for the morning. Actual numbers were less, with about thirty people coming in the evening and seven in the morning.

The first class engaged new members in telling their "Jewish Journeys" prior to joining the temple. What made them join? What kind of background did they have? What were their hopes and dreams for their new temple? This was done in small groups and shared with the larger group. A brief history of the temple was given, and *Parashat Lech L'cha*, in which Abraham leaves his father and journeys forth, was taught and discussed.

The second class discussed the *Sh'ma* prayer in detail, again breaking up into groups and answering questions about the meaning of the prayer and its relevance for us today. This discussion brought out many basic questions about our religion and time was too short for an in-depth discussion. Attendees were encouraged to study further, as this was but a taste of the basic foundations of Judaism.

The third class dealt with the meaning of a Jewish community, and the text from Exodus that talks about the making of the *Mishkan* was discussed as a segue into meeting heads of the committees of the temple. Representatives from Sisterhood, Brotherhood, Caring Community, Ritual and Outreach, CCC, and Mark Biderman came and said a few words about their groups and encouraged people to get involved. Lists of contact names and numbers were distributed.

Evaluations were completed. The comments were overwhelmingly positive. Attendees felt they were properly welcomed into the temple and loved the study aspect of the course. They were impressed with the level of content, not expecting to "learn" at all. Their comments were very helpful and will assist us in planning the next group of classes, which will take place in the spring.

My sincere thanks to Rabbis Matt and Randy and to Irwin and Kerith for their time and energy spent on preparation and execution of these new classes. They were all wonderfully helpful, scholarly as usual, and enthusiastic about participating in the classes. I look forward to these classes becoming a fixture at Rodeph Sholom.

Sandy Abramson
Membership Chair

The Outreach and Membership Idea Book

Next New Member Wokshop:
Wednesday November 3rd
7:15 p.m. —8:30 p.m.
For more info, call extension 1317

New Members Shabbat Dinner:
November 19th, services 6:00 p.m.
dinner follows
For more info, call extension 1317

UPCOMING EVENTS AT RODEPH SHOLOM

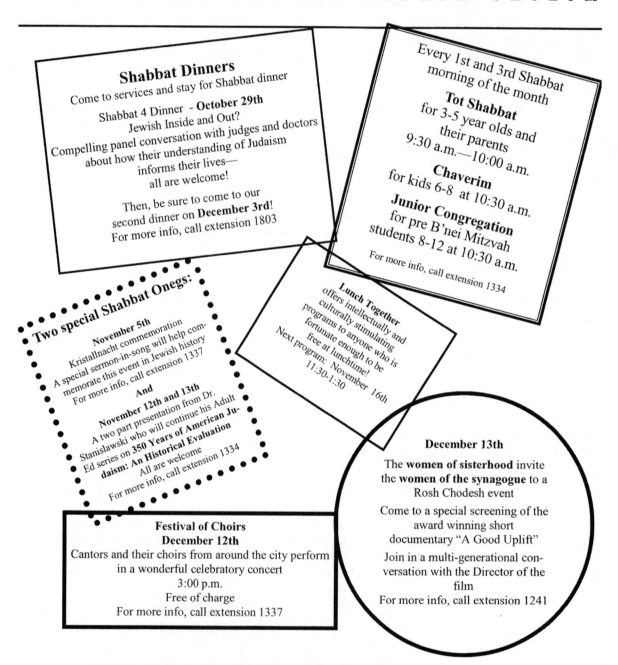

Shabbat Dinners
Come to services and stay for Shabbat dinner
Shabbat 4 Dinner - **October 29th**
Jewish Inside and Out?
Compelling panel conversation with judges and doctors about how their understanding of Judaism informs their lives—
all are welcome!

Then, be sure to come to our second dinner on **December 3rd!**
For more info, call extension 1803

Every 1st and 3rd Shabbat morning of the month
Tot Shabbat
for 3-5 year olds and their parents
9:30 a.m.—10:00 a.m.
Chaverim
for kids 6-8 at 10:30 a.m.
Junior Congregation
for pre B'nei Mitzvah students 8-12 at 10:30 a.m.
For more info, call extension 1334

Two special Shabbat Onegs:
November 5th
Kristallnacht commemoration
A special sermon-in-song will help commemorate this event in Jewish history
For more info, call extension 1337
And
November 12th and 13th
A two part presentation from Dr. Stanislawski who will continue his Adult Ed series on **350 Years of American Judaism: An Historical Evaluation**
All are welcome
For more info, call extension 1334

Lunch Together
offers intellectually and culturally stimulating programs to anyone who is fortunate enough to be free at lunchtime!
Next program: November 16th
11:30-1:30

Festival of Choirs
December 12th
Cantors and their choirs from around the city perform in a wonderful celebratory concert
3:00 p.m.
Free of charge
For more info, call extension 1337

December 13th
The **women of sisterhood** invite the **women of the synagogue** to a Rosh Chodesh event

Come to a special screening of the award winning short documentary "A Good Uplift"

Join in a multi-generational conversation with the Director of the film
For more info, call extension 1241

And, always remember to check our website for more information on programs, services and upcoming events! **www.rodephsholom.org**

Congregational Life

On any given day or night, our temple buildings are bustling with people who invest their time, minds, and hearts in our committees and auxiliaries. Our programs and activities respond to and reflect the pulse and population of New York City and the needs of our congregants and community. A policy of inclusiveness makes Rodeph Sholom a welcoming place for everyone.

- **Sisterhood** enriches lives with special friendships, spiritual fulfillment, community service, Rosh Chodesh and Torah study, support of women's issues, and more.
- **Brotherhood** provides camaraderie, sponsors informative programs and social events, and supports the Jewish Chatauqua Society.
- **RSYP** holds a monthly Shabbat participatory service and dinner for Rodeph Sholom Young Professionals ages 25 to 40, and also sponsors social activities, study, and community projects.
- **Youth Groups** composed of our teens and preteens plan and participate in shul-ins, retreats, and social, educational, and social action projects.
- **The Caring Community's Mitzvah Corps** responds to congregants in need through visits and telephone calls.
- **The Community Concerns Committee** sponsors programs that feed the hungry, shelter the homeless, assist women and children as they move from shelters to their own homes, and help persons with AIDS and their families. They conduct blood and clothing drives and a congregational Mitzvah Day. Through a subcommittee, they reach out to the gay and lesbian community. They sponsor joint programs with two black churches in Harlem and have recently become involved in advocacy relating to contemporary issues of public importance.
- **Re: Union** offers socializing opportunities for single Jewish parents and sponsors both family and adults-only events.
- **The Outreach Committee** welcomes intermarried families and provides support to converts to Judaism by sponsoring classes, workshops, and discussion groups.
- **The Shop at 7 West** is our Judaica and gift shop located in the temple lobby and operated by Sisterhood volunteers for the benefit of the congregation.
- **Facilities** of various sizes are available to rent for all occasions. Please contact the administration office at 212-362-8800.
- **Our rabbis, cantor, and professional staff** look forward to knowing you, sharing your joys and sorrows, and offering guidance, comfort, and encouragement.
- **Union Field Cemetery** is owned and operated by Rodeph Sholom. For information about this beautifully maintained cemetery in Queens, please call 718-366-3748.

Chavurah Program and Guide

Congregation:	Congregation Beth Israel
Address:	9001 Towne Centre Drive San Diego, CA 92122
Phone Number:	(858) 535-1111 ext. 3112
Contact's Name and E-mail:	Bonnie Graff, Program Director, bgraff@cbisd.org
Number of Member Units:	1,350
URJ Region:	Pacific Southwest Council
Rabbis:	Paul Citrin, Sheila Goloboy
Outreach Chairperson:	Debbie Weiner

Brief Description: The Chavurah Program at Congregation Beth Israel provides a wonderful shared Jewish experience for everyone who participates. It is one of the many ways to enhance a congregant's experience as a member of Congregation Beth Israel. A *chavurah* is a group of ten to twelve couples or families averaging twenty individuals who get together on a regular basis to celebrate Jewish life. The difference between a *chavurah* and any other social group is that all members must make a commitment to the group to meet regularly once a month. Each *chavurah* determines the types of activities it wants. For example, some activities involve celebrating Jewish holidays, hosting speakers and discussions on Jewish topics, or joining together to participate in social action activities. *Chavurot* can become extended family for group members, especially during life cycle events, such as hosting a Shabbat dinner when a member celebrates a bar or bat mitzvah.

Program Goal: The goal of the Chavurah Program is for members of the synagogue to feel connected to others. Getting to know people in a larger congregation can be intimidating for some members. A *chavurah* is a terrific way to become acquainted with other members who have children, are empty nesters, or have similar interests. Members of a *chavurah* can feel like extended family for each other, particularly in California where so many are here without family. This is especially important for new member integration and retention. It is imperative that we encourage new members to join a small group so that they find an instant "home" within our vast temple. This greatly enhances the likelihood that they will maintain their membership and often leads to other involvement on committees as well.

Target Population: The target population is every member of Congregation Beth Israel who is interested in becoming part of a smaller group within the synagogue. *Chavurah* applications are included in all prospective member packets and are sent out a second time when the individuals join CBI. They are then displayed at prospective member Shabbat, new member orientations twice a year, and at new member Shabbat. Reminders are also placed in the synagogue newsletter "Tidings," our annual "Preview," which is given out at High Holy Days, and on our Web site.

Some *chavurot* have been in existence for more than twenty-six years. New members can be added to an existing *chavurah* as vacancies arise. New synagogue members are especially targeted to join either an existing *chavurah*, depending upon space or needs, or new *chavurot* are formed for them.

Number of Participants: There are twenty-five *chavurot* at Congregation Beth Israel averaging ten to twelve families (twenty people). This equals approximately 650 people (adults and children) who are actively involved in *chavurot*.

Number and length of session(s): Each *chavurah* meets approximately one time per month throughout the year for a program or a planning session lasting approximately two to four hours each.

Staffing Required: Bonnie Graff, program director, acts as the coordinator of the *chavurot*. Clergy are asked from time to time to meet with individual groups as well.

Total Cost of Program: Cost of printing the "Chavurah Program Guide" and other program materials: $350/year. Administrative/assistant: approximately one hour per week throughout the year. Staff allocation to include: photocopying and mailing applications, putting the application into the new member packets, composing and mailing pending letters, database work, scheduling orientation meetings, mailing orientation meeting notices, updating the "Chavurah Program Guide," and making arrangements for printing of books.

Source of Funding: *Chavurot* are self-supporting and do not rely on the synagogue for program costs.

Fee for Attendees: All members of *chavurot* must be members of Congregation Beth Israel. There is no separate fee for becoming a member of a *chavurah*. Some *chavurot* choose to have each family pay a small amount ($5 or $10 per month) for a collective fund to pay for speakers' honoraria, special presents, donations to honor a member, charitable functions, or to save toward a *chavurah* weekend. This is up to each *chavurah* and no member is excluded for not being able to pay this nominal fee. All *chavurot* are self-supporting and do not rely on the synagogue for program costs.

Logistics: The logistics of administering the *chavurot* are the program director's responsibility. All *chavurah* applications are sent to the office of the program director. Applicants are either placed in existing groups as openings arise or are invited to become part of a newly formed *chavurah*. The process of assigning people to a *chavurah* is complex. Great pains are taken to make sure that the applicants are matched with a group that is compatible with the information recorded on the *chavurah* application. *Chavurot* inform the program director of the need for new members instead of selecting members independently. That way people are generally put in a *chavurah* in chronological order and not made to feel that others were placed into a group before they were.

Each *chavurah* designates one person to act as the liaison between the *chavurah* and the synagogue. When information of interest to *chavurah* members needs to be disseminated, the program director typically sends out e-mails to each of the *chavurah* liaisons, who then forward the e-mail to each of the *chavurah*'s members.

Every group plans its own activities, usually having a planning meeting once every six months to plan its activities. The group brainstorms possible program ideas to reach a consensus of ideas and activities that will satisfy the majority of the members. Responsibilities are divided up and each family volunteers to host one of the activities. Dates are chosen for the activities and then one of the members volunteers to prepare a calendar of events and distribute it (usually via e-mail) to the *chavurah* members. Each member of a *chavurah* is the host of at least one monthly program per year and is responsible for coordinating the activity, materials needed, and the refreshments. Refreshments are usually handled in a "pot luck" fashion with everyone bringing something. Most programs are at *chavurah* members' homes, although the synagogue is always available for larger gatherings such as a Passover seder.

Sometimes the program involves attending a synagogue activity or other community event together. *Chavurot* celebrate Jewish holidays together, for example, breaking the fast together on Yom Kippur. *Chavurot* also celebrate life-cycle events of their members, for example, if a child of a member is celebrating a bar or bat mitzvah, the other families of the *chavurah* can join together in hosting a Shabbat dinner or making hotel welcome bags for out-of-town friends and family.

Instructions to Facilitator: Starting a new *chavurah* is a well-structured and time-tested process. A letter is sent out to all candidates inviting them to a meeting that is held at the synagogue and led by the program director. It is suggested that this first meeting be adults only so that people can participate in the meeting without distraction. Time is allotted for socializing both before and after the meeting. There is an icebreaker session and then the program director gives a brief introduction about the history and practice of *chavurot* at CBI and explains the decision-making process on placement in *chavurot*. The emphasis on commitment to the group and connection to the synagogue is highlighted. An explanation is given for the many ways in which the *chavurah* can define itself as a group and establish its own identity via the type of programming the group elects to do. Of course, substantive Judaic programming is stressed, which includes Jewish holiday celebrations, life-cycle events, mitzvah projects, and Jewish discussion topics.

The group takes time to look through the "Chavurah Program Guide" and is reminded of important methods for the long-term success of the group. The program director describes the "how to" of building the infrastructure of the group, how to lead a meeting, and helps with details of the next organizational meeting of the group. Participants are given *chavurah* membership rosters and icebreaker exercises that can be used at the next meeting to help in the process of getting to know each other. The program director is then available to help with questions, program ideas, and any concerns that occur during the life of the group. There are even occasions when the program director is asked to meet with an already existing group that is suffering from malaise, attrition, or other such difficulties and needs to be reenergized.

Evaluation of Program: *Chavurot* have been integral to Congregation Beth Israel for more than a quarter of a century. There are groups that have been in existence for that entire time, and the children and grandchildren are now forming their own *chavurot*. Although not all groups succeed and not all individuals who are placed in *chavurot* stay in the group, on the whole the *chavurah* program is considered essential in attracting, integrating, and retaining members. It is significant that placement in a *chavurah* is taken very seriously so that the fewest possible mismatches occur. A great deal of attention is paid by the program director to people's needs, interests, backgrounds, and stages of life. This bodes well for a cohesive group, especially when contrasted with many *chavurah* networks that place any ten families together without regard to these factors.

Follow-up: The program director handles follow-up for issues regarding *chavurot* in terms of placing or changing members of *chavurot* and is always available to *chavurot* for program ideas and acts as a consultant/problem solver as the *chavurah* evolves and new needs arise.

CHAVURAH PROGRAM GUIDE

Everything You Wanted To Know But Were Afraid To Ask!

What is a Chavurah?
Membership Policy
Long-Term Planning Guide
Favorite Chavurah Tips
Program Ideas
Sample Calendar
Resource Guide
Speakers
Discussion Triggers

Compiled by
Bonnie Graff
Program Director

Congregation Beth Israel
9001 Towne Centre Drive
San Diego, CA 92122
(858) 535-1111

Table of Contents

Chapter   **Page**

What is a Chavurah? 1

Membership Policy and Procedures 2

Ten Favorite Chavurah Tips 3

"How To" Guide: Long-term Planning 4

How to Successfully Chair Your Assigned Chavurah Meeting 5

Program Ideas 7

A Sample Calendar of Activities 12

Chavurah Resource Guide 14

Library Resources 15

Speaker Resources 16

The Seven "C's" of Chavurah 19

Sample Planning Questionnaire 20

What's Your Name? A Guide to Naming Your Chavurah 21

Notes 22

Whom to Call at the Synagogue 23

What is a Chavurah?
A chavurah is a group of 10-12 couples or families or up to 20 individuals who get together on a regular basis to celebrate Jewish life. The difference between a chavurah and any other social group is that all members must make a commitment to the group to meet regularly once a month.

What's the advantage of a Chavurah?
Getting to know people in a larger congregation can be intimidating for some. A chavurah is a terrific way to become acquainted with others who live near you, and have similar interests.

What kinds of activities does a Chavurah do?
It's up to you! Your group can enjoy a Shabbat dinner together, have a Chanukah party, build a Sukkah, even go camping if you're so inclined. Each chavurah determines the types of activities it wants... some involve children, some do not. You can ask one of our clergy to attend your monthly meeting to discuss a variety of topics related to Jewish life. Congregation Beth Israel's Program Director, Bonnie Graff, is available to help with programming ideas.

How do you get a Chavurah together?
After returning a completed chavurah application, you will be "matched up" with others who have similar qualifications. At the first meeting of your new chavurah, the CBI Program Director will be there to help break the ice and to explain more about how a chavurah is organized.

What if I don't like everyone in my group?
In any group of that size, there may very well be one or two individuals you can't seem to get to know. The best advice is to stick with it! You'll be surprised what can happen over time. Some of the Congregation's chavurot have been together for almost 17 years! If it's just not working out though, you can speak to the Program Director about your options.

Membership Policy and Procedures

1. Using group consensus as a model, discuss your group's optimal membership at a time when no new membership is currently at issue.

    a. Establish your group's minimum and maximum size (in either number of families or number of persons).

2. All chavurah members must be members of Congregation Beth Israel.

    a. Call the Program Directors office with the qualifications and characteristics of the "ideal" new member(s).

    - ◆ number of people
    - ◆ ages of children
    - ◆ ages of adults
    - ◆ checklist of basic interests you'd like them to have in common with your group
    - ◆ regularly scheduled meeting dates and times

    b. In the event that a chavurah wishes to reach out into the congregation and invite a person or couple to join them, their names must first be cleared with CBI's Program Director.

3. Once a chavurah invites an applicant to one of it's meetings, he, she or they are to be considered a member of that group, if the applicant so chooses. Welcome and include new members. Let them share in the decision making and responsibilities of the Chavurah.

4. Each chavurah is urged to advise CBI's Program Director of any changes in membership in order to keep our mailing lists accurate.

Ten Favorite Chavurah Tips

1. Decide what you want to do, and what your general goals will be, based on a combination of social activities, Jewish issues, holiday celebrations, etc.

2. Try and reach a consensus which satisfies the majority of people. This requires patience and "give and take" (see Seven C=s of Chavurah).

3. Plan a monthly schedule with dates, locations, and programs in advance... at least six months, preferably a year.

4. Send out a copy of the entire schedule to each member, and then send out monthly meeting cards 10 days to two weeks before each meeting with RSVP required and adhered to by all.

5. Fulfill your commitment to each other by doing your share.

6. Attend regularly and make it a priority. Work together to make the meetings something you look forward to.

7. TALK things over if there are conflicts, but be sensitive to the feelings of others.

8. Recognize the dynamics of your own chavurah, and be realistic about what you do. Some groups will become real extended families; others will develop some close friendships within the group but share a common bond with everyone, enjoying a variety of experiences together. Others will be united in their dedication to Judaic study. Don't compare yourselves but strive for the elements which make your chavurah special to you... with the following exception:

   What everyone in each chavurah should have in common is a desire to strengthen your Jewish ties and those of your family, to enrich yourself Jewishly, to reach out to other synagogue members, and to enjoy!

9. Remind your chavurah of coming events of interest at the synagogue and in the Jewish community. Check the *Tidings* and the Jewish press for details. Some of the events may prove to be great activities for the entire chavurah to attend together. (Perhaps one member of the chavurah may choose to research this information on a monthly basis.)

10. Appoint an chavurah liaison as a way of keeping in touch with CBI and other chavurot.

How To Guide for New and Ongoing Chavurot
Long-Term Planning

1. Program Planning Meeting
Hold meeting approximately every six months.

a. Brainstorm possible programs. Try to reach a consensus of ideas and activities which will satisfy the majority of your membership. For the yearly schedule, consider a combination of social, educational, cultural and religious events. You may wish to include discussions of Jewish issues, inviting a guest speaker from the synagogue or community, view an interesting video tape as prelude to discussion, attend a specific CBI function or service, etc. REMIND each member in advance to bring his/her personal calendar to this planning meeting to clear all dates.

b. Divide up responsibilities for the program planning meeting; secretarial work, telephoning, refreshments, etc.

c. Decide on a specific time for monthly meetings, (for example, every third Sunday of the month.) Plan a monthly schedule of meetings with dates, locations and program ideas in advance for at least the next six months but preferably for one year.

d. Decide who wants responsibility for each program function. This can be done alphabetically by last names, or by interest in a specific program. If the host family, "A" is suddenly unable to hold its assigned meeting, the next family on the list should be immediately contacted to substitute. If this is not feasible, then the yearly schedule should continue as planned. The original host family, "A" will miss its turn and, therefore, await the next rotation of assignments.

e. Send out a copy of the finalized schedule of programs to each member. Include a roster of membership with directions to each home. You may also wish to include a list of members' birthdays, and wedding anniversaries, etc.

2. Handling Finances
Some chavurot collect monthly dues; $5.00, $10.00, whatever. This could be used for speakers honoraria, special presents, donations to honor a member, charitable functions, or perhaps, to save towards a Chavurah Weekend.

3. Chavurah Synagogue E Mail Connection
In lieu of Chavurah Liaison meetings, all chavurah communication is conducted via e-mail. Please select a liaison, preferably someone who will remain the representative for a year at a time. This maintains much needed continuity with CBI. In this way chavurot can be apprised of events which might interest their group. There are times when your chavurah may wish to share an activity with another chavurah and this can more easily be arranged via the Internet. Each chavurah liaison can be given a chavurah list with names, addresses, phone numbers and e mail addresses of others so that groups can get together to plan shared events. This is also an effective way of communicating new ideas, brainstorming creative programming and problem solving between our chavurot.

Successful Chavurot are made up of members who make it a priority to attend all of its meetings.

How To Successfully Chair Your Assigned Chavurah Meeting

1. When monthly meetings are planned in advance, each chavurah member/family should be given a copy of the calendar for the year. This not only clarifies the specific program assignments but hopefully should increase interest in attendance.

2. Mail a reminder postcard ten days or two weeks before your meeting or send an email to members of your chavurah. Request some form of RSVP and include travel directions to your home if you feel it helpful.

3. When you are in charge of a program, prepare early, plan ahead. If research of a topic is necessary, utilize the advice of the Chavurah Steering Committee, the Rabbis or Cantor, the CBI Librarian or other resources available in the community. Do your homework and try to present a quality program. Consider mailing relevant reading materials to the members of your chavurah at least ten days ahead of time. This will assure their involvement and participation in the program as well as stimulate interest in attending. Prepare in advance some key questions or helpful information to help start the discussion, if needed.

4. Encourage your members to arrive on time and begin your meeting promptly. The person or couple responsible for the program for that evening might choose to act as chairpersons and conduct the meeting or program. If a guest speaker is involved, you might wish to call him/her a week prior to make sure time and travel directions are clear, and to inquire if any aids will be required.

5. Plan ahead as to how refreshments will be handled and at which point in the evening they will be served. You may wish to invite others to help with refreshments to free you to supervise the program. Consider these possibilities for handling refreshments:

   a. Members chairing program in their home to provide refreshments.

   b. When you have program responsibility, hold the program in another member's home with them handling refreshments.

   c. Preparation of any food to be shared by all members in a potluck fashion.

6. Try to conduct the program in an organized manner. You might consider this simple agenda: Welcome time, call meeting to order, discuss old and new business, time for announcements, and then presentation of pre-planned program with opportunity for discussion. Finally, social time with refreshments served.

7. Remind your chavurah of coming events of interest at Congregation Beth Israel and in the Jewish comm. unity. Check the Tidings newsletter and the Jewish press for details. Some of the events may prove to be a great activity for the entire chavurah to attend together. Perhaps one member of the chavurah may choose to research this information on a yearly basis, or the host will do it.

8. When planning your assigned program, consider asking others to help you. Utilize any resources available to you and don't hesitate to delegate responsibilities if it will make the program more interesting or easier for you. Draw from your own inner desires to strengthen your Jewish ties. You will then enrich yourself and every member of your chavurah.

Program Ideas

At Congregation Beth Israel

Purim Carnival
Sponsor and run a booth at the carnival... a fun activity for chavurot of any age. Provide baked goods for sale.

Scholar-in-Residence Weekend
A wonderful opportunity for your chavurah to learn in an atmosphere that is stimulating and intimate. Call Bonnie Graff's office at 858 535-1111 ext. 3800 for topics and dates, or check CBI brochures or web site for programs that might interest your group.

Becoming An Extended Fomily

Hanukat Habayit (Dedication of the Home)
When a member moves into a new home, have everyone bring both food and a special wish for the new homeowners. Affix the mezuzah with the traditional blessing.

Making a Donation
Giving tzedakah on behalf of the chavurot can be done to honor any special simcha (happy occasion) or to memorialize a loss. The synagogue has many funds which would appreciate your support. Times to make a donation include: births (of children or grandchildren), graduations, retirements, recovery from illness, deaths, yahrzeits.

Preparing the Meal After a Funeral
So that the mourners do not have to worry about providing a meal at their home after a funeral, have the chavurah assume this responsibility (actually a mitzvah), and be there to help relieve some of the burden.

Shabbat Hosting for a Bar/Bat Mitzvah
When a member celebrates a Bar or Bat Mitzvah, have the whole chavurah in attendance on Friday night to welcome family and friends. Request Shabbat Hosting for the dates in advance.

Celebrate Together

Chanukah
This is a wonderful time for a party, with or without children. Don't forget the latkes and dreidels. On a more serious note, this holiday raises questions about the "December Dilemma' (explaining the celebration of Christmas in a secular society to a Jewish child) as well as the historic struggle of the assimilationists vs. the traditionalists. Lots of food for thought and discussion.

Havdalah
Done on Saturday night, traditionally after three stars are visible in the sky, this is a beautiful, simple and very short service marking the end of Shabbat. Song sheets in English, Hebrew and transliterated Hebrew are available. It is a wonderful way to begin a Saturday night program.

High Holy Days
Often the chavurah comes back together after a short summer break around holiday time. Join at a member's home after Rosh Hashanah services for lunch and to catch up with each other. Have a chavurah Break-Fast on Yom Kippur, even if some of the members have local family. Join CBI's Tashlich service at the beach.

Lag B'omer
On the 33rd (LaG) day between Passover and Shavuot, this holiday is traditionally celebrated with a picnic, outdoor games and haircuts. This is a great excuse for a chavurah to have a day at the park.

Passover
Though many families have plans for a first seder, chavurot often celebrate a second, third or seventh seder together. It does not have to be a sit-down meal. Rather, decide which parts of the Haggadah you would like to include, involve children (if applicable) in preparing a skit about life in the wilderness, talk about associations Passover has for you, etc. Be creative!

Purim
Revive the practice of giving shalach manot (gifts of food) to each other and to those who are less able to enjoy the holiday, e.g., shut-ins, elderly, those in nursing homes. Spend a meeting preparing the packages of treats (don't forget the hamantaschen) and then deliver them yourselves.

Shabbat
1. Split the chavurah up for Friday night dinner in a few different homes, then all meet together for dessert and singing.
2. Meet at the synagogue for a Shabbat service on Friday night or at our Shabbat Morning Minyan.
3. Have Shabbat dinner at an Israeli restaurant with candies, challah and wine.

Shavuot
A perfect time for a discussion of the Ten Commandments (why not have everyone rank them in order of importance?) followed by a traditional dairy meal.

Sukkot
Building a sukkah together is a great challenge and a wonderful project which really gives the chavurah a sense of accomplishment. Don't forget the decorations and a potluck meal to eat inside the sukkah. In keeping with the customs of inviting ushpizin (symbolic guests), have everyone think of someone they'd like to invite "in spirit" to join the chavurah in the sukkah and explain their choices.

Tu B'shevat
As the holiday of the trees, this is the time to do some planting. A wonderful idea is for the chavurah to plant a small tree, bush or garden each year at a different member's home. Over the years, the chavurah will enjoy seeing tangible evidence of its growth. Or arrange with the Parks system to plant trees in areas where they are needed, either in town or in Julian.

Yom HaAtzmaut
Israeli Independence Day can be celebrated by doing anything connected with Israel, eg., Israeli wine and cheese party, inviting a speaker to talk about an issue related to Israel, have someone show and explain their photographs or video from a recent trip, etc.

Yom HaShoah
Holocaust Memorial Day can be observed by talking with a survivor, discussing an article on a Holocaust related subject, or attending CBI's Yom HaShoah service.

Discussion Triggers

Chavurot are often frustrated by the futility of small talk. In an effort to get people to reveal themselves a bit, and to encourage discussion of personal values and experience, these topics are sure to work. Try using unfinished sentences by going around the room asking people to complete the same sentence. Examples are:

- My most significant book, poem, play or person...
- My most memorable Jewish moment...
- If I won a million dollars in the lottery I would...
- A good Jew is one who...
- I hope my children remember me as...
- The Jewish Community's most pressing problem is...

Family Activities

Children can be included in most chavurah programs as long as accommodations are made. If kids know their opinions are valued, they will feel comfortable partaking in discussions on a variety of "adult" topics. Nonetheless, the following programs have been found to be particularly fun when done with whole families in the chavurah.

Social Action Projects
Visit the sick on holidays with songs and food.

Create a Game Show
Small groups of adults and children are asked age-level questions from either the Jewish Jeopardy board game or one of several Jewish trivia books available.

Family Retreat
Plan a weekend away at a camp, rustic hotel, camping on the beach, etc. Include Shabbat dinner, discussion groups, recreational activities, Havdalah. Divide up responsibilities for organizing, programming, meals, services. Have some activities for adults and children together, others separate.

Chavurah Picnic
Have each family bring their own food and organize parent/child sports activities. Perhaps invite another chavurah with the same age children.

Roots
Have each family trace its history back as far as possible and make a presentation to the chavurah. Include information such as birth places, dates, name changes, ports of entry, occupations, etc. Use a world map to plot migration patterns.

Learning

Choose an interesting topic to discuss or study. Lead the discussions yourselves by utilizing resources from CBI's library or choosing a knowledgeable speaker.

Comparative Religions

How much do we really understand about the other religions of the world? How are they similar to Judaism? How are they different? How does one's religion affect one's outlook on life?

How Other Jews Practice

What are the real differences between Orthodox, Conservative, Reform and Reconstructionist beliefs and practices?

The History of Jewish Customs and Traditions

Why do we do what we do? How much of our practice comes from Jewish law (halachah), and how much is custom that has been passed down through the ages? How much room is there to continue adding to that heritage?

The Jewish Holidays

The Jewish holidays are rich in history and practice, and discussion always enhances our appreciation of them. Excellent books on the subject which are easy to read are "The Jewish Holidays" by Michael Strassfeld (coauthor of "The Jewish Catalog") and "Seasons of Our Joy" by Arthur Waskow.

The Jewish Life Cycle

From birth to death, what are the meanings behind the many Jewish practices we associate with these important events?

What Judaism Says About... (any social issue)

Our Jewish tradition, with all its various branches, often has more than one opinion on almost any contemporary Jewish issue. For example, ever thought about how an Orthodox astronaut would know when to pray in space...?

A Sample Calendar of Activities

September:
(For Adults) Share stories about your varied Jewish upbringings. Bring in ceremonial objects, pictures, or a memory to share... OR...

(With Children) Sunday brunch including apples and honey. Arts and crafts project: Make one poster for each family with wishes for the New Year. Display them, read them out loud, then take home as a decoration for Rosh Hashanah or Sukkot.

October:
Build a Sukkah and eat brunch or dinner in it. Have everyone prepared to share who (real or imaginary) they would like to invite to join them in the Sukkah. OR...

All go to Simchat Torah at CBI.

November:
Invite a speaker to talk and lead a discussion on "Coping with the Changing Family" (or any topic). OR...

Volunteer to prepare and serve food to the homeless at CBI's Hunger Project.

December:
Chanukah party with candies, food, games, small gifts for children's grab-bag. OR...

Collect toys and clothes for a shelter.

January:
Hang a mezuzah at a member's new home, with a short dedication ceremony (available from the CBI office), light meal, good wishes and shmoozing.

February:
Tree planting for Tu B'Shevat. You might want to plan a fun Tu B'Shevat seder with symbolic foods of Israel, plus songs and stories about trees and nature.

March:
Organize a Jewish Tour of Los Angeles, Jewish-related art exhibit, or other cultural trip. OR...

Make up a Purimscpiel (funny play). OR...

Make up baskets of hamentaschen and sweets to take to a retirement home, and sing songs with the seniors.

April:
Make a Passover seder of your own creation on the second or third night. Don't feel restricted to the Haggadah for ideas or readings.

May:
The perfect month to focus on Israel. Stage a debate about Israel's future. Invite a speaker from the Israeli Consulate. Go out to dinner at an Israeli restaurant.

June:
Plan a Shabbat experience at a home, on the beach, in a park. Every family has its own set of candles and kiddush cup. A good time to reflect on the year's activities, successes, challenges.

July:
Have a Saturday night barbecue. End with Havdalah service in a circle in the garden.

August:
Hold a family picnic with Macabiah games or attend Summer Pops.

NOTE:
A Planning Meeting needs to be scheduled in addition to the regular activities in order to plan for the upcoming year. You do not have to meet each month, but the more regular your meetings, the more "built-in" to your schedule the chavurah becomes.

Hosts of scheduled events should notify chavurah members of details in writing two to three weeks in advance of the scheduled event. Sometimes phone calls are necessary to answer questions or to make sure members are attending.

Chavurah Resource Guide

The following list of program ideas, topics for discussion, and speaker resources are meant only as a guide to help stimulate your thinking, and add depth to your chavurah experience. Your suggestions for additional ideas and speakers are welcome. If you need help locating a resource, contact Bonnie Graff at CBI at 858 535-1111 ext. 3128 or bgraff@cbisd.org.

Program Ideas
Jewish Trivial Pursuit
Spend a Shabbat at the Military Bases
Jewish Charades
Visit the Chabad House, Hebrew Home, Israel Cottage in Balboa Park
Camping at Mataguay or weekend retreat at Brandeis Bardin Institute
An Armchair Tour of Israel
Have a Macabiah Day
Havdalah at the Beach
Work at the Hunger Project (Call CBI ext. 3500)
Celebrate the Jewish Holidays:
- Sukkah building party
- Chanukah party
- Share a seder together
- Purim costume party

Discussion Topics
Jews of the Diaspora
Making Jewish Art Objects
Jewish Women in History
Singing Jewish Music for Fun
Jewish Humor
Jewish Life Cycle Events
Judaism and Medical Ethics: Genetic Engineering
What is a Jew?
The Politics of the Jewish Community
Ethical Wills
Biblical Archaeology
Contemporary Jewish Authors/Books
Jewish Values Clarification
The Yiddish Theatre
Raising a Jewish Child
Jews in Politics, Sports, Entertainment
The Holocaust for the Second and Third Generations
A History of Jews in America, California, San Diego
Extremist Groups
Tracing your Jewish Roots
AntiSemitism: Then and Now

Library Resources

The following is a sampling of what is available in the CBI Library.
Contact Liz Goldstein, the librarian for guidance.

Periodicals:
Commentary
Hadassah Magazine
Jerusalem Report
Keeping Posted, a monthly publication of URJ
Lillith, the Jewish Women's Magazine
Moment Magazine
Reform Judaism
Shma, A Journal of Jewish Responsibility

Reference Books and NonFiction
An entire book, a chapter or even a meaningful paragraph can serve as a springboard for discussion.

The Chavurah, A Contemporary Jewish Experience, Bernard Reisman
The Jewish Experiential Book, Bernard Reisman
The Jewish Catalogue, First, Second, Third, by Siegel and Strassfeld
A Do-it-yourself Kit. Third catalogue has cumulative index.
The Jewish Family Book, Sharon Strassfeld
Jewish Values and Social Crisis, Albert Vorspan
The Jewish Encyclopedia
Life Is With People, M. Zborowski
The Jewish Directory and Almanac, Ivan L. Tillem, ed.
Explaining Christmas to the Jewish Child, Lois Miller Weinstein
The Shabbat Catalog, Ruth Brin
The Jewish People's Almanac, David Gross
When Bad Things Happen to Good People, Rabbi Harold Kushner
God Wrestling, Arthur Waskow
The Jewish Trivia and Information Book, Trivia Judaica, Ian Shapolsky
Generation Without Memory, Anne Roiphe
An Orphan in History, Paul Cowan
A Certain People; American Jews and Their Lives Today, Charles E. Silberman
Back to the Sources; Reading the Classic Jewish Texts, Barry W. Holtz, ed.

Basic Jewish Philosophy
The Nine questions People Ask About Judaism, Prager & Telushkin, (200)
Basic Judaism, Steinberg (250)
What is a Jew?, Rabbi Morris Kertzer. A guide to beliefs, traditions and practices of Judaism. (200)
Pirke Avot: Sayings of the Fathers, Hertz (232.1)
Philosophies of Judaism, Guttman (259)
The Story of Jewish Philosophy, Blau (259)

Jewish Practices
Festivals of Jews, Schauss (240)
The Jewish Home Advisor, Kolatch (240)

Jewish History
Jews, God and History, Dimant (900) Wanderings, Potok (900)
Wanderlings, Potok (900)
My People: The Story of the Jews, Eban (900)
Any book by Grayzel, Sachar, Roth or Bamberger (900's)

Holocaust
The Abandonment of the Jews, Wyman (940.4)
The War Against the Jews, Dawidowiez (940)
Rise and Fall of the Third Reich, Shirer (940)

Mysticism
Major Trends in Jewish Mysticism, Scholem (283)

Immigrant History
World of our Fathers, Howe (325)
Our Crowd, Birmingham (973.8)

Israel
The Israelis, Elon (950.01)
O Jerusalem, LaPierre and Collins (950.11)
Arab and Jew: Wounded Spirits in a Promised Land, Shipler (953.23)

Marriage
Sex, God and the Sabbath, Green (304.2)

Yiddish
The Joys of Yiddish, Rosten (480)

Biography
The Labyrinth of Exile: A Life of Theodor Herzl, B.H. Pawel (BH)
Begin: The Haunted Spirit (BB)
Einstein: The Life and Times (BE)
Freud: A Life for our Times, Gay (BF)

Classic Fiction
The Island Within, Lewison (F L)
As a Driven Leaf, Steinberg (F S)
The Source, Michener (F M)
Exodus, Uris (F U)
The Last of the Just, Schwartzbart (F S)

Fiction
The Slave, I.B. Singer
The Source, James Michener
Reconciliations, Elizabeth Klein
Conversations with Rabbi Small, Harry Kemelman

Video
Our Library has many videos on a wide variety of Judaic subjects too extensive to list. Please call Liz Goldstein, the librarian at 858 535-1111 ext. 3118 for information.

Speaker Resources

Torah and Talmud and other Jewish Texts
Dr. Al Ray
Joseph Roditi, CBI Staff
Sydney Wexler

San Diego Jewish History
Dr. Arnold Gass
Laurel Schwartz (+)
Stan Schwartz (+)
Jewish Historical Society of San Diego
(+ *for groups of 30 or more*)

Creating a Jewish Library
Liz Goldstein, CBI Librarian

Jewish Education
Noah Hadas

Jewish Geneology
Audrey Karsh

Jewish Mysticism
Ita Sheres, S.D.S.U.
Joseph Roditi, CBI Staff

Israel and the Middle East
Jewish Community Relations Council of Jewish Federation - Tina Friedman
American Jewish Committee Speakers Bureau

Church-State Issues
Anti-Defamation League - Morris Casuot
Jewish Community Relations Council

Soviet Jewry
Jewish Community Relations Council
American Jewish Committee

Jewish Arts
Jacqueline Jacobs

The History of Jewish Music
Cantor Arlene Bernstein
Cantor Emeritus Sheldon Merel

Holocaust
Gussie Zaks, Survivor, The New Life Club
Lou Dunst, Survivor
Dr. Laurence Baron, SDSU Lipinsky Institute

Children of Holocaust Survivors
Sheldon Bleiweiss

Women in Judaism
Jackie Tolley, SDSU
Ita Sheres, SDSU

Miscellaneous
Rabbi Paul Citrin
Rabbi Sheila Goloboy
Cantor Arlene Bernstein
Morris Casuto, ADL
Rabbi Lisa Goldstein, Campus Issues
Anita Hosenpud*, Beyond War
Jill Spitzer*, Executive Director, JFS
Dan Schaffer, Middle East History; Politics-
Jackie Tolley, SDSU Campus Issues
(* CBI member)

We encourage your suggestions for additional speakers in order to expand this list. It is suggested that chavurot or other such groups join together to invite speakers. Contributions to the appropriate agency or Congregation Beth Israel would be welcomed. For additional information, call Bonnie Graff, Program Director at 858 535-1111 ext. 3128.

The Seven C's of Chavurah

1. Commitment
It is essential to a Chavurah. Commitment involves each group member taking time, energy, and responsibility in the planning, execution, and participation in the group's activities.

2. Cooperation
Groups become cohesive through interaction of all members. Decisions should be reached through consensus, not through default. All participants (including silent ones) should be encouraged to voice their opinions without giving long speeches or monopolizing.

3. Communication
For a group to be gratifying to its members, it is important that each member become an effective communicator. This means developing both active listening and speaking skills. Listening involves hearing not only the words used, but observing the manner in which they are said and grasping the meaning behind the words. Speaking involves expressing yourself directly, honestly and appropriately.

4. Conflict
Even with good communication, conflict in a group is unavoidable. Conflict is a necessary part of group process and the working out of conflict leads to a more cohesive group. Differences between members are inevitable, both in personality and in needs, and are a challenge to increasing one's tolerance and flexibility. One cannot expect either to like everybody or to have all of one's needs met all the time. However, differences that are causing resentment and dissatisfaction should be both articulated and worked out.

5. Confrontation
When there is a conflict, it is important to confront the situation before it saps energy from the group. There are several rules to follow for effective confrontation:

- Confront directly; do not gossip, complain, or talk about the person outside the group.
- Confront with care, concern, honesty, and directness.
- Confront the behavior of the person, and be concrete and specific when you are describing what bothers you. Speak for yourself and from yourself.
- Confront during the appropriate time at a group meeting. Usually an antagonism between two or more people affects the rest of the group and is best worked out in front of the group.
- Confront with receptivity. Be open to feedback from the person you are confronting. Use your active listening skills.

6. Companionship
It is important to know when you join a Chavurah group whether you are seeking or avoiding an extended family situation. If you know your own needs and those of the other members, you can derive the kind of companionship and degree of intimacy that you desire from the group.

7. Change
Becoming a cohesive Chavurah is a continuous process. The needs of group members, both individually and collectively will change. Periodically, the group should set aside some time just to review its goals and expectations, to see if they are current and meeting the needs of all its members most of the time.

Sample Planning Questionnaire
(Send in advance of the Program Planning Meeting)

To help our planning meetings proceed in a more orderly way, and to make certain that our chavurah is doing what you want, please read, fill out, and bring the following information to our next upcoming planning meeting.

Please think about the direction in which you would like the chavurah to move, i.e.,

more of _____

or less of _____

We will discuss your ideas at our upcoming meeting. This is your/our group and we want to be involved in activities that are mutually rewarding to all.

Please list which month you would like to sponsor an event:

First Choice: _____ Second Choice: _____

Please list two or more activities you would like the chavurah to be involved in for the coming year:

1. _____

2. _____

Should we expand on topics that have been brought up in the past for discussion?
❏ Yes   ❏ No
If yes, please indicate which ones:

_____

Do we have a good balance of family and adult meetings?   ❏ Yes   ❏ No
If no, please give brief explanation:

_____

Other thoughts or ideas?

_____

_____

_____

What's Your Name?

Each chavurah has a special identy. At your first meeting, as you discuss your goals for the group, it can be a lot of fun to decide on a name that reflects some aspect of your group's personality. It also is a lot easier to refer to the group by name in any correspondence from the synagogue or in an article for CBI's newsletter or web site.

The following are a few suggestions for names. Feel free to choose one of these, or make up your own. Please check with the Program Director, Bonnie Graff, to make sure a name has not already been chosen.

Aba and Ima (Father and Mother)
Achdut (Unity)
Achei Nefesh (Soul Brothers)
Achvah (Fraternity)
Ahavah (Love)
Ahleezim (Funny Ones)
Aleph (or any other Hebrew letter)
Anachnu (We)
Barak (Lightning)
Berit Yedidut (Friendly Alliance)
Chai (Life)
Chatzufeem (From Chutzpah)
Chaverim (Friends)
Chayim (Life)
Chevrah (Association)
Chug (Circle)
Emet (Truth)
Etz Chaim (Tree of Life)
Fressers (Yiddish for "love to eat')
Garin (Nucleus)
Gesher (Bridge)
Gila (Joy)
G'ulim (The Redeemers)
Hatikvah (Hope)
Hava Nagila ("Let's Be Joyful," also the name of a folk dance and song)
Havanah (Understanding)
Jerusalem (or any city in Israel)
Kesher (Communication)

Kevutzah (Group)
Kibbitzers (Advice givers)
Kinus (Gathering)
L'Chaim (To Life)
Limud (Study)
Maagal (Circle)
Maven (Expert)
Maziks (Yiddish for "cute little troublemakers")
Shalom (Peace)
Shemesh (Sun)
Shevet (Tribe)
Shira (Song or Poetry)
Shomrim (The Watchmen)
Shpielers
Tikkun (Spiritual work, repairing the world)
Tzadikim (Righteous)
Tzibur (Community)
Yachad (United)
Yom Rishon (Sunday, literally, 'first day')
Zahav (Gold)
Zion

Notes

CONGREGATION BETH ISRAEL CONTACT DIRECTORY
Phone: (858) 535-1111, plus extension below.

ACTIVITY	PERSON(S) RESPONSIBLE
Worship services, pastoral needs, Bar/Bat Mitzvah program and/or date setting, weddings, baby namings, funerals, Outreach to interfaith families	Rabbi Paul Citrin or his Assistant, Gail Malkus, Ext. 3110 Rabbi Sheila Goloboy or Cantor Arlene Bernstein or their Assistant, Susan Hutchison, Ext 3116
Administration, Capital Campaign, Endowment, Property Management, Insurance, Budget & Finance, Master Calendar	Stuart Simmons, Executive Director or his Assistant, Beverly Miller, Ext. 3113
Religious School, Day School, Bill & Sid Rubin Preschool, B.I.B.S., BITTS, My Family & Me, Tot Shabbat	Dr. Harvey Raben, Director of Education Tammy Vener, Early Childhood Education Director, (858) 535-1144, Ext. 3123. Rhona Gordon, Religious School Secretary, (858) 535-1144, Ext. 3121 Leslie Leshnick, Schools Administrative Asst., Ext. 3120
Library	Liz Goldstein, Librarian, Ext. 3118
Congregational Programming: Chavurah, Continuing Education, Kehillah (Caring Community), Makom, Social Action, Women of Beth Israel, Yasher Koach	Bonnie Graff, Program Director, Ext. 3112, or Myra Bressel, Program Assistant, Ext. 3128
Program/Event Reservations	Extension 3800
Music, Bar/Bat Mitzvah Training, Volunteer Choir Children's Choir, Shabbat Singers	Cantor Bernstein or her Assistant, Susan Hutchison, Ext. 3116
Membership Information, Master Calendar	Beverly Miller, Ext. 3133 or Stuart Simmons, Executive Director, Ext. 3113
Use of Facilities & Event Planning	Regina O'Callaghan, Facilities Coordinator, Ext. 3106
Youth Programs	Rabbi Sheila Goloboy Susan Hutchison, Assistant, Ext. 3116
Accounting/Business Office: Accounts Payable/Receivable; Credit Card Usage; Stock Transfers; Scrip	General Accounting, Ext. 3900 Bridget Weiss, Accounting Manager, Ext. 3144; Barbara Thompson, Accounting Assistant, Ext. 3115, Belinda Williams, Accounting Assistant, Ext. 3129
Tidings & SDJT Newspage	Debbie Simmons, Editor, Ext. 3126
Hunger Project	Joan Kutner, Ext. 3111
Mount of Olives Memorial Lawns at El Camino Home of Peace Mausoleum at Cypress View	Nelson Cohen, Mount of Olives Lawn Sales at (858) 452-5684 (619) 264-3168
Women of Beth Israel	Ellen Edwards or Elaine Simon, Co-Presidents (call temple to leave message)
Men's Club	Larry Krause, President or David Dahl, Executive Vice President (all temple to leave message)
Gift Shop	Janice Schuffman, Ext. 3107
Website	Webmaster Emily Jennewein emily@jennewein.org

CHAVURAH

CONGREGATION BETH ISRAEL
of San Diego

ABOUT US   CALENDAR   CONTACTS   EDUCATION   MEMBERSHIP   PROGRAMS   WORSHIP   SITEMAP

Photo: Stuart Simmons

CHAVURAH

Quick Links:
Chavurah "Chappenings" from Mishpacha Chavurah
Kadimah Chavurah Conducts Shabbat Services
The Chavurah Program
Chavurah Application

PROGRAMS
RSVP FORM
ADULT EDUCATION
BEREAVEMENT
BITY & NOAR
CARING COMMUNITY
CEMETERY
CHAVURAH
EMPTY NESTERS
FUNDRAISERS
HUNGER PROJECT
STAND WITH ISRAEL
MEN'S CLUB
OUTREACH TO INTERFAITH
SCHOLAR IN RESIDENCE
SENIORS
SINGLES
SOCIAL ACTION
WOMEN OF BETH ISRAEL
YOUNG ADULTS

Chavurah "Chappenings" from Mishpacha Chavarah

A very long time ago, we dubbed our Chavurah "Mishpacha" indeed the group has become "extended family." From our children's b'nai mitzvot to our children's weddings and grandchildren's births, we qvell and often celebrate together. At the other end of the life cycle, in times of grief, we hug and "do for."

Each month a designated couple hosts our get-together, and that couple is entrusted to create the evening's program. Programs vary widely, including fun and games, Israeli dancing, guest speakers, spirited discussions on current events or spiritual subjects, and an occasional outing. Having honed the art of the potluck dinner, we are, arguably, CBI's best-fed Chavurah.

You can be a part of our Chavurah network. Print and complete a Chavurah Application or contact Bonnie Graff, Program Director at 858-535-1111, ext. 3128.

go to top

Kadimah Chavurah Conducts Shabbat Services

We value spiritual enrichment, social justice, and meaningful Jewish education.
– From Our

Starting in March 2003, Kadimah Chavuraha, began officiating at monthly Friday night Shabbat services at the

Mission Statement

Classic Residence, a senior hi-rise in La Jolla. The chavurah created a wonderful siddur and the service is led by Don Greenberg, Herb Hein and Leta Gold. It started with a small group of residents, but has grown to almost 20 regulars and they are very grateful for CBI's interest in keeping them connected to the Jewish communty.

go to top

Shabbat Chavurah always starts with lunch after Minyan. The Talmud says that food sustains serious students.

Chavurah Shabbat is an Active Group
Chavurah Shabbat meets monthly at one of our member's or members' home for lunch after Shabbat services. Following lunch, we have some kind of Jewishly oriented study and/or discussion program, which is planned by a different member or couple than the lunch host(s), so we spread the responsibilities around.

About 85% of our members also frequently attend the Saturday morning Minyan service, so we see each other most Saturdays and don't have to wait for our monthly Chavurah meeting. The fabric we've woven in our Chavurah has bound us together in wonderful and meaningful ways. We are in many ways an extended family."

Serious study beings, but the food continues. This month's program was a highly competitive game of Jewish Trivial Pursuit.

The Chavurah Program
A chavurah is a small group of up to 20 CBI members who join together to celebrate Jewish life. Through programs of study, observances of holidays and festivals, socializing and sharing of simchas, and participating together

in synagogue life and community concerns, members personalize and vitalize their Jewish experience. We currently have 27 chavurot, some of which have been in existence for 26 years. Applications are available to form a new chavurah or to join an existing one.

Four of Shabbat Chavurah's most serious students, refreshed and ready for the Jewish Trivial Pursuit challenge

The Chavurah Program at Congregation Beth Israel provides a wonderful shared Jewish experience for everyone who participates. It is one of the many ways to enhance your experience as a Temple member. We encourage you to join a Chavurah.

What is a Chavurah?
Chavurah (plural is Chavurot) comes from the Hebrew word, chaver, meaning friend, or fellowship. Each Chavurah is a small group of Temple members who come together to learn, to socialize and to enjoy Jewish living with their families. They study together, worship together, celebrate Jewish holidays together, eat together. For many, the chavurah is an extended family.

2. What Does A Chavurah Do?
The Chavurah celebrates Jewish life. Through programs of study, observances of holidays and festivals, socializing and sharing of simchas, members personalize and vitalize their Jewish experience. They also participate together in Temple life and in community concerns.

A Chavurah provides a unique opportunity for self-growth, involvement, friendship, and for a feeling of true belonging. The programs are self-directed. Responsibility for activities rests with the members of the Chavurah.

3. When And Where Does A Chavurah Meet?
A Chavurah usually meets once a month, in the homes of the members, in rotation. Each group decides on the most convenient dates and times for themselves.

4. How Large Is A Chavurah?
Each group should have approximately twenty people. However, there are no hard and fast rules about the size. Chavurot exist for families and for individuals.

5. How Do I Join A Chavurah?
Print and complete a Chavurah Application. You will be contacted soon afterwards. New Chavurot are formed on the basis of age, children, spheres of interest, etc. You will be placed in a Chavurah

CHAVURAH   Page 4 of 4

just as soon as enough applications are received to form a new group, or if there is an opening in an existing Chavurah which fits your needs.

Contact Program Director Bonnie Graff at 858-535-1111 ext. 3128 if you have any further questions.

go to top

Home | About Us | Calendar | Contacts | Education | Membership | Programs | Worship | Sitemap

Congregation Beth Israel
9001 Towne Centre Drive
San Diego, CA 92122
(858) 535-1111 Fax (858) 535-1130

Dear Congregant:

The Chavurah Program at Congregation Beth Israel provides a wonderful shared Jewish experience for everyone who participates. It is one of the many ways to enhance your experience as a temple member. This letter will provide answers to some frequently asked questions and hopefully encourage you to join a Chavurah.

What is a Chavurah?
Chavurah (plural is *Chavurot*) comes from the Hebrew word *chaver*, meaning friend or fellowship. Each *chavurah* is a small group of temple members who come together to learn, to socialize, and to enjoy Jewish living with their families. They study together, worship together, celebrate Jewish holidays together, and eat together. For many, the *chavurah* is an extended family.

What Does a Chavurah do?
The *chavurah* celebrates Jewish life. Through programs of study, observances of holidays and festivals, socializing and sharing of simchas, members personalize and vitalize their Jewish experience. They also participate together in temple life and in community concerns.

When and Where Does a Chavurah Meet?
A *chavurah* usually meets once a month in the homes of the members, in rotation. Each group decides on the most convenient dates and times for themselves.

How Large is a Chavurah?
Each group should have approximately twenty people. However, there are no hard and fast rules about the size. *Chavurot* exist for families and for individuals.

How Do I Join a Chavurah?
Complete the application on the reverse side and mail it to me at the temple. You will be contacted soon afterwards. New *chavurot* are formed on the basis of age, children, spheres of interest, etc. You will be placed in a *chavurah* just as soon as enough applications are received to form a new group, or if there is an opening in an existing *chavurah* that fits your needs.

If you have any questions or desire additional information, feel free to call me for an appointment. I look forward to hearing from you and meeting you in person.

Sincerely,

Bonnie Graff,
Program Director

CHAVURAH APPLICATION

Participation in a Chavurah is limited to members of Congregation Beth Israel

MEMBER

Mr. Mrs. Ms. Miss Dr.

Last Name:_____

First Name:_____

Birthday: Mo.____Day____Year_____

Residence Address:_____

City, State, Zip:_____

Residence Phone:_____

Occupation:_____

Business Phone:_____

MEMBER

Mr. Mrs. Ms. Miss Dr.

Last Name:_____

First Name:_____

Birthday: Mo.____Day___Year____

E-mail Address(s):_____

Occupation:_____

Business Phone:_____

CHILDREN

Name	Age	Sex	Live at Home? (Y/N)	Name	Age	Sex	Live at Home? (Y/N)
_____				_____			
_____				_____			

1. Describe your Jewish background and interests:

2. Describe your other special interests:

3. Are the ages of other children in the *chavurah* important to you? Explain:

4. Are the ages of other members in the *chavurah* important to you? Explain:

5. What kind of activities would you like to do in a *chavurah*?

6. Describe the kind of people you would like to meet in a *chavurah*.

7. Do you have any other helpful information to assist us in placing you in a *chavurah* that will meet your needs and interests?

Date Submitted: _____

Discussion Triggers:
These topics can be very helpful in getting people to reveal themselves a bit and encouraging discussion of personal values and experience:

- My most memorable Jewish moment (experience, person, book, story . . .)
- A good Jew is one who . . .
- I hope my children remember me as . . .
- What I received as Jewish learning was . . . ; what I am giving my children is . . .
- The Jewish community's (or Israel's) most pressing problem is . . .
- If I could establish a million dollar fund or new institution it would be for . . .

Jewish Identity Icebreaker

Jewish Identity

Step 1 - Ask members of the group to imagine that they had to relocate and the community they are moving to is an island on which they will be the only Jews.

Step 2 - Ask them to think what items they would pack to maintain their Jewish identity, culture, heritage, and observance.

Step 3 - Have participants share their packing list and say why they felt those items were significant in this situation.

Jewish Artifacts I

Step 1 - Ask the participants to bring a personally significant Jewish artifact or object to the meeting.

Step 2 - Have them share the object and its meaning with others in the group.

Jewish Artifacts II

Step 1 - Pass a selected group of artifacts from person to person. Each one touches, smells, etc. Each object as it goes around the circle.

Step 2 - Ask participants to discuss how they felt, what they sensed, and what they remembered.

Jewish Artifacts III

Step 1 - Give each participant one Jewish artifact and then go around the room asking each one to talk about the object.

Step 2 - Put all objects in center and have group discussion.

MEET THE CHAVURAH

- Someone born in the same state or country as you.
- Someone born on the same day as you.
- Someone with two children.
- Someone with grown children.
- Someone with green eyes.
- Someone with the same size shoe as you.
- Someone who has been to Israel.
- Someone who has been a temple member for over 10 years.
- Someone who wears glasses.
- Find someone with the same favorite holiday.
- Someone who has the same favorite color as you.
- The person who lives closest to you.
- Someone who has not been bar/bat mitzvah.

Kehillah: The Caring Community

A congregation is only a community when those who are most frequently left out – new members, intermarried couples, the elderly, and the sick – feel included. The Kehillah Committee works with the clergy and other committees to foster the concept of community, providing social action within the congregation.

Kehillah offers: *Bikkur Cholim* (visiting the sick) providing emotional and spiritual support from fellow congregants in concert with the pastoral support from the clergy • Kehillah Callers, telephone contact by congregants to keep in touch with fellow congregants • Project *Chai*, in cooperation with Jewish Family Services, provides social activities in a Jewish context for young adults with developmental delays • Share your Holidays, a matching program for those who would like to celebrate holiday meals with a family • Contact and Cards, communication with those in our congregation who are not well or have suffered loss, to express condolence and support • Programs featuring experts in the field of physical and emotional support and care.

Outreach: *Bringing Judaism Into Your Life*

This series of programs and classes is designed for those who want to learn more about Judaism, whether they were born Jewish, are considering Judaism, have chosen Judaism, or are raising Jewish children.

We offer: Hebrew *Aleph Bet* 101: Beginning Hebrew . . . and so much more, Sundays, Sept. 12 - Dec. 12 • Hebrew Made Easy, Mondays, Sept. 27- Dec. 13 • My Family & Me, Sundays beginning Oct. 3 • 20+ Ideas to Enhance Your *Shabbat* Celebration, Nov. 20 • *Chanukah* Gifts From Your Kitchen, Nov. 30 • Light Up Your *Chanukah*, Dec. 1 • Basic Judaism, Tuesdays, 15 weeks, beginning Jan. 11 • Outreach to Interfaith *Shabbat*, Mar. 18 • How to Raise a Jewish *Mensch*, Thursdays, Apr. 14, 21, May 5, 12 Primer & Practice Passover, Apr. 13 • Taste of Judaism I: Are You Curious?, Thursdays, May 5, 12, 19 • Got Shabbat (and *Havdalah*)?, May 14

ALEINU: Adult Learners Network

Where there is learning there is wisdom!

Expand your mind and your circle of friends with our *ALEINU* year-long offering of adult learning opportunities. Through the efforts of a tireless committee of volunteers, we are pleased to offer the most comprehensive array of courses available without enrolling in a university.

In addition to our 15-week Basic Judaism course, we offer classes in fields ranging from philosophy, theology and contemporary Jewish thought to biblical study, Jewish creative arts and Hebrew, basic and beyond. Classes are offered weekly and monthly and special speakers and events are offered throughout the year. Classes are scheduled on weekday evenings and Sunday mornings.

To obtain a brochure, call (858) 535-1111, ext. 3128, or pick up a copy in the lobby at the Civic Theatre.

Empty Nesters Social Group

As the Sandwich Generation, we are grandparents, parents and children at the same time. Join our Empty Nesters group consisting of temple members whose children have recently left the nest and who are between the ages of 45 and 60, to *schmooze*, *nosh* and make new friends.

Programs will include: Ice cream Social with Rabbi Paul and Susan Citrin, Nov. 7 • Special Guest Speaker Rabbi Paul Citrin, Jan. 23 • Film Fest & Discussion with Andy Friedenberg, director of the Cinema Society of San Diego and Rabbi Paul Citrin, Apr. 10

Tikkun Olam/Social Action

As part of *K'lal Yisrael* (the entire Jewish community), we support the State of Israel and value our connection to world Jewry. We seek dialogue and joint action with people of other faiths in the hope that together we can bring peace, freedom and justice to our world.

We are dedicated to pursuring *tzedek* (justice) and righteousness and to performing *mitzvot* (commandments), acts which bring us closer to translating the words of the Torah into the work of our hands. We use our individual consciences and collective strengths to help solve social problems wherever they may exist.

We are partners with God in *Tikkun Olam* (repairing the world) through education, advocacy and performing *mtizvot*.

Programs include: Scott Silverman of Second Chance STRIVE will speak • HIPPY (Home Instruction Program for Parents of Preschool Youngsters) Book Drive and HIPPY Reads Week • Breast Cancer 3-Day Walk • Thanksgiving Interfaith Service and Mama's Kitchen Food Collection • Voices for Children Winter Coat Collection • Volunteer for a Volunteer • Martin Luther King Jr. All People's Breakfast • Hunger Project • Mental Health Luncheon with JFS • and more

Chavurah Program

A *chavurah* is a small group of up to twenty CBI members who join together to celebrate Jewish life. Through programs of study, observances of holidays and festivals, socializing and sharing of *simchas*, and participating together in synagogue life and community concerns, members personalize and vitalize their Jewish experience. We currently have 27 *chavurot*, some of which have been in existence for 26 years. Applications are available to form a new *chavurah* or to join an existing one.

Stand With Israel Committee

The Committee's mission is to uphold and strengthen the solidarity of Congregation Beth Israel with the State of Israel and its people. It advocates support of Israel and the involvement of our CBI community through outreach and educational programs, creating and publicizing opportunities to enhance the spiritual, social and financial well being of Israel.

The Committee's goal is to increase awareness of the importance of Israel's existence to our lives and to our shared future by providing a forum for speakers and writers. It actively encourages our congregants to become engaged in the American political arena to maintain a strong relationship between the United States and Israel, a relationship based on the democratic ideals that both nations share. (See the back cover of *Tidings* and the website for a listing of programs and activities.)

Check us out on the web at www.cbisd.org

CONGREGATION BETH ISRAEL
9001 Towne Centre Drive
San Diego, CA 92122

FOR IMMEDIATE RELEASE
Contact: Bonnie Graff, Program Director
(858) 535-1111, ext. 3128

THE SPIRIT OF TIKKUN OLAM IS ALIVE AND WELL AT CBI

On Sunday, March 21, approximately 23 CBI members gathered in the social hall to sort and box all the donations made at the Purim carnival on March 7. Five charities received our donations with the largest recipient being the Hunger project with 80 cartons of sorted clothing, shoes, household items and toys. Other charities were: Mr. Bookman, New Alternatives, Rachel's House and Mama's Kitchen.

Irwin Herman (Mr. Bookman) was terribly appreciative of the donation of 18 cartons of wonderful books and videos that were boxed and delivered to him. *Todah Rabah* to *B'Lishem Chavurah* who coordinated the effort with Robert and Judy Metz handling the collections and supplies and Glenn & Maxine Farber in charge of the sorting and packing operation. The project coordinators were assisted by members of the *Chavurah* and other congregants who helped both in sorting and boxing all the collectibles on two Sunday mornings.

photo caption:

A few of the packing crew admire the Hunger Project bounty. From left: Glenn Farber, Maxine Farber, Audrey Friedman, Anita Hosenpud, Alec Schiller, and Barry Friedman

CONGREGATION BETH ISRAEL
9001 Towne Centre Drive
San Diego, CA 92122

FOR IMMEDIATE RELEASE
Contact: Bonnie Graff, Program Director
(858) 535-1111, ext. 3128

MITZVAH MAKERS AT CONGREGATION BETH ISRAEL

Starting in March 2003, *Kadimah Chavurah* began officiating at monthly Friday night Shabbat services at the Classic Residence, a senior hi-rise in La Jolla. The chavurah created a wonderful *siddur* and the service is led alternately by Don Greenberg, Herb Hein and Leta Gold. It started with a small group of residents, but has grown to almost 20 regulars and they are very grateful for CBI's interest in keeping them connected to the Jewish community.

Achim Men's Group

Congregation:	Temple Isaiah
Address:	55 Lincoln Street Lexington, MA 02421
Phone Number:	(781) 862-7160
Contact's Name and E-mail:	Mitch Tyson, mitch@tyson.net
Number of Member Units:	800
URJ Region:	Northeast Council
Rabbi:	Howard Jaffe

Brief description: The Achim Group is a men's spiritual group that encourages the men of our congregation to get together to worship, study, get to know each other better, and discuss the issues important to us as men. We use Jewish texts as a jumping-off point for sharing our life experiences and to talk about the issues we face. The events we hold include an annual weekend retreat, Sunday morning *kallot*, and occasional dinners. Topics in 2002 included "The Roles Men Play in Life" (as sons, fathers, spouses, etc.), "The Stages in a Man's Life," and "Finding Courage in Our Lives" (to make the right personal and career decisions).

Program Goal: Provide an opportunity for men to get together in order to nurture our spirituality, build friendships, strengthen our ties to Judaism, and create an opportunity for more male members to get involved in the life of our temple.

Target Population: All men in our temple.

Number of Participants: Approximately fifty have signed up and have participated in one or more of our activities.

Number and Length of Session(s): The annual Men's Weekend Away runs from Friday night to Sunday noon, *kallah* events run about four hours on Sunday morning, and occasional dinners last about two and a half hours.

Staffing Required: The rabbi runs several of the study sessions. The services, mixers, and logistics are done by volunteers.

Total Cost of Program: The weekend costs approximately $6,000; the *kallot* cost between $100 and $1,000, depending on whether we have an outside speaker.

Source of Funding: The program is funded by the participants.

Fee for Attendees: Per attendee the weekend costs approximately $300, each *kallah* is $20 to $30, and the dinners $15 to $20. We have offered discounted fees to those who cannot afford to pay the full amount.

Logistics: We form planning committees for each event. The committee arranges the room, the restaurant, or the retreat location; selects the theme and the speaker/facilitators; and solicits participants and collects the money.

Instructions to Facilitator: The facilitators are encouraged to start with material that the men can identify with and relate to in their lives. Once people start sharing their experiences, asking the group for advice, or sharing problems they are facing, we encourage the facilitator to step back and let the group proceed on its own.

Evaluation of Program: After each program we send out an e-mail asking for feedback. We get a lot of comments back about how much participants enjoy it and look forward to it. We also get feedback that the programs trigger a reassessment of relationships or career choices. Everyone is always surprised and gratified to find out how much we have in common and that we are all struggling with the same issues.

Follow-up: After each event we look for volunteers to plan the next event. Our last dinner on the topic of interfaith relationships drew more than forty-five people, many participating for the first time. We are currently planning a June *kallah* on Jewish ethics and next year's annual Weekend Away will be on the topic of listening.

We're Looking for a Few Good (and Thoughtful) Men!

Please join us for the first Temple Isaiah "Men's Weekend Away," Friday, November 1–Sunday November 3.

Join Rabbi Gropper, Rabbi Jaffe, and a group of Temple Isaiah men at the Warren Conference Center and Inn in Ashland, MA, a 45-minute drive from Lexington, for a weekend of discussion, Torah study, worship, camaraderie, and outdoor activity.

We will be exploring how we might balance our roles as Jewish husbands, fathers, sons, workers, members of communities, and see if in the process we can find ourselves!

The weekend begins in Ashland at 5 P.M. on Friday, November 1, and ends by noon on Sunday, November 3. The cost for this event is approximately $325 and includes housing and all meals.

Participation will be limited to the first 32 persons who sign up by completing and returning the attached registration form. A commitment to participate in the full program is required (no "drop ins" please).

For questions or more details, please call or e-mail Mitch Tyson at 781-862-6065 or mgtyson@att.net, or any other member of the planning committee: Bruce Lynn, Daniel Sheff, David Smerling, or Danny Watt.

Registration Form for Men's Weekend Away (Please Print)

Please fill out completely and mail with your check for $325 made out to Temple Isaiah with a note saying that it is for the Men's Weekend Away,

Temple Isaiah, 55 Lincoln Street, Lexington, MA 02141.

Name:

Address:

Telephone:

E-mail:

Willing to drive carpool from Lexington to Ashland and back?　　　　_____

Would like a ride from Lexington to Ashland and back?　　　　_____

Would like to join "planning committee," please call me.　　　　_____

Please describe any dietary restrictions:

A package of logistical details, including an agenda for the weekend and "homework assignment," will be sent prior to the event.

Session I: Introductory Session

Men's Retreat 2002—Rabbi Daniel Gropper

Welcome:
1. Who are we (make a list)—fathers, sons, husbands, unemployed, etc.
2. Share our pies (we are all of these yet we are very different).
3. Text: I'm searching for my brothers.
4. What are we doing here? Reading from Salkin.

Genesis 37: 12-16

One time, when his brothers had gone to pasture their father's flock at Shechem, Israel said to Joseph, "Your brothers are pasturing at Shechem. Come, I will send you to them." He answered, "I am ready." And he said to him, "Go and see how your brothers are and how the flocks are faring, and bring me back word." So he sent him from the valley of Hebron.
When he reached Shechem, a man came upon him wandering in the fields. The man asked him, "What are you looking for?" He answered, "I am looking for my brothers. Could you tell me where they are?

Resources:
Salkin, Rabbi Jeffrey K. (1999) *Searching for My Brothers: Jewish Men in a Gentile World.* New York: Putnam Publishing Group, pgs. 6, 7, 9.

Session II: Our Roles as Workers

Time: 1 hour

Opening Thoughts: Acknowledge that we are all in different stages as workers: self-employed, employees, employers, unemployed, and retired. What is common is a cultural emphasis on work. Our task is to examine how and where we can find meaning in that work.

Goals:
To explore what Judaism teaches about work
To understand how we are to work
To discuss if we should strive for more balance and if so, then how

I. Set Induction
1. Pass out copy of *mein yingele*—share responses
2. Take Workaholics Anonymous Test:

How Do I Know If I'm a Workaholic?

1. Do you get more excited about your work than about family or anything else?
2. Are there times when you can charge through your work and other times when you can't?
3. Do you take work with you to bed? on weekends? on vacation?
4. Is work the activity you like to do best and talk about most?
5. Do you work more than 40 hours a week?
6. Do you turn your hobbies into money-making ventures?
7. Do you take complete responsibility for the outcome of your work efforts?
8. Have your family or friends given up expecting you on time?
9. Do you take on extra work because you are concerned that it won't otherwise get done?
10. Do you underestimate how long a project will take and then rush to complete it?
11. Do you believe that it is okay to work long hours if you love what you are doing?
12. Do you get impatient with people who have other priorities besides work?
13. Are you afraid that if you don't work hard you will lose your job or be a failure?
14. Is the future a constant worry for you even when things are going very well?
15. Do you do things energetically and competitively, including play?
16. Do you get irritated when people ask you to stop doing your work in order to do something else?
17. Have your long hours hurt your family or other relationships?
18. Do you think about your work while driving, falling asleep, or when others are talking?
19. Do you work or read during meals?
20. Do you believe that more money will solve the other problems in your life?

How did we do?

What is a Jewish response?

Work is essential to our lives. Work also provides an essential arena in which to live a life of Torah, ethics, and caring. Yet work is only a part of life, not the whole thing. To be a workaholic means to be an *oveid avodah zarah*, "an idol worshiper." It is to place acquisition of money, possessions, fame, or power above all else. But there is only one thing that is above all else, the Holy One who asks us to be partners in creation. We are to spend our week working at creating like God. Work has a sacred weekly limit, Shabbat, which was created to remind us not to lose perspective.

Blu Greenberg's poem: "Six Days Shall You be a Workaholic"

These tell us that we should work, why we should work, and even when we should work. But they don't tell us how we should work.

II. Viewing work as a spiritual practice (choice text study in small groups)
(Copy texts individually and place in large envelopes with questions. Paste text without question to outside of envelope. Let people mill and read and select the text they want to discuss.)

3 Texts:

Be satisfied with who you are and what you do.
A favorite saying of the Rabbis of Yavneh was: I am God's creature and my fellow is God's creature. My work is in the town and his work is in the country. I rise early for my work and he rises early for his work. Just as he does not presume to do my work, so I do not presume to do his work. Will you say, I do much and he does little? We have learned: One may do much or one may do little; it is all one, provided he directs his heart to heaven.

- What do you think this text is trying to convey?
- How can you feel satisfied with who you are and what you do when your neighbor seems to have so much more?

All of work is prayer and a way of coming closer to God.
Rabbi Yitzhak of Vorki told of how once he was together with his master, Rabbi David of Levov, at sunrise. The Rebbe was enrobed in a *tallit* and crowned in *tefillin*, ready to pray the Morning Prayer, when a gentile came in, pounded on the table and asked that he sell him a quantity of liquor. (His house was also an inn.) There was no one else in the house to sell it to him, so the Rebbe himself went with alacrity, measured it out himself, and put it before the man. (When asked about why he left his prayer preparation to do business,) the Rebbe explained to him softly, "Listen to me, my sweet friend. My path in the service of God is 'Know God in all your ways.' . . . So when I went to measure out the liquor, my whole intention was to fulfill the Torah's mitzvah about honest measures and to give pleasure to God by this; and that is why I happily ran to do it with such haste." [*Kodesh Hillulim*, pp. 150-151]

- What is the true meaning and purpose of our work? Why do we do it?
- How can we view it as such?

What's it really all about?
Rava said: When they escort people to their Heavenly tribunal after their death, the tribunal asks: "Did you conduct your business transactions faithfully? [only then are you asked] Did you set aside fixed times for Torah study? [Talmud, *Shabbat* 31a]

- How would you answer this if you were asked it today?
- If you answered in the affirmative to part 1, what about to part 2? How could you change this?

Practice
Before you go to work, have a time of preparation to make yourself ready to be careful about all forbidden things and ready to fulfill God's warning, and not transgress, God forbid, such things as theft and robbery, fraud, lying, cheating, false weights and measures.

After eating the midday meal, and before you go back to work, prepare yourself again as you did in the morning, going over in your mind the various things to avoid. And happy are you if you fulfill all this. [R. Hayyim Yosef David Azulai, *Avodat hakodesh*, Moreh b'Etzba 3-97 and 3-122]

Individual Exercise: Write a personal prayer that you can say each morning before you begin your workday, and each evening as you are about to leave for home.

Session III: Our Roles as Fathers

Time: 1.5 hours

Goals:
For participants to consider their own obligations as fathers
To view how Judaism views the role and obligations of a father
To explore Jewish biblical narratives with an eye to the father-son relationships explored within

Set Induction:
Ask participants to think for a few minutes about their children and their roles as father.
Ask them to share the roles that they have as father (list on board).

Hand out Jewish texts that describe the role and obligations of a parent.

Kiddushin 29a: "Our Rabbis taught: The father is bound in respect of his son, to circumcise, redeem, teach him Torah, take a wife for him, and teach him a craft. Some say, to teach him to swim too."

Discuss:
In what ways did your father do this for you?
In what ways do you do this for your children?

Read Akeidat Yizhak together:

Large group questions:
1. What do we (or don't we) learn about parenting from these texts?
2. Imagine you are Abraham, how might you have handled this situation differently?

Bibliodrama: We are going to make midrash by becoming some of these characters and adding our voices to theirs. In small groups, I am going to ask you to become either Abraham, Isaac, or one of the servants. What is important is that you speak in character but that you speak as yourself in the present. You know your past but not your future.

1. Set the scene
   a. Get into groups of three—Abraham, Yitzchak, One of the servants.
   b. Triangle chairs: actor, director, observer
      Text: "And Abraham said to his young men, Stay here with the ass; and I and the lad will go yonder and worship, and come back to you. 6. And Abraham took the wood of the burnt offering, and laid it upon Isaac his son; and he took the fire in his hand, and a knife; and they went both of them together."

   And Abraham, what are you thinking?
   And Isaac, what are you thinking?
   And Mr. Servant, what are you making of this entire scene?

   Switch

   Write two to three sentences as your character expressing what you have learned about yourself.

Share with the entire group: hear from the Abrahams, the Isaacs, and the servants.

The Akeida—Genesis Chapter 22

1. And it came to pass after these things, that God tested Abraham, and said to him, Abraham; and he said, Behold, here I am. 2. And he said, Take now your son, your only son Isaac, whom you love, and go to the land of Moriah; and offer him there for a burnt offering upon one of the mountains which I will tell you. 3. And Abraham rose up early in the morning, and saddled his ass, and took two of his young men with him, and Isaac his son, and broke the wood for the burnt offering, and rose up, and went to the place of which God had told him. 4. Then on the third day Abraham lifted up his eyes, and saw the place far away. 5. And Abraham said to his young men, Stay here with the ass; and I and the lad will go yonder and worship, and come back to you. 6. And Abraham took the wood of the burnt offering, and laid it upon Isaac his son; and he took the fire in his hand, and a knife; and they went both of them together. 7. And Isaac spoke to Abraham his father, and said, My father; and he said, Here am I, my son. And he said, Behold the fire and the wood; but where is the lamb for a burnt offering? 8. And Abraham said, My son, God will provide himself a lamb for a burnt offering; so they went both of them together. 9. And they came to the place which God had told him; and Abraham built an altar there, and laid the wood in order, and bound Isaac his son, and laid him on the altar upon the wood. 10. And Abraham stretched out his hand, and took the knife to slay his son. 11. And the angel of Adonai called to him from heaven, and said, Abraham, Abraham; and he said, Here am I. 12. And he said, Lay not your hand upon the lad, nor do anything to him; for now I know that you fear God, seeing that you did not withhold your son, your only son from me. 13. And Abraham lifted up his eyes, and looked, and behold behind him a ram caught in a thicket by his horns; and Abraham went and took the ram, and offered him up for a burnt offering in place of his son. 14. And Abraham called the name of that place Adonai-Yireh; as it is said to this day, In the Mount of Adonai it shall be seen. 15 The angel of the Lord called to Abraham a second time from heaven, 16 and said, "By Myself I swear, Adonai declares: Because you have done this and have not withheld your son, your favored one, 17 I will bestow My blessing upon you and make your descendants as numerous as the stars of heaven and the sands on the seashore; and your descendants shall seize the gates of their foes. 18 All the nations of the earth shall bless themselves by your descendants, because you have obeyed My command." 19 Abraham then returned to his servants, and they departed together for Beer-sheba; and Abraham stayed in Beer-sheba.

Small Group Questions:

1. Do you, in any way, see yourself (as a father or as a son), reflected in the Akeida text? If so, how? If not, why not?
   a. How do you respond to this text as a father?
   b. How do you respond to this text as a son?
2. Can you think of a time in your life when you might have treated your child(ren) in a similar way to how Abraham treated Isaac? Do you feel that you may have, in some way, sacrificed your child? For what?
3. If you could rewrite the past, what, if anything, might you have done differently as a parent? What do you wish your father did differently with you? Can you change the past?

Gather to share discoveries with the large group.

As a Large Group:

A final thought: From Rabbi Norman Cohen, *Voices From Genesis*

Commenting on the Akeida—Genesis 22
At the denouement of the episode, Isaac was awakened to the fragility of life and to his father's true nature. He was no longer the naïve young person who thought that his father could do no wrong and in whom Isaac had total confidence, assuming that his judgment and his ability to protect his son were impeccable. He now saw Abraham as a human being, with the same frailties as every other person. In discovering his father's humanness, he discovered himself. This was a powerful moment of maturation for Isaac, as it is for every young adult who witnesses his or her parents' frailty for the first time. Isaac would never be the same. The mark of this experience would remain with him throughout his entire life. What he had seen and felt would shape his whole being.

The Isaac who ascended Mount Moriah with his father did not come down from the mountain. A more mature, wiser Isaac descended in his place—one who, having experienced a near-death trauma at the hand of his father, was no longer umbilically connected to him. Isaac had become an individual in his own right.

1. How did you feel when you discovered your father's frailties? How did you respond?
2. Have your children discovered your own frailties? If so, how did they respond? How did you respond? If not, what sort of thoughts have you had about this impending moment for your child?
3. When our children discover our frailties do our obligations as fathers change? If so, how?

Activity: Write a letter to your child(ren) explaining why you made the choices that you made when you and they were younger. Or alternatively, write a letter to your father telling him some of the things you wish he had done for you.

Saturday Evening Session: Stories of Our Elders

This would probably work best as a fireside chat format:

- Pass out index cards to all the participants. Have them write a question they would like to ask a man who is older than they: something they always wanted to ask their father or an older man (or if their father is deceased, something they wish they had asked).
- Ask two to three older members of the community to attend the retreat. Ask them in advance to prepare some introductory thoughts on who they are and one or two things they have learned or gleaned from life.
- Have a moderator (rabbi) ask the senior members the questions and see where it goes.

Final Session (Sunday Morning)

Our role as ourselves: How do we put the "I" back in the Pie?

Adam I vs. Adam II

Goals:
To have participants take some of what they learned and apply it to their own lives
To consider how they might re-balance their own lives

Activity One: Meditation to get rid of the stuff we want to get rid of.

Activity Two: Small groups
1. Take out the pie graph that people made to come here.
2. Assuming that you can't change anything here, brainstorm simple ways (some might do some things already) to put the fullness of yourself into each part of the pie AND how might you take your ego out of a situation *(bitul ha'neshamah)* to allow the event to be in you instead of you being in the event.

Adam I & Adam II—Rav. Joseph Soloveitchik

Adam I: sees the world as an object to be mastered:

Text:
God (Elohim) blessed them and God said to them, "Be fertile and increase, fill the earth and master it; and rule the fish of the sea, the birds of the sky, and all the living things that creep on earth." God said, "See, I give you every seed bearing plant that is upon all the earth, and every tree that has seed-bearing fruit; they shall be yours for food."

1. According to this text, what is the role of human beings?
2. What does this do for our self-esteem? What is the problem with that? What does it do to our relationships?

Adam II: From Genesis, Chapter 2

Adonai (YHWH) God formed man from the dust of the earth. God blew into his nostrils the breath of life, and man became a living being.

Adonai God planted a garden in Eden, in the east, and placed there the man whom God had formed. Adonai God took the man and placed him in the garden of Eden, to till it and tend it.

Adonai God said, "It is not good for man to be alone;
Adonai God called out to the man and said to him, "Where are you?"

"The world is not an object to be controlled, but a reality to be experienced with a sense of wonderment, puzzlement, and surprise. It is the qualitative framework of being, rather than the functional question, that Adam the second brings to nature.... Human dignity is now seen in the quest for purpose, meaning, and relationship....

In seeking to discover purpose and significance, one likewise seeks a God who can address the human being and provide a frame of reference for total dedication and passion of love. One is not satisfied with knowing Elohim, the impersonal God of the cosmos; one seeks a God who has a personal name, YHWH.

What you bring to the relationship is not a common goal to master helplessness and to achieve dignity. Rather, you bring a quest to overcome loneliness, to achieve friendship, or, to use theological language, to achieve redemption. (Redemption in this context is not an otherworldly yearning to be liberated from the body, but a desire to overcome the sense of loneliness that haunts those who experience their own uniqueness and singularity.)

From: David Hartman, *Love and Terror in the God Encounter: The Theological Legacy of Rabbi Joseph Soloveitchik,* pp. 106–108

How do we move from being Adam I to becoming Adam II?

End: Find a partner to talk to in the weeks ahead.

Meditation for Finding the True Self Within

To use after progressive relaxation

You are now ready to go deeper within—entering into a place of deep knowingness—the true source of your awareness and knowingness.

(Deepening script follows)

Reaching the inner self deepening

I'm going to count from ten down to one now, and as I do, you will actually feel yourself going within—into the very core of your awareness.

Ten—Releasing and relaxing more with each breath

Nine—Moving deeper; turning to your inner self

Eight—Moving into who it is that you are

Seven—Softly , gently moving down inside yourself

Six—Going into your inner essence—whatever you sense that to be

Five—Moving down into your place of wisdom

Four—Beginning to sense the core of your own wisdom—the wisdom that brought you here because on a deeper level your knowingness tells you that giving birth gently and easily is your birthright—to trust in yourself and in your body

Three—Moving to the place where your knowingness will reveal to you the determination, the strength, the confidence, the wisdom, and the trust that you seek to gently and easily bring your baby into the world

Two—Now at the level of your inner being

One—You are now at one with your inner being and have reached your own special place of power. That power that's been within you always—it's your birthright, claim it now and make it yours again You are now ready to go deeper into your own place of wisdom and the true source of your own awareness and knowingness.

Fear release script
(This script should be preceded by reaching the inner self induction)
And now that you are so thoroughly relaxed, take yourself in your mind's eye to a wonderful healing room at the very core of your subconscious. This is a beautiful room of soft blues and greens. As you look around the room, you see a large cushy chair. Sit in this chair and make yourself comfortable. By

your side is a large white book. This book is the history of your life and your beliefs as they are recorded in your innermost mind. It's a lovely book, but some of the pages of the book contain images and experiences that may have planted seeds of doubt or fear in your mind regarding your role as a father, as a son, as a worker, as a lover or as a member of the Jewish and global community. Some of these pages hold images of experiences, stories, relationships, fears that may linger from things your parents have said, movies you've seen, conversations you've had, literature you've read, and even comments that well-intentioned friends are passing on to you now.

To protect you from any emotion that you may see . . . so that you can observe the scene as though you were simply an onlooker, there is a large sheet of plexiglass between you and the book. What images you recall, you will witness without feeling any deep emotion that may have surrounded the event.

See yourself now, opening the book. Take your time; search through the pages of the book one by one. When your subconscious reveals a picture that depicts a fear or a concern that you may have, any limiting thoughts about work or parenting or partnering that portrays those parts of your life in a negative way—a comment, experience, or whatever—pause and study that page. See it for what it is . . . study the thoughts that are looming on that page . . . bring them up. Make them larger. See how they colored your thinking . . . now, quickly, take all of the color out of that image. Let it turn to gray . . . getting lighter . . . fainter . . . fuzzy . . . smaller . . . and now the picture seems to be disappearing right into the surface of the page. Now all you can see is the beautiful texture of the paper. The page is absorbing all of the emotion surrounding the hurtful image . . . like a sponge, the texture is drawing away all of the negative emotion. Now as you look, all you can see is the beautiful, clear texture of the page.

That page no longer belongs in the book of your life or your thoughts. (Rip the page right out of your book. Tear it out; crumple it up as tightly as you can; and now put it aside. Continue to search through your book.) Maybe there are other memories in your life that you may want to eliminate. Here is your chance. Any event, person, experience that you want to release, find it. Each time you come to a page that contains some image that you want to release, continue to do as you did before. Let the image come up, and watch it fade and disappear into the page. You can move right along. Your subconscious works quickly.

Keep searching . . . take your time. Continue the process.

Continue to search and identify those pictures that could create tension or fear—questions surrounding the roles you play in your life.

(Repeat softly some of the sources of fear—comments, experiences, etc.)

Now prepare to bring your work to an end . . . don't worry . . . if there are still more images, we can go back and pick them up at another time.

Now that you've ripped the negative pages from your book . . . you're ready to move on. Now, gather all the little wads of crumpled paper together . . . all those pages that carry the emotions and fears you've released . . . in your mind's eye now, place those pages into a disposable tote bag. Stash them into that bag with all your might. Push them down into the bag.

You become aware that to your right there is a cabinet in the wall...a cabinet that's sort of like a kitchen cabinet. Open the cabinet and throw the bag into it. But now you see that this cabinet has no shelves. Instead, there is a long chute, similar to a laundry chute. Watch as the bag goes down...down...down...down...and now it's landing in a huge incinerator. Watch as the flames completely envelop the bag. It's difficult to see the outline of the bag now. It's all turning into gray ash. The bag has disappeared. Now watch as the flames engulf each of your wads of paper. Their shape is disappearing...the emotions and fears are being destroyed. First red flame, then black, and now everything is just flat, gray ash. Becoming fuzzy, so fuzzy that you can hardly see anything but flat gray ash.

Now the chute is turning into a wind tunnel, and it's blowing the small, minute pieces of ash out over the landscape of your mind. Watch then go up, up, up and out over the landscape of your mind...they are getting lighter and lighter now...fuzzier and fuzzier...and now you can hardly see them at all. Now they are gone...they have fallen over the horizon. The emotions attached to those negative thoughts and events have been completely destroyed. They are gone from the landscape of your mind. Gone forever. You feel so calm and free.

And now I'd like you to see yourself returning to your chair and your book. Take the book again and open to the middle of the book.

What a wonderful scene! Look—it's you and you look wonderful. You look radiant. You feel on top of the world. Your eyes are sparkling, and there's a beautiful light all around you. You look so relaxed, refreshed, and happy. Your work life, your family life, your own life are very fulfilled. You are so elated. See yourself in your favorite colors. Let those colors and that scene come up big. This is one picture that we are not going to release and destroy. We're going to save this and think on it many times. From now throughout your life you will be able to return to this scene as a place of calm and serenity. Enjoy this scene.

Now that your success is so large, it's lifelike. See yourself in your mind's eye, getting up from your soft cushy chair and stepping right into that wonderful scene. Step into that page. This is no longer a picture. It's you standing in this body. There is but one body, now. The body of success. Feel it; sense it; let the feelings of happiness permeate your entire body. Feel your arms wrapped around this new feeling.

And now I'd like you to take just a moment to choose in your mind just what you will experience through your life. Will it be tightness? Pressure? Stress? Discomfort? Or will it be joy, serenity, relaxation, fulfillment, contentment and peace? It's your choice. Choose now. (Pause.)

I'm going to count from one up to five now, and at the count of five, you will come back to the room, feeling refreshed, alert, and assured, filled with a new sense of excitement, confidence, and trust in your body and nature's way of birthing. One...two...three...feeling the energy beginning to return.

Finding Meaning in Our Work

Here are five simple things we can do on a regular basis, at home and at work.

First, get a life. We know the expression, all work and no play makes Jack a dull boy. It's true. Some of the most relaxed and fulfilled people I know are those who do as much out of work as at work. They exercise, they travel, they study, they cook. They explore life and its endless variety. Most importantly, they don't define themselves by their careers. If you ask an American what he does, you'll generally get an occupation as a response. Ask an Israeli the same question and the response will be a quizzical look. "What do I do? I hike, I spend time with friends, I cook, I travel." "Yes, but what do you do for work?" "For work? I work." Want to make work meaningful? Begin by making life meaningful.

Second, discover Shabbat as a potential for real rest. One of the greatest advancements we as a people brought to the world is the notion of rest. Not only rest for Jews but for every person and animal in the community. Just as we rest, so too must everyone and everything that works for us. Unfortunately, the notion of Shabbat is synonymous with restriction, not relaxation. Begin to define Shabbat for yourself. Perhaps it's a day without e-mail or television. Perhaps it's one day where you hide your wallet.

Third, pray daily. I'm not talking about a daily minyan where we stand wrapped in *talit* and *t'filin* (but it wouldn't hurt). I'm talking about spending a few moments every day reflecting on who we are, where we have been, and where we are going. I'm talking about saying a little prayer thanking God for giving us bodies that work and the strength to persevere. At the very least before checking our voicemail and e-mail we can say, "Dear God, give me the strength and the wisdom to think clear thoughts, to make wise decisions, and to speak compassionately to all."

Fourth, give back. We are the most affluent and the best-educated Jewish community, ever. If we work only to benefit ourselves, what worth does our work have? When we give generously of our funds to help projects, when we use our valuable time to make a difference, the work we do might become more fulfilling.

Finally, remember who you work for. When the king of Israel came to sit on his throne, a courtier would say to him, "*Da lifenei mi atah yoshev*—know before whom you sit" (*Esther Rabbah 1*). When our ark is opened to display the Torah Scrolls, the words above read, *Da lifnei mi atah omed*, know before whom you stand. When we start our day, it might be beneficial to ask, just as the watchman asked the Rebbe, "*Da lifnei mi atah oved*, know before whom you work."

E-mail Traffic the Week
after the 2002 Men's Weekend Away

Friends,

Thank you all for an incredible weekend. There is so much to process. It's hard to transition back. But my wife and kids are very eager to know what it was like and I am eager to start some new dialogues with them. I also put in a call to my father and left a message for him to call me back.

We will schedule another planning session to examine ways of following up. When we have a date I will e-mail everyone. Everyone is invited to participate. If you can't make it, e-mail your ideas and suggestions.

I've attached the final list of attendees. The "Reply All" button should start the dialogue!

I also found it was an incredible weekend. It would also be interesting to see if people want to find a way to continue the discussions and the process without waiting 12 months for another big weekend event. Would monthly evening sessions (dinners? breakfasts?) be of interest to allow us to continue to talk?

Morning coffee, the Boston Globe, and this e-mail. What a way to start my Monday! I'm refreshed, invigorated, and committed to maintaining the new sense of self and center that you all helped me regain this weekend. Thank you all! I hope that we'll find a way to get together on a regular basis as a large or small group to keep up the momentum of what we started.

Have a great week and remember to hold tight to that grain of sand as the tidal wave washes over you.

Amen and Amen. As we spent more time together, I began to understand why so much of our liturgy uses masculine language. While I am the first to argue for gender sensitivity, I appreciate that if the authors of this liturgy were male, they used language that made sense for them. Therefore, Avinu Malkeinu (Our Father, Our King) makes sense.

I also called my dad. Thanks again to everyone who made this weekend so wonderful. It is because we were all truly present with one another that we were able to make it work. Just knowing you are all there and available makes life that much more calm.

Mah Tov Helkeinu, how great is our portion! L'Shalom

MWA Achim –

My wife just reminded me that we should be careful to avoid being exclusionary with our newly discovered "achim group"—that we should be sure to keep the door wide open to anyone who for one reason or another was not able to join us last weekend, or who would like to join in the experience that we now share.

I think that there's an important pitfall we want to avoid here—the tendency toward clique perception of the small group within a larger community.

Is there a way to do that without diluting the intensity of our newly found closeness?

L'chaim!

Achim (Brothers),

It's hard to believe that it has been only a week since our Weekend. The flow of e-mails has been fantastic and certainly indicates that it was no ordinary weekend. Whether we've made any actual changes in our lives it seems that many of us view some things about our lives differently and we have definitely started a new dialog and created new bonds among 24 men. And I think we also have found a way to share our energies and draw energy from the group.

It is a journey that we want to continue to take together. There have been many good ideas on how to continue what we have started. There have also been some discussion about how to involve others. In that spirit, we have set up a meeting on Tuesday, November 19th at 8:00 at the Temple to discuss next steps. Everyone is invited. If you can't make it please send out an email with any ideas you may have.

Achim,

While some of the group were out of town or ill we still got 16 of us together tonight to discuss the next steps. We saw the future with the following activities:

Fall weekend – We'll start planning this in the spring

Kallah/Program – This will be a day or half day program on a Sunday similar to our weekend but shorter. XXXXX will start planning for this program to be held in the March timeframe.

Dinner – This will be on a weekday night (probably Wednesday or Thursday) at a Chinese restaurant with a private room, nearby to Lexington. The planning group will develop a short program that includes some study (maybe prereading) and discussion, as well as just social interaction. The first dinner will be in January and the planning group will be XXXXX.

Coffees - These would be impromptu. Anyone can send an e-mail, pick a day and time, and pick a Starbucks or equivalent place.

The two planning groups will preannounce their meetings and anyone is welcome to join them in the planning and preparation for these fellow-on events.

We spent some time talking about the issue of opening our group to others. We agreed that events will be open to all Temple men. We will set limits on the number of participants where appropriate and accept the first applications to come in. We will describe the event, the topics, and set the expectation that participants will be expected to share themselves. In this way we will be open to the entire community but we will rely on a self-selection process to ensure that we can maintain the high level of spirituality and sharing that we had in the first event.

Thanks to everyone who participated and thanks to everyone who forwarded suggestions prior to the meeting. It felt good to be together again even though we were just planning and not studying, worshipping, or sharing. But I think we've established a framework to continue the wonderful connections we established at the Warren Center.

2003—Achim Group to Meet for Dinner Program

The November Men's Weekend Away was such a fulfilling experience for those who attended that its participants have organized themselves as the Achim Group, with the objective of providing similar men's study, worship, and sharing activities throughout the year. The first of these ongoing sessions will be a dinner program on Wednesday, January 22 at 7 P.M. It will be held in conjunction with an informal dinner at a Chinese restaurant in the area. Participants will be provided with a reading on the program theme, "Defining Moments in Becoming a Man," in advance of the session. The group is open to all men who are interested in participating in such activities on an ongoing basis, even if they were unable to attend the Weekend Away, but attendance at this dinner will be limited by the restaurant room capacity, so those interested in attending should call or e-mail Steve Deutsch (781-863-2044; jsedeutsch@rcn.com) in advance.

Achim Kallah 2003
March 16, 2003

The God of My Father

I. God as Father (God, no matter what we do with language is gendered. The question is, how do we portray that gender? As Jeff Salkin writes, "When your daughter stubs her toes, she does not run into the house yelling, 'Parent! Parent!'"

Read Mary Daly quote: "If God in his heaven is a father ruling his people, then it is the nature of things and according to the divine play and the order of the universe that society be male-dominated."

Ken Woodward (It's hard to be a father):

"These are tough times to be a father. The media are full of stories about abusive fathers, fatherless children, and deadbeat dads – and about New Fathers who are trying to do better. But in general this is an age when fathers get little respect, and you don't have to look farther than the biggest father figure of them all, God. Few theologians these days seem to want a God who takes charge, assumes responsibility, fights for his children, makes demands, risks rebuffs, punishes as well as forgives. In a word, a father."

    a. Prayers: (don't do here. Save for later)
       i. Avinu Malkeinu
      ii. Anim Zmirot
         1. How do these prayers portray God?

How does a fatherly image of God teach men about fatherhood?
1. Jewish God is not oppressive.
2. God is firm and fair, active when necessary, and compassionate when desirable. The Jewish God is a creative combination of distance and intimacy, of the urge to love and the need to control.

Exodus 34:4: *Adonai, Adonai,* a God compassionate and gracious, slow to anger, abounding in kindness and faithfulness, extending kindness to the thousandth generation, forgiving iniquity, transgression and sin; yet He does not remit all punishment.

3. God can be wrong—and loves it (Baba Metzia 59b)
    a. It has been taught: On that day R. Eliezer brought forward every imaginable argument, but they did not accept them. Said he to them: "If the halachah agrees with me, let this carob-tree prove it!" Thereupon the carob-tree was torn a hundred cubits out of its place—others affirm, four hundred cubits. "No proof can be brought from a carob-tree," they retorted. Again he said to them: "If the halachah agrees with me, let the stream of water prove it!"

Whereupon the stream of water flowed backwards—"No proof can be brought from a stream of water," they rejoined. Again he urged: "If the halachah agrees with me, let the walls of the schoolhouse prove it," whereupon the walls inclined to fall. But R. Joshua rebuked them, saying: "When scholars are engaged in a halachic dispute, what have ye to interfere?" Hence they did not fall, in honour of R. Joshua, nor did they resume the upright, in honour of R. Eliezer; and they are still standing thus inclined. Again he said to them: "If the halachah agrees with me, let it be proved from Heaven!" Whereupon a Heavenly Voice cried out: "Why do ye dispute with R. Eliezer, seeing that in all matters the halachah agrees with him!" But R. Joshua arose and exclaimed: "It is not in heaven." What did he mean by this?— Said R. Jeremiah: That the Torah had already been given at Mount Sinai; we pay no attention to a Heavenly Voice, because Thou hast long since written in the Torah at Mount Sinai, After the majority must one incline. R. Nathan met Elijah and asked him: What did the Holy One, Blessed be He, do in that hour?—He laughed [with joy], he replied, saying, "My sons have defeated Me, My sons have defeated Me."

4. God Weeps

   God said: "So long as I am within the Holy Temple, the peoples of the world will be unable to touch it. However, I will shut My eyes and swear that I will have nothing to do with it again till the messianic end of time. Meanwhile, let the enemies (the Romans) come and devastate it." At once the Romans entered the Temple and burned it. After it was burned, the Holy One said: "I have no dwelling place in the Land of Israel. So I shall remove My Presence from it and go up to My former residence [the heavens]."

   God wept and said: "Woe is Me! For Israel's sake I caused My Presence to dwell below. But now that Israel sinned and I am returning to My former place, I have, Heaven forbid, become a laughingstock of the nations, an object of derision for mortals."

   In that instant, the angel Metatron came, fell upon his face, and spoke before the Holy One: "Master of the universe, let me weep, but You must not weep." God replied: "If you do not let Me weep, I will go into a place where you have no authority to enter and weep there" (Lamentations Rabbah, 24).

5. God Nurtures (Deut. 32:10 ff): "He found him in a desert land, and in the waste howling wilderness; he led him about, he instructed him, he kept him as the apple of his eye."

II. The God of My Father
   a. When is it used in Torah? What is its purpose/power?
      i. Genesis 26:24—God appears to Isaac: protection and blessing
      ii. Gen. 28:13-15—God as cheerleader, booster, protector, comforter. "I will never leave you."
      iii. Gen. 46: 1–4—Don't be afraid to go to a scary and dark place because I will be with you and I will bring you up.
      iv. Exod. 3:6–14—Figuring out just who this God is (Ehyeh Asher Ehyeh). It's always somewhat ambiguous.
      v. I Chron. 28:9—God is always there but you must maintain your part of the relationship.

III. For Small Group Discussions:
   The God/Gods of my father...
   1. Did my father have an understanding of God? What was it? How did he share it with me?

2. What were some of my father's gods? (What was really important to him?) What or whom did he worship? Why? How do I feel about his choices?
3. How did he consciously and unconsciously make these gods known to me?
4. Are his gods my gods? Which are different? Why?

IV. Individual Writing Exercises:
1. What are my gods?
2. What of my gods do I want to pass onto my children or someone whom I mentor and care for?
3. If someone asked my children what is important to me (i.e., what are your father's gods?) what would they say? How would I feel about their answers?
4. What do I hope they come to see is of importance to me? How have I let them know this? How do I continue to let them know?

TEMPLE ISAIAH
ACHIM

CONSIDERING: STAGES OF A MAN'S LIFE

PROGRAM 11/1-11/2 2003

	SATURDAY	
8:30-9:00	Arrival, coffee/pastry	Telechron Room Warren House
9:00-9:45	**Service**	"
10:00-10:45	**Mixer**	"
1:00-12:30	**Program 1—** Stages of a Man's Life	
12:30-1:30	Lunch & check in	Hayden Lodge Dining Room
1:30-2:30	**Program 2—** On Being a Spouse/Partner	Telechron Room Warren House
2:30-3:30	**Program 3—** Parenting—What It Means to Be a Father	"
3:30-5:30	Free	Grounds
5:45-6:00	**Havdalah**	
6:00-6:30	Drinks	Maple Room Warren House
6:30-7:45	Dinner	"
8:00-10:00	**Program 4—** The Role of Work in Our Lives and Identities	"
10:00 +	Scotch/Cognac/Port	
	SUNDAY	
7:00	Lake Walk/Exercise Optional	Lake/Exercise Rm
8:00-9:00	Breakfast	Hayden Lodge Dining Room
9:00-9:45	**Service**	Telechron Room Warren House
10:00-11:30	**Program 5—** Mortality and Immortality—What It Means to Be Mortal and How We Achieve Immortality	" "
11:30	**Good bye**	

Achim,

Thank you all for a wonderful weekend. Thank you for being willing to share and engage in a conversation that men don't do easily or often. Listening to you helped me to think about a number of issues from different angles. Listening to you reconfirmed for me I'm not alone in struggling with these issues and also that these are the right issues to struggle with. And like last year's weekend this weekend deepened old friendships and created new ones.

I want to express again my thanks to Bruce who managed all the details and logistics, Daniel for leading the beautiful service on Saturday morning, Rabbis David Wolfman and Howard Jaffe for leading the programs and helping to launch our discussions, Jake for leading the mixer, Don for bringing the sports gear, and George and Irving for their support on the planning committee.

Many of you expressed an interest in continuing these conversations. We will schedule a planning session to initiate follow-up activities. Last year we had a dinner at a local restaurant where we held a short program and we also held a half day Kallah at the Temple. We talked about doing more of these shorter events and hopefully after this weekend we will have new energy to do so. If you'd like to help organize a dinner, a Kallah, or another kind of event we'd love to have you join us. I will e-mail everyone when we have a date.

The address above is Achim 2003 group. If you have any comments, suggestions, or want to send an e-mail to the group just hit the "Reply All" button.

I also feel energized about this effort, and find myself wanting to have more of these meetings. Someone mentioned in the course of the weekend that monthly discussion meetings might be a good idea. In any event, I would be interested in participating in the planning sessions for what we do next (so long as the meetings are not on Tuesdays!).

Thanks so much for your efforts in organizing this event and for helping to guide it.

Thanks to all for a memorable and wonderful weekend . . . I look forward to many more together. . . . It was great strengthening old friendships and making new ones.

And thank you for making this a reality. It has touched many men's lives in deep and important ways. It was wonderful for me to have the opportunity to lead the service. This is a setting in which I feel safe and confident, and I felt the difference in leading a service there—it allowed me to offer what flows through me. So, from my heart to yours, thank you.

Thanks to everyone for a wonderful weekend. When I returned home it hit me

how much I missed you all. I learned a lot about myself this weekend, about what's important in life, about how much we all have in common. I'm looking forward to seeing you soon.

As a first time participant in the Achim and someone rather new to the temple, it was a joy to meet so many fine men. The weekend raised many questions for me that I will delight in exploring over the next few months. The openness, respect, intelligence, and spirit that was shown, particularly during some spirited debates, was exhilarating. I looked forward going through the many years ahead, strengthening my relationships with you all. Until we meet again.

Remembering where we all were a week ago—

The challenge is in continuing to live from that space. We are reminded of it when we see each other, and we can help each other retain that in our daily lives.

Sign Up for 3rd Annual Temple Isaiah Men's Weekend Away

Please join us for the 3rd Annual Temple Isaiah "Men's Weekend Away," Friday Evening November 5 –Sunday Midday November 7 sponsored by the Temple Isaiah Men's Achim Group.

A group of Temple Isaiah men will gather at the Warren Conference Center and Inn in Ashland, MA (a 45 minute drive from Lexington), for a weekend of discussion, Torah study, worship, camaraderie, and outdoor activity. This year Rabbi Jaffe, Rabbi Ullman, and Daniel Sheff will lead us through an exploration of the concept of "courage." How do we find the courage we need in our personal and professional lives? We want to encourage and welcome men who have not participated in any of our past programs to join us for the weekend!

LOGISTICS: The weekend begins at the Warren Conference Center at 6 P.M. on Friday, November 5 for Shabbat dinner and will end by noon on Sunday, November 7 after brunch. The cost for this event will be $325 and includes housing and all meals. Financial assistance is available to ensure that everyone who wants to participate can.

SIGN UP: Participation will be limited to the first 32 persons who sign up by sending an e-mail to Mitch. A commitment to participate in the full program is preferred (no "drop ins" please).

PAYMENT: Please send a check to Temple Isaiah, 55 Lincoln Street, Lexington, MA 2421, made out to Temple Isaiah for $325 and please remember to mark the envelope <u>Attention: Achim</u>.

QUESTIONS: For questions, to receive a list of last year's participants, or to discuss financial assistance, please call or email us:
Mitch Tyson   781-862-6065   Mitch@tyson.net (to discuss financial assistance)
Bruce Lynn   781-861-9023   Lynn33@rcn.com

A more detailed program with logistics and more details will be sent out in October.

TEMPLE ISAIAH ACHIM
FINDING COURAGE IN OUR LIVES

PROGRAM 11/5-11/7 2004

Goals—For a group of Jewish men associated with Temple Isaiah to . . .
1.) Spend a Shabbat together
2.) Explore the role of courage in our personal and professional lives
3.) Learn from each other
4.) Examine what Jewish tradition says about courage
5.) Create community

FRIDAY   **NIGHT**
	5:00-6:30 PM	Arrive and Check in	Reception
	6:30-7:30	Dinner	Dining Room
	7:30-8:30	**Shabbat Services – Daniel Sheff**	Reservoir Room
	8:30-9:30	Mixer	"
	9:30-10:30	**Program I – Rabbi Jaffe**	"
	10:30+	BYO Libations – Scotch/Cognac/Port/etc.	Cabin 4

SATURDAY   **ALL DAY**
	7:00 AM	Optional Lake Walk/Exercise	
	8:00-9:00	Breakfast	Dining Room
	9:00-9:45	**Shabbat Service – Daniel Sheff**	Reservoir Room
	9:45-12:00	**Program 2 – Daniel Sheff**	"
	12:00-1:00	Lunch	Dining Room
	1:00-3:00	Free Outdoor Time	Grounds
	3:00-5:00	**Program 3 – Rabbi Jaffe**	Reservoir Room
	5:00-6:00	Break	
	6:00-6:30	**Havdalah** – George Foote	Warren House – Telechron Room
	6:30-8:00	Dinner and Cocktails	"
	8:00-10:00	**Program 4 – Rabbi Ullman**	Reservoir Room
	10:00 +	BYO Libations – Scotch/Cognac/Port/etc.	Cabin 4

SUNDAY   **MORNING**
	7:00 AM	Optional Lake Walk/Exercise	
	8:00-8:45	Breakfast	Dining Room
	9:00-9:30	**Morning Service**	Reservoir Room
	9:30-11:00	**Program 5 – Daniel Sheff**	"
	11:00-11:30	Pack, Photos, and Good Bye	
	11:30	**Back in plenty of time to see the Patriots beat the Rams**	

Comments after the 2004 Men's Weekend Away— Temple Isaiah Achim

And thanks to you! It was a remarkable experience.
See you next year, and earlier.—

Thanks for organizing this wonderful event. I really enjoyed it and I'm still mulling over stuff.
Harvey

Thank you all. This was a great weekend. Each year it gets better. I look forward to future programs.

Just wanted to say that it was really great to see some new faces... at the retreat this year. I can't express how much I had been looking forward to the weekend, and it did not disappoint. Thanks to everyone for their gracious comments about my role; it means a lot to me.

I have been thinking how much this gathering marks, for me, a new beginning of my year of future growth.... This weekend truly marks a personal growth event for me. As I write this, I am reminded that this is the 39th anniversary of the great blackout of the northeast U.S. (where were you?). If the lights went out then, they truly blazed stronger in the event this weekend. Thanks to everyone for making my life that much richer.

I want to add my thanks to all who arranged and participated in such a great and meaningful weekend!

Thank you for organizing the weekend and thanks to everyone for making it such a rich and rewarding time.

Faces of Reform Judaism

Congregation:	Temple Beth Sholom
Address:	2625 N. Tustin Ave. Santa Ana, CA 92705
Phone Number:	(714) 628-4600
Contact's Name and E-mail:	Monica Engel, sovta11@cox.net
Number of Member Units:	600
URJ Region:	Pacific Southwest Council
Rabbis:	Shelton Donnell, Heidi Cohen
Outreach Chairperson:	Monica Engel

Basic Description: Using the URJ "Faces of Reform Judaism" poster (**www.urj.org/outreach**) as a model, our congregants, representing those on the poster, were invited to read the words expressed by their model. A brief introduction for each participant told their story as it related to their model, i.e., an interfaith couple raising their four children Jewish, unmarried Jew-by-choice aspiring to be a rabbi, a single Jew-by-choice mom raising an adopted multiracial child, etc.

The program took place during our *Shir Shabbat* service using our usual siddur. The readings were interspersed into the service at appropriate "breaks," i.e., after the candlelighting, after the *Chatzi Kaddish*, etc. The participants were called up to the bimah after their introduction was read by the outreach chairperson. The Shabbat bulletin contained the names of the participants as well as a copy of Lisa Bock's poem "The Stranger."

Program Goal: To bring to the attention of our congregation the diversity that exists among our congregants as a reflection of the entire Reform Jewish community.

Target Population: Our entire congregation, including born Jews, interfaith families, Jews-by-choice, and those considering conversion.

Number of Participants: Thirteen adults, six children.

Number and Length of Sessions: One Shabbat service, approximately one and a half hours.

Staffing Required: Clergy and outreach chair.

Total Cost of Program: $20

Source of Funding: Outreach budget.

Logistics: Posters, scripts, festive *Oneg*.

Instructions to Facilitator: Use your poster from the URJ and place prominently. Select members of your congregation who, as closely as possible, represent the poster stories. Prepare introductions for each participant describing how he or she reflects those on the poster. Advertise in newsletter, flyers, etc.

Evaluation of Program: Highly successful, positive comments from both participants and audience. No negative feedback.

Follow-up: Ongoing personal contact, articles in temple newsletter, i.e., Journey to Judaism article, submitted by Jews-by-choice.

OUTREACH SHABBAT

FRIDAY, MAY 21st, 8:00 P.M.

You've seen the URJ *"face* of Reform Judaism" posted in the Library and Entry Lobby…

NOW ENJOY
Temple Beth Sholom's
FACES of Reform Judaism

Join us for an enlightening, exciting Shabbat Service and meet our very own Jews by Choice, Interfaith and/or Interracial families, Born Jews, Singles and Single Parents *ALL* committed to Reform Judaism.

Dear Friends:

I am looking forward to our Faces of Reform Judaism program celebrating 25 years of Outreach and I truly appreciate your agreeing to participate. We at TBS are very fortunate to have a broad diversity of congregants, which will make our Shabbat presentation so meaningful. I think this diversity is also what makes TBS so special.

Enclosed is the paragraph you will be reading. In each case, I have tried to select readings that reflect the reader in some way. (I wasn't always successful, but hope you like the reading). I have also enclosed the introductions for your approval. If you would like to change the intro, please let me know asap.

In an effort to have a smooth transition between readers, I have given you all the "parts" in the order they will be read so that you can be prepared to come up to the bima as soon as the previous reader has completed his/her reading. I suggest that you sit as close to an aisle as possible.

Thank you so much for agreeing to participate. I think this program will enlighten many people and will be a great benefit to Outreach.

B'Shalom

Monica

P.S. Please feel free to call me at 949 458-8732

P.P.S. I have also enclosed a photo pin of the person/s you are representing. Please be sure to wear it on the 21st.

96 The Outreach and Membership Idea Book

Shabbat Shalom!
Friday, May 21, 2004 - 8:00 PM
Shir Shabbat - Choir Performing
Interfaith-Outreach Shabbat

Officiating: Rabbi Shelton J. Donnell
 Rabbi Heidi M. Cohen
 Cantorial Soloist Mark Thompson
 Frank Holtzman, Organist

Bimah Guest: Sylvan Swartz, President
 Temple Beth Sholom

Blessing of Shabbat Candles: Norri, Warren, Matthew, Nathan and Daniel Hennagin

Kiddush: Matthew Hennagin

Pre-Nuptial Blessing: Sharon Nise and Bob Miller

Blessing of High School Graduates

Presentation of L'Taken Seminar Certificates

Participants in Outreach Service:
Bruce & Lyn Liby, Eric & Gaylin Goodman, Lucille & Millie Satler, Jim & Juliet McKenzie, Melanie Hoshall, Brendan Howard, Elias Villegas, Mel & Gerri Schusterman.

Norri and Warren Hennagin, in honor of their son, Matthew, becoming a Bar Mitzvah cordially invite you to enjoy the Oneg Shabbat to be held in the Social Hall at the conclusion of tonight's service. Hostesses are: Nancy Fox, Joy Palmer, Elaine Schwartz and Monique Schwartz.

Saturday, May 22, 2004
9:15 AM Weekly Torah Study Group meets in the Library

10:30 AM
Matthew Hennagin will be called to the Torah As a Bar Mitzvah

Next Week's Service Schedule

Friday, May 28, 2004
8:00 PM in the Sanctuary

CONFIRMATION

Our Confirmation Service will be held on Sunday, May 23rd, at 10:00 A.M., followed by brunch in the Social Hall.

TORAT SHOLOM

The Torat Sholom opening ceremony will take place on Sunday, May 23rd, at 3:30 in the afternoon in the Sanctuary. Join your family and friends for an afternoon of music and spirituality as we take the first steps in the yearlong journey of writing Torat Sholom, our own Sefer Torah. All congregants – from the youngest to the oldest – are invited to attend our gala opening ceremony. Scribes Neil Yerman and Rabbi Shmuel Miller will be present. Beth Shafer, leading songwriter and singer, will follow the ceremony with a concert. Hors D'oevres will be served following the ceremony.

May 24th is the first writing day for Torat Sholom – Contact Melanie at 714-628-4620 to set up your appointment. Pledge cards are available in the TBS Lobby.

OUR 60TH ANNIVERSARY CELEBRATION!

Please join us on Saturday evening, June 5th, as we celebrate 60 years of Temple Beth Sholom. Get a table together with your family and friends and join us for a night to remember at the historic Santa Ana Performing Arts Center. The night will include dinner, dancing, entertainment and a live and silent auction. Some of the live auction items are: Turnip Rose Silverdome Dinner for 10; Five course gourmet dinner for 10 with entertainment provided by a performance from OCHSA at the home of Liz and Stu Silverman; Disneyland and California Adventure for 8 plus gourmet meal at Club 33; Parties by Panache Catered Brunch for 25; A Day at Santa Anita for 2 with lunch at the Turf Club, a private tour of the grounds, box seats at the finish line, $30 each to wager, and your very own personal handicapping expert; and a private evening reception at Chemers Gallery for 20 – 30 people, including wine, desserts and an artist demonstration. For more information, call Ann Miller at 714-921-9284, or Ellen Glasser at 714-998-0780.

COME HOME TO CAMP SHOLOM!

Join us for another exciting summer! For more information call the Religious School office at 714-628-4600.

The Stranger   by Lisa Bock

I was the stranger.
A strange young girl from an uncertain background.
I met your son.
We fell in love.
You were patient,
You held your breath, waiting.
Waiting for puppy love to go away.
But the love grew stronger,
And the stranger became less strange.

I grew to love you, too.
Your ways were never strange to me.
I saw the bonds within the family,
I was awed by your commitment to the House of Israel,
I was inspired by your love of Torah, and of God.
Perhaps you saw this; perhaps you just hoped-

You invited me to Chanukah,
To Passover. To Passover again.
To Shabbat dinner. I loved the holidays.
I watched while you lit the candles.
I imagined that I could do the same.
I fell in love with your son,
With you,
And with your people.
I was no longer a stranger.
You welcomed me.

In the Book of Ruth,
Ruth says to Naomi,
"Do not urge me to leave you,
to turn back and not follow you.
For wherever you go, I will go;
wherever you lodge, I will lodge;
your people shall be my people;
and your God my God."
You became Naomi to my Ruth,
I became your daughter.

You gave us, the newlyweds,
gifts- Shabbat candles, a Chanukiah,
A mezzuzah for our new home,
All the food and planning for your grandson's bris;
A new baby dress for your granddaughter's baby-naming;
A beautifully tattered, well-used Jewish cookbook,
(with the stains on the pages so I could tell which recipes
were the family favorites),
boxes of matzah bought on sale for Passover,
you gave us your love and advice.
But your love of Judaism was the biggest gift of all.

Thank you, mom.

Bruce and Lyn Liby
Brian and Cindy Kanarek Culver are a unique blend. Cindy was born in Nicaragua and grew up in Miami, where her Jewish father and Christian mother raised her as a Jew. Brian is a native of Georgia and grew up in the African Methodist Episcopalian Church. Brian and Cindy state "we are fortunate to have supportive families that have embraced our decision to have a Jewish home and to raise our 20 month old daughter, Katerina, with the Jewish faith. Participating in Outreach classes like Bridge to the Home has helped us to continue to learn more about the traditions and everyday things that we can do to have a Jewish home—and that's our goal."

Eric and Gaylin Goodman
Marra Gad was born a Jew and raised a Jew. She says "I have always been proud to take an active part in Jewish community, beginning as a child and continuing in high school as president of my youth group and vice president of CFTY youth group, blooming each time I visited Israel. I'm a religious school teacher and youth group adviser. Unfortunately, my Jewish life has been peppered with adversity because of the color of my Jewish face. I've been called 'nigger' and 'exotic looking' and many things in between. My pale brown skin and curly dark hair have led strangers to ask 'how can you be a Jew.' For centuries Jews have lived in every corner of the world creating a beautiful tapestry of Jewish life and culture that is not defined by race or color. This 'Face of Reform Judaism' project is a beautiful expression of what I have always been taught and known. It is not my face that identifies me as a Jew, it's my soul."

Lucille and Millie Saller
Lily Bender became a Jew-by-choice at her bat mitzvah after having been "dipped" in the Aloha Jewish Chapel Mikveh, Pearl Harbor, at age 8, when Rabbis Plaut, Goldfarb and Leibovitz witnessed her conversion to Judaism. Subsequently, she has attended the UAHC Camp Swig during four summers and was a counselor there last summer. She and her Jewish friends from Honolulu established "HOOTY," the youth group at Temple Emanu-El, where she also attends services. Lily is currently a student at the University of Oregon.

The McKenzies
Patricia Marshall and Jon Rosen are an interfaith couple with grown children from prior marriages. Pat comes from a Midwestern mainstream Protestant background with forays into Catholicism and Christian fundamentalism. Jon grew up as a Reform Jew on Long Island, spent his early adult years purposefully unaffiliated and joined a temple as a way to expose his children to Judaism so that they could choose a spiritual path with the benefit of some knowledge of Judaism. Jon slowly became involved in synagogue life, finding it increasingly attractive and rewarding. He is now immediate past president of his synagogue, whose inclusiveness has made Pat feel valued and loved. Outreach has allowed Pat and Jon to share a special close relationship with his synagogue while respecting their very different backgrounds.

Melanie Hoshall
One of Annie Fantasia's first forays into Judaism was through "A Taste of Judaism: Are You Curious?" Then, she states "the morning following my conversion to Judaism, I started studying Hebrew full time in order to make application to HUC-JIR a reality." Annie is now a fourth year student at Hebrew Union College–Jewish Institute of Religion in Cincinnati, Ohio and is serving a bi-weekly student pulpit at

Temple Beth El in Muncie, Indiana. She says, "I remain devoted to my home Temple community and am still nurtured and supported by them as they accompany me on this second dream."

Brendan Howard and Elias Villegas
Adam Shapiro struggled with Judaism most of his life after his father died at a young age. He states "My search for Judaism was a conscious choice in my mid 20s, when I realized I lacked something on the inside. I wanted to learn how to keep up with the tradition of passing on my Jewish heritage from generation to generation as ancestors did before me. I found comfort at Central synagogue where I fit nicely with the congregation whom I've grown to love. I studied and realized my bar mitzvah at 28 and then went on to lead the 20s/30s group. I very much look forward to creating my own Jewish home when I have kids of my own."

Rabbi Donnell
"We are Victor Appel, Rabbi of Temple Emanu El of Edison, New Jersey and Colin Hogan, teacher at Princeton Charter School. Outreach means creating a Judaism that is welcoming. As a gay Jewish couple, this means a congregation that recognizes our anniversary. As a family, this means that our Religious School teacher will talk about all types of families. As Jews, Outreach means that Reform Judaism welcomes us with outstretched arms."

Mel and Gerri Schusterman
Amy and Robert Heller met at Eisner Camp and are lifelong Reform Jews. They are the new first family of the UAHC (new URJ). Mazel tov to Bob on his election as Chairman of the Board. He said, "Our congregations are committed to embracing you when you are ready to be embraced. That is what Outreach and Synagogue Community are all about. I'm proud to say that welcome and inclusion are core values of Reform Judaism."

Shabbat Shalom!!! Tonight we celebrate the 25th Anniversary of Outreach and the many faces of Reform Judaism. Just as the United States of America is recognized as a melting pot for people from other lands, so is Reform Judaism a melting pot for welcoming the stranger. On this bima tonight we will be honored by the presence of congregants who represent the various faces of Reform Judaism at TBS – born Jews and Jews by Choice, interfaith families, single parent families and all the other designations consistent with today's society. Gone is the stereotypical Jew – dark, swarthy faces, long noses, brown eyes. We are now also blonde, redheaded and brunette (and some are actually bald) with blue, green and hazel colored eyes and brown, black and white complected. We are of European, Hispanic and Asian descent. We are the Faces of Reform Judaism.

Statistically, 50% of all marriages today are interfaith. How blessed we are to have non Jewish parents willing to raise their children in Jewish homes and give them the best Jewish education available. How blessed we are to have people of all ages and stages converting to Judaism because they believe in what we teach and live by and who have gone on to become Presidents, Vice Presidents and members of the Sisterhood, Brotherhood and Temple Boards, active volunteers and generous supporters of TBS. How blessed we are.

Our participants tonight will read the words of the people who represent the Faces of Reform Judaism on the now familiar poster displayed in our library and the lobby. Some of you have been given pins with photos of these same people. I hope they will help you to always give a warm welcome to the stranger who comes through the doors of TBS.

INTRODUCTIONS

Our first speakers are:

Bruce, Lyn, Nick and Elyse Liby – Lyn was born Jewish; Bruce chose Judaism. They are the loving parents of Nick, Bruce's teenage son, who adheres to his Christian beliefs, and Elyse, a bi-racial little doll who thoroughly enjoyed being dunked in the mikvah. Elyse will not be joining us tonight. Being a rambunctious 2 years old, at this point she can only handle Tot Shabbat. I'm sure her proud parents will be happy to show you her photo at the oneg.

Eric, Gaylin and Gabrielle Goodman – Eric and Gaylin had Jewish grandparents, but were both raised in rather secular homes. They explored Judaism shortly after they married and completed conversion prior to the birth of their adorable redheaded daughter, Gaby.

Lucille and Millie Saller – Lucille is a single mom of Millie, a multi racial beauty. Lucille was attracted to Judaism when she was a secretary in our Religious School office 8 years ago and recently she and Millie completed conversion.. In addition to her "real job", Lucille is now the Design Editor for the Kol Sholom. Millie celebrated becoming a Bat Mitzvah two weeks ago.

Jim and Juliette and their children, Thomas, Alicia, Eli and Leah are an Interfaith family who maintain a Jewish home. They and their four lovely children are an integral part of our TBS family.

Melanie Hoshall – Many of you know Melanie in her capacity as assistant to Rabbi Cohen and our Religious School Director, Mindy Davids. Relatively new to Judaism, Melanie has embraced Judaism with her whole heart and is a Hebrew scholar to be reckoned with.

Brendan Howard – Brendan is a recent convert to Judaism, and along with Melanie and several others was instrumental in organizing our lay led Shabbat Library minyan. He is also reorganzing our Temple Library with Wendy Bocarsky. Brendan is seriously considering the Rabbinate.

Elias Villegas – As our Custodian extraordinaire, Elias encompasses the true spirit of Judaism as a giving, caring member of our Temple family. Not raised as a Jew, his vague childhood memories of a grandfather who practiced Jewish rituals have kept Elias on his sometimes bumpy journey to Judaism. He received his Hebrew name, Elyahu Nahum, a few short weeks ago. I guess we can no longer call upon his help with custodial matters on Shabbat.

Rabbi Donnell – A person who needs no introduction, he represents the bald as well as the bold – those in the gay community who have had the courage to make themselves known.

Mel and Gerri Schusterman – Mel and Gerri have been active members of TBS since 1962. Along with their son and daughter, they have celebrated and shared many lifecycle events with their TBS family. They are currently putting together the photo album for our upcoming 60th Anniversary fundraiser on June 5th.

Membership Retention Phase—Transition Mentoring

Congregation:	Congregation Emeth
Address:	PO Box 1430
	Gilroy, CA 95021
Phone Number:	(408) 847-4111
Contact's Name and E-mail:	Rabbi Yitzhak J. Miller, Rabbi@emeth.net
Number of Member Units:	61
URJ Region:	Pacific Central West Council
Rabbi:	Yitzhak J. Miller
Outreach Chairpersons:	Debbie Zajac, Denise Weyl-Flynn

Brief Description: Having developed a successful mentoring program to integrate new members, we adapted this program to attend to the needs of members transitioning their relationship with the congregation at times such as:

- Children completing religious school and going to college
- After a bar/bat mitzvah
- After a marriage or divorce
- After a conversion, birth, or death

Through a direct, person-to-person chat (with one of the "Open Arms" Outreach Committee's trained mentors and/or the rabbi), the program helps members to recognize that their primary focus for being part of the congregation may be changing, and helps them evaluate additional opportunities they have for engagement with the congregation, its members, and its programs.

Target Population: Existing members at risk for dropping out of the congregation.

Number of Participants: Five to ten households a year, three to five mentors active at any given time.

Number and Length of Sessions: Ongoing program.

Staffing Required: Similar to typical integration mentoring program.

Total Cost of Program: None, other than time.

Logistics: Needs to be attended to regularly as part of an ongoing evaluation of the status of every congregation member by the Open Arms "member care" committee. Major lifecycle events automatically trigger an assessment.

The "Mentoring Handbook" by Arlene Chernow, printed in the *2004 Outreach Idea Book* in the "Mentoring with Menschlekeit" program of Temple Beth El, Las Cruces, New Mexico, is the primary resource used for training mentors. Questions are then revised to suit transition mentoring instead of conversion or integration mentoring.

Evaluation: A simple and successful program—very worthwhile use of time and energy directed specifically at those member units most at risk for leaving the congregation once their "perceived needs" are fulfilled. The biggest challenge is feelings of guilt on the part of mentors when a household chooses to leave the congregation anyway. Mentors need to set clear expectations that the goal is not to "save" every member, but to help make sure all members of the Jewish community know that there is a place for them within the congregation and are aware of all the opportunities the congregation has for them. Their goal is to help break the mindset of a congregation that "provides services to people," rather than a community that is an integral and ongoing part of every Jewish household.

Transition Mentoring Guide: Questions and Discussion Topics

Discussion Text: The following text about Moses making transitions in his life will provide a Jewish context for your discussion about making transitions in congregational life:

> Moses left Egypt and went the land of Midian; and he sat down by a well. [Jethro], the priest of Midian had seven daughters. They came [to the well] and drew water, and filled the troughs to water their father's flock. The [other] shepherds tried to drive them away; but Moses stood up and helped them, and watered their flock. And when they came home to their father, he said, "How is it that you have come so soon today?" They said, "An Egyptian delivered us from the hand of the shepherds, and also drew enough water for us, and watered the flock." He said to his daughters, "And where is he? Why is it that you have left the man? Call him, that he may eat bread."
>
> Moses was content to dwell with the man; and he gave Moses Zipporah his daughter. She bore a son, and he called his name Gershom; meaning, "I am a stranger in a strange land."
>
> ... Moses kept the flock of Jethro his father-in-law, the priest of Midian; he led the flock far away into the desert, and came to the mountain of God, to [Sinai]. A messenger of God appeared to him in a flame of fire out of the midst of a bush; he looked, and, behold, the bush burned with fire, but the bush was not consumed. Moses said, "I will now turn aside [from the flock], and see this great sight, why the bush is not burnt." When God saw that Moses had turned aside [from his beloved flock] to see, God called to him out of the midst of the bush, and said, "Moses, Moses!" And Moses said, "Here I am." And God said to Moses, "Come now, and I will send you to Pharaoh, that you may bring forth my people the children of Israel out of Egypt." Moses said to God, "Who am I, that I should go to Pharaoh, and that I should bring forth the people of Israel out of Egypt? O my Lord, I am not eloquent, neither yesterday nor the day before, nor since you have spoken to your servant; but I am slow of speech, and of a slow tongue." God said to him, "Go, and I will be with your mouth, and teach you what you shall say. Aaron the Levite, your brother speaks well. You shall speak to him, and put words in his mouth; and I will be with your mouth, and with his mouth, and will teach you what you shall do. He shall be your spokesman to the people." (Exodus 2:15–4:17)

Discussion Questions (in the order they appear in the text):
- What congregational "land" are you currently "leaving"? Where do you think you are "headed"? Where have you chosen to "sit down"?
- What unforeseen opportunities for interactions have you already found while "sitting by the well"?
- Who or what in the congregation has "called to you"?
- In what ways do you feel like a "stranger" in this "new land"?
- What new roles have you taken on to "shepherd" in this "new land"?
- What unexpected things in the congregation have you "seen" that "captured your attention"?
- What "higher purposes" in the congregation have "called to you"?
- What anxieties do you feel about this new direction?
- Who/what is around you to help you bridge this transition and facilitate your new direction?

Initial discussion:
The initial discussion should likely focus on three areas:

1. What has been the primary focus of this person/family for the recent past?
    a. Was their experience generally positive?
    b. What did they most value about their experience?
    c. Is there any "unfinished business" that needs to be cared for before they can move to the next phase of their relationship with the congregation?
2. Is this focus what originally brought the person/family to the congregation?
    a. If so, some discussion will likely be needed to overcome the "health club mentality" of paying "fees" to a congregation when "services" are needed.
    b. If not, discussion about previous transition(s) may prove helpful.
3. To what level does this person/family feel inclined to remain part of the congregation?
    a. Do they simply need help finding new direction in the congregation, or are they, left to their own devices, likely to leave the congregation?
    b. Has the person/family found "unforeseen benefits" to being part of the congregation?

It is virtually impossible to move on to subsequent discussion unless there is some sincere desire on the part of the person/family to remain part of the congregation.

If your assessment is that the person/family DOES NOT wish to remain part of the congregation, work simply to educate them about other opportunities, and ensure the door is left open for future interaction. Remember: A "bad taste in the mouth" is worse than the person/family leaving the congregation!

Subsequent discussion:
- If the person/family has made transitions in the congregation before, use the following to guide discussion to reflection about previous successful transitions.
- If the person/family has never made a transition before, you will need to spend much more time discussing the fundamental concept of a lifelong relationship with a synagogue, and how to make transitions.

The following questions may help guide your discussion:
1. What initially drew you to the congregation? What "benefits" have you found in being part of the congregation that you didn't foresee? (Communicate that additional unforeseen benefits likely also will be in the future.)
2. What programs or aspects of the congregation have you wanted to participate in, but haven't yet found the time? (Often people/families have been so focused on their initial goal that they forgot there were other things they wanted to "try out.")
3. In what ways can you already see "needing" the congregation in the future (e.g., funeral, counseling, religious school, children's wedding, continued learning, etc.)?
4. In what ways have you felt you benefited from being part of the congregation? Are there additional potential benefits you would like to explore?
5. In what ways have you felt you contributed to the congregation? Are there additional opportunities you would like to explore?
6. With whom have you made connections in the congregation, and in what ways does being part of the congregation help provide a catalyst for those relationships?
7. In what ways do you feel the congregation is "richer" because of your presence? In what ways would the congregation be "poorer" if you were not such an active part, or not a part at all?
8. What tangible steps can the congregation take to help make this transition as meaningful as possible?

Chapter Two

Honoring Our Interfaith Families and Inviting Conversion

Interfaith families have long been a part of our congregations. Recognizing non-Jewish partners and acknowledging their involvement in our community is central to their connection to our synagogues. From a program for grandchildren and their non-Jewish grandparents to a program that answers all questions about the conversion process, this chapter provides excellent examples of ways to engage your interfaith families, and invite and support conversion.

Sharing Shabbat: A Program for Jewish Children and Their Non-Jewish Grandparents is an adult education offering for interfaith families that introduces Shabbat to non-Jewish grandparents who share this experience with their grandchildren through crafts and discussion. This program is a wonderful opportunity to engage the parents of your interfaith couples who have chosen to raise their children as Jews or are exploring the idea.

Walking the Interfaith Family Through the Jewish Year is a program that meets regularly during the year to discuss the holidays and to provide support for interfaith families. These sessions are a gift of time that is dedicated to discussion and learning, processing and identifying the issues that are associated with the decision to raise Jewish children.

Everything You Wanted to Know about Judaism is a full spectrum of educational and experiential programs for interfaith couples, interfaith families, and the entire congregation to help congregants feel more comfortable with the Jewish holidays and learn creative ways to celebrate. Programs include "Find Out How to Build a Sukkah" and "Just in Time for Passover."

Do your members understand the process and rituals of conversion? **The Many Voices of Conversion** presents different perspectives on Reform Jewish conversion along with a clear explanation of the history and requirements of this life-cycle event. By debunking the misconceptions about conversion, this program provides a safe environment in which dialogue about this significant life-cycle event can occur.

Sharing Shabbat: A Program for Jewish Children and Their Non-Jewish Grandparents

Congregation: Temple Sharey Tefilo-Israel
Address: 432 Scotland Road
South Orange, NJ 07079
Phone Number: (973) 763-4116
Contact's Name and E-mail: Jennifer Larson, jrltsti@comcast.net
Number of Member Units: 900
URJ Region: New Jersey–West Hudson Valley Council
Rabbis: Dan Cohen, Ellie Miller, Harvey Goldman (Emeritus), Herbert Weiner (Emeritus)
Outreach Chairperson: Jennifer Larson

Brief Description: Introduce non-Jewish grandparents to the Shabbat experience by sharing Shabbat with their grandchildren through discussion and crafts.

Program Goal: To foster a greater understanding of the Jewish Sabbath experience for the non-Jewish parents of interfaith couples who have decided to raise their children as Jews or who are exploring the idea.

Target Population: Interfaith families, interfaith families with children in religious school or those deciding how to raise their children, and the unaffiliated interfaith community.

Number of Participants: Eight to fifteen family pairs (grandparent/grandchild).

Number and Length of Sessions: One two-hour session.

Staffing Required: One facilitator and if possible one clergy member.

Total Cost of Program: $300

Source of Funding: Programming budget and clergy discretionary fund.

Fee for Attendees: None, but a $10 donation per family was suggested to cover some costs.

Logistics:
- Room set up to accommodate the eight to fifteen family pairs (grandparent/grandchild)
- Four round tables for eight with seating for each of the four activities
- A table on the side for the resources/take-home materials
- A table for the refreshments
- A table for additional supplies, if necessary
- For the discussion, set up a circle in another room for the eight to fifteen family pairs and the facilitator

Materials:
- Name tags
- Aluminum foil (for candle holders)

- Clear plastic cups (for *Kiddush* cups)
- Clear contact paper, construction paper (for Shabbat place mats)
- White handkerchiefs (for challah cover)
- Markers (washable), glue (glitter and regular), scissors, buttons, ribbon, and tissue paper (colored) for the decorations
- White *kippah* to decorate
- Polaroid camera and film

Gift Bags:
- Shabbat candles
- Kosher grape juice
- Challah recipe
- Blessings in both Hebrew and English with transliterations
- List of resources at temple and in community available for interfaith families
- Temple bulletin
- List of library resources for information

Instructions to Facilitator: Welcome grandparents and grandchildren. Thank grandparent(s) for taking the time and joining their grandchild(ren) for a shared Shabbat experience. Reiterate what a wonderful relationship grandchildren and grandparents have. Ask adults how the Sabbath was celebrated in their home growing up, and how they celebrated with their children. Introduce Shabbat—a day of rest—to the group. Show and explain the ritual items of Shabbat and their meanings. Recite the Shabbat table blessings and explain them in English. Discuss the idea of *tzedakah*, and how important mitzvot are for Shabbat, how important "rest" is in the meaning of Shabbat. Note: Make sure to define the words for the group.

Ask grandparents: What does Sabbath rest mean for your family? Growing up? With your children? How has it changed? How do you think your children share the Sabbath rest with their children? After the introduction, introduce the project part of the program.

- *Kiddush* cup—using a clear plastic wine cup, decorate with tissue paper and gouache paint.
- Challah cover—using a precut cover (made of muslin, linen, or felt) give out felt pieces shaped like the Star of David, *Kiddush* cups, and other Jewish ritual objects. You can also give the option of handprints using craft paint (make sure to have water/wipes to immediately wipe off the paint). Also have trim available, and a precut "Shabbat" word in both English and Hebrew.
- Candlesticks—using aluminum foil and two Shabbat candles, allow the family to make candlesticks.
- Shabbat place mat—using construction paper, precut designs with *Kiddush* cup, candles, etc.; also handprint can be cut out. The photo of child/grandparent goes here! Using contact paper, cover the front and back, creating a "seal" for the artwork on the place mat.
- *Kippot*—If possible, making with leather or satin white/cream *kippot* and decorating. (You will need a fifth craft table if you choose to do this project.)

Evaluation of Program: Formal evaluation questionnaires were given to the participants. They filled out and returned them while the children played and had refreshments.

> *(Personal Evaluation of Facilitator)* To set a good relaxed mood, I decided to play Peri Smilow's CD *Freedom Project: Music of the Civil Rights Movement and Passover*. Families arrived, children took some of the refreshments. I set up the program in two

rooms. After the initial discussion about how the grandparents celebrated their Sabbath growing up, the original plan was to continue and discuss the various blessings and symbols of Shabbat; however, the children were restless, and we convened in another room to start the projects and the symbols and blessings were discussed while the projects were being done. There were four projects set up: Shabbat place mat, challah cover, *Kiddush* cup, and candlesticks. After the children/grandparents completed the projects, had refreshments, and filled out the questionnaire, everyone took home a bag with resource information, the blessings for Shabbat, a recipe for challah, and their projects. The feedback was very positive.

Follow-up: Each family was invited to the Interfaith Family Discussion Group series and is continually included on the mailing list for interfaith events.

432 Scotland Road
South Orange, NJ 07079
973-763-4116

TSTI's Interfaith Outreach Committee
invites you to join us for:

"Sharing Shabbat: A Program for Jewish children & their non-Jewish Grandparents"

Come spend an afternoon with family,
share old stories, make new friends,
create lasting memories, and **ask questions**.
Refreshments served.

This event is free and open to the public.

Sunday, November 14th
3:00–5:00 pm

For information and a reservation, call the Temple office.
973-763-4116 x 221

Temple Sharey Tefilo-Israel ~ We welcome you home.

Temple Sharey Tefilo-Israel Bulletin — Page 11

Shop Sharey
Holiday Bazaar
Thursday, November 11
7-10 P.M. in the Ballroom

The Iris Family Preschool invites you to our fall fundraiser. Come and enjoy a night of shopping, wine and dessert.

custom framing
pocketbooks
jewelry
home decor
kid's clothing
toys
stationery
gourmet cookware
art
gifts and treasures
of all kinds

INTERFAITH OUTREACH

The following is from the URJ website:
According to the 2000 National Jewish Population Study, about half of contemporary North American Jews marrying today will enter into interfaith relationships and one-third of their children will be raised as Jews.

This summer, I attended the URJ Outreach Fellows Program for Interfaith Family Certification at HUC-JIR in Cincinnati, Ohio. The URJ's commitment to outreach is very strong. Their mission statement says, "As Reform Jews we are committed to actively welcoming all and building vibrant, inclusive congregational communities. We seek to perform the mitzvot of *ahavat hager* (loving the stranger) and *keruv* (drawing near all those who are far.)" My personal experience as a partner in an interfaith marriage gave me the perspective I needed to attend the program and to bring back to TSTI a renewed conviction to help our families continue on their path Jewish learning in an open, comfortable environment.

As an extension of the Membership Committee on which I have served for the past two years, I am beginning an Outreach Committee and would like to invite any member of TSTI who is interested to join. This fall we will be offering our first program, "Sharing Shabbat: A program for Jewish children and their non-Jewish grandparents." Later this winter, we will be offering an Interfaith discussion group. If you are interested, please contact me, **Jennifer Larson** via email: jrltsti@comcast.net. If you have more questions about Interfaith Outreach and the URJ, please check out their website: www.urj.org/outreach.

INTERFAITH OUTREACH PROGRAMMING

Join us on
SUNDAY, NOVEMBER 14
from 3-5 p.m.
for the
KICK-OFF EVENT
to an exciting year
of programming.

SHARING SHABBAT:
A Program for Children
and their non-Jewish
Grandparents
(for 4 year olds and up,
grandparents of any age!)

RSVP to Rabbi Miller's
assistant, Susan at
973-763-4116 ext. 221

RSVP's are a must to ensure
that everyone has supplies
necessary for a
great program.

Temple Sharey Tefilo-Israel Bulletin

INTERFAITH OUTREACH

INTERFAITH DISCUSSION SERIES:
ENCOURAGING JEWISH CHOICES

FIRST SESSION
SUNDAY, JANUARY 9 FROM 3-5 P.M.

A great opportunity to explore interfaith family dynamics for parents, grandparents, or anyone contemplating an interfaith marriage. Space is limited and babysitting is available, but an RSVP to Jen Larson at jrltsti@comcast.net is imperative.

RESOURCE LIBRARY
LITERATURE FOR INTERFAITH FAMILIES AND LIFE-CYCLE EVENTS

Open to all members of TSTI. Donations of books are most welcome. Contact Jen Larson at jrltsti@comcast.net

INTERFAITH OUTREACH PROGRAMMING

Join us on
Sunday, November 14
from 3-5 p.m. for the
KICK-OFF EVENT
to an exciting year of programming.

SHARING SHABBAT:
A Program for Children and their non-Jewish Grandparents
(for 4 year olds and up, grandparents of any age!)

RSVP to Rabbi Miller's assistant, Susan at 973-763-4116 ext. 221 RSVP's are a must to ensure that everyone has supplies necessary for a great program.

Fifth Annual Turkey Drive

For the fifth year in a row, Temple Sharey Tefilo-Israel will serve as the South Orange drop-off site for the annual Thanksgiving Turkey and Food Drive of the Community FoodBank of New Jersey. This year's Drive will be held on Saturday, November 20, 2004 from 9:00 am to 2:00 pm. The TSTI site makes it easy for local residents – and particularly for our members – to help the FoodBank provide a traditional Thanksgiving dinner to those in need. In response to the request of community members, this year our turkey site will again be equipped to collect any and all non-perishable foods that you may wish to donate. Canned and packaged goods (including such Thanksgiving staples as canned vegetables, cranberry sauce, stuffing, and gravy) will be gratefully accepted.

To make the Turkey Drive even more convenient for our members, frozen turkeys may also be brought to TSTI's Friday evening services on November 19, 2004. Place your frozen (never thawed) turkey in the freezer in the main kitchen (look for the turkey sign on the freezer).

If congregants prefer, financial donations can instead be made to enable the FoodBank to purchase turkeys for the Drive at wholesale prices. Checks can be sent to the Community FoodBank of New Jersey, 31 Evans Terminal Road, Hillside, NJ 07205. Please mark "Turkey Drive" on the outside of the envelope. If you prefer to help electronically, a "virtual turkey drive" is available online at www.njfoodbank.org. You can purchase a turkey and even dinner fixings by credit card!

Sharing Shabbat: A Program for Jewish Children and Their Non-Jewish Grandparents

Supply List

Name tags
Aluminum foil—for candle holders
Clear plastic cups—for *Kiddush* cups
Clear contact paper, construction paper—for Shabbat place mats
White handkerchiefs—for challah cover
Markers (washable), glue (glitter and regular), scissors, buttons, ribbon, etc. for decorations
Tissue paper (colored)
White *kippah* to decorate
Polaroid camera and film

For place mat—use Polaroid camera and take photo of grandchildren with grandparent. Decorate construction paper with Shabbat items (pre-cut *Kiddush* cups, candlesticks, challah), place photo on paper, cover with clear contact paper. Cover back.

For candlesticks holders—use candles to make a holder with Model Magic; let dry.

For *Kiddush* cup—with glitter and regular glue and tissue paper, decorate clear plastic cup.

For challah cover—decorate handkerchiefs with buttons, fabric scraps, and glitter glue.

For *kippot*—decorate with glue and fabric markers.

Gift bag for grandparents/grandchildren to take home:
Shabbat candles
Kedem grape juice
Challah recipe
Blessings in both Hebrew and English with transliteration
List of resources at temple and in community available for interfaith families
Temple bulletin
List of library resources—books

Sharing Shabbat: A Program for Jewish Children and Their Non-Jewish Grandparents

Resource List

Temple Clergy—Our clergy members are always willing to discuss issues that arise for all of our temple families. An appointment can be made with Rabbi Cohen or Rabbi Miller through the temple office, 973-763-4116.

Outreach Fellow—Temple Sharey Tefilo-Israel is fortunate to have an interfaith outreach fellow as a member of our congregation. Outreach fellows are trained by the Union for Reform Judaism to facilitate programming and assist with interfaith issues. Jennifer Larson, our outreach fellow, is available to answer questions. Please contact her via e-mail: jrltsti@comcast.net.

Interfaith Outreach Library
A new resource open for our members will include texts covering issues on marriage, parenting, life-cycle events, and Judaism in general. Information from the Union for Reform Judaism is available in the library as well. Pamphlets on issues such as conversion, inclusion, and intermarriage are included. The library is being housed in the upstairs office hallway. Please see the office secretary for more information.

On the Web—www.urj.org
www.interfaithfamily.com
www.Jewishfamily.com

Some texts that you may like to read for further information:

Older, Effin	*My Two Grandmothers* (Fiction for grandchildren of interfaith families)
Freedman, Greenberg & Katz	*What Does Being Jewish Mean? Read-Aloud Responses to Questions Jewish Children Ask About History, Culture & Religion*
Diamant, Anita	*Living a Jewish Life: Jewish Traditions, Customs and Values for Today's Families*
Einstein & Kukoff	*Introduction to Judaism: A Sourcebook*

Sharing Shabbat: A Program for Jewish Children and Their Non-Jewish Grandparents

Shabbat Blessings: On Friday night, when the Sabbath begins, begin with the lighting of the Sabbath Candles, followed by the *Kiddush* (blessing the wine), and the *Motzi* (blessing the bread). A prayer for the children may also be included in Shabbat evening blessings.

Lighting the Shabbat Candles

Move your hands around the flames several times and bring them toward your face. This gesture symbolically welcomes the Sabbath into your home.

Place your hands over your eyes, so that you will not see the Sabbath lights until you have recited the blessing.

Hebrew with transliteration below. (Hebrew is read from right to left.)

Baruch atah Adonai Eloheinu   בָּרוּךְ אַתָּה יְיָ אֱלֹהֵינוּ
melech ha-olam   מֶלֶךְ הָעוֹלָם,
asher kidshanu b'mitzvotav v'tzivanu   אֲשֶׁר קִדְּשָׁנוּ בְּמִצְוֹתָיו וְצִוָּנוּ
l'hadlik ner shel Shabbat.   לְהַדְלִיק נֵר שֶׁל שַׁבָּת.

Blessed are You, *Adonai* our God, Ruler of the Universe, Who has made us holy through your commandments and commanded us to kindle the Sabbath lights.

Kiddush for Shabbat
(Blessing over the Wine)

Hold the wine cup in your right hand as you recite the blessings:

Hebrew with transliteration below. (Hebrew is read from right to left.)

Baruch atah Adonai Eloheinu   בָּרוּךְ אַתָּה יְיָ אֱלֹהֵינוּ
melech ha-olam,   מֶלֶךְ הָעוֹלָם,
borei pri hagafen.   בּוֹרֵא פְּרִי הַגָּפֶן.

Blessed are You, *Adonai* our God, Ruler of the Universe, Who creates the fruit of the vine.

HaMotzi
(Blessing over the Bread)

Baruch atah Adonai Eloheinu
melech ha-olam,
ha-motzi lechem min ha-aretz.

בָּרוּךְ אַתָּה יְיָ אֱלֹהֵינוּ
מֶלֶךְ הָעוֹלָם,
הַמּוֹצִיא לֶחֶם מִן הָאָרֶץ.

Blessed are You, *Adonai* our God, Ruler of the Universe, who brings forth bread from the earth.

Blessing Your Children

Place your hands on your child's head and say the following:

For a daughter:

Y'simeich Elohim
k'Sarah Rivkah Rachel v'Leah.

יְשִׂמֵךְ אֱלֹהִים
כְּשָׂרָה רִבְקָה רָחֵל וְלֵאָה.

May God make you like Sarah, Rebecca, Rachel, and Leah.

For a son:

Y'simcha Elohim
k'Efrayim v'chiM'nasheh.

יְשִׂמְךָ אֱלֹהִים
כְּאֶפְרַיִם וְכִמְנַשֶּׁה.

May God make you like Ephraim and Menasseh.

The blessing continues for all children:

Y'varech'cha Adonai v'yishm'recha.
Ya'er Adonai panav elecha vichuneka.
Yisa Adonai panav elecha, v'yaseim
l'cha shalom.

יְבָרֶכְךָ יְיָ וְיִשְׁמְרֶךָ.
יָאֵר יְיָ פָּנָיו אֵלֶיךָ וִיחֻנֶּךָּ.
יִשָּׂא יְיָ פָּנָיו אֵלֶיךָ וְיָשֵׂם
לְךָ שָׁלוֹם.

May God bless you and keep you. May God's light shine upon you and be gracious to you. May God's face be lifted upon you and give you peace.

Sharing Shabbat: A Program for Jewish Children and Their Non-Jewish Grandparents

Challah Recipe

Makes 2 loaves

1 pkg. active dry yeast
¼ cup warm (110°F) water
2 cups hot water
1 tablespoon salt
1 tablespoon sugar

2 tbs. vegetable oil
2 eggs, beaten
8 cups flour
1 egg yolk, beaten
poppy seeds (optional)

1. Dissolve yeast in warm water and allow to stand 3-5 minutes until tiny bubbles appear on the surface.
2. In a mixing bowl, pour hot water over the salt, sugar, and vegetable oil. When cooled to lukewarm, add dissolved yeast, eggs, and gradually beat in the flour.
3. Toss onto a floured board and kneed until smooth and elastic (or in a mixer fitted with the dough hook attachment).
4. Put dough in a greased bowl, cover, and let rise until doubled in bulk.
5. Punch dough down and divide in half. Cut each half into four equal parts and roll each piece 1 ½ inches thick. Twist three lengths into a braid; fasten ends well and place in a floured loaf pan. Repeat with three more lengths. Cut each remaining quarter into three parts, roll each part ½ inch thick and braid. Lay each braid on top of the loaves in the pans, cover, and let rise until doubled in bulk.
6. Preheat oven to 400 degrees F. Brush loaves with beaten egg yolk and sprinkle with poppy seeds (optional). Bake for 15 minutes, reduce heat to 350 degrees F and continue baking until done, about 45 minutes. For a hard crust, cool unwrapped.

Category	Author	Title	Price	
Basic Judaism	Einstein & Kukoff	*Every Person's Guide to Judaism*	$13.95	
Basic Judaism	Einstein & Kukoff	*Intro to Judaism: A Sourcebook*	$17.95	X
Basic Judaism	Prager & Telushkin	*The Nine Questions People Ask about Judaism*	$10.40	
Basic Judaism	Shenker	*Welcome to the Family: Opening the Doors to the Jewish Experience*	$10.47	X
Basic Judaism	Silver	*Where Judaism Differed: An Inquiry into the Distinctiveness of Judaism*	$16.00	
Basic Judaism	Telushkin	*Jewish Literacy: The Most Important Things to Know about the Jewish Religion, Its People and Its History*	$23.80	
Chidrearing	Diamant	*The New Jewish Baby Book*	$13.27	X
Childrearing	Diamant	*Living a Jewish Life: Jewish Traditions, Customs and Values for Today's Families*	$11.17	X
Childrearing	Diamant & Kushner	*How to Be a Jewish Parent*	$10.50	X
Childrearing	Mogel	*The Blessing of the Skinned Knee*	$11.20	X
Children's	Freedman, Greenberg & Katz	*What Does Being Jewish Mean? Read-Aloud Responses to Questions Jewish Children Ask About History, Culture & Religion*	$8.80	X
Children's	Kushner	*When Children Ask about God*	$9.60	X
Children's	Olitzky, Rosman & Kasakove	*When Your Jewish Child Asks Why: Answers for Tough Questions*	$24.94	X
Children's	Shaffer	*Chag Sameach: A Jewish Holiday Book for Children*	$5.95	X
Children's	Wolpe	*Teaching Your Children about God: A Modern Jewish Approach*	$10.40	X
Children's Cooking	Nathan	*The Children's Jewish Holiday Kitchen*	$16.80	
Conversion	Berkowitz & Moskovitz	*Embracing the Covenant: Converts to Judaism Talk about Why*	$11.87	
Conversion	Diamant	*Choosing a Jewish Life*	$10.64	X
Conversion	Epstein	*Questions & Answers on Conversion to Judaism*	$23.00	X
Conversion	Epstein	*Conversion to Judaism: A Guidebook*	$23.00	X
Conversion	Kukoff	*Choosing Judaism*	$10.95	X
Etiquette	Magida	*How to be a Perfect Stranger, Vol. 2: A Guide to Etiquette in Other People's Religious Ceremonies*	$13.97	
Grandparents	Levin	*Mingled Roots: A Guide for Jewish Grandparents of Interfaith Families*	$13.95	X

Category	Author	Title	Price	
Grown Children	Goodman-Malamuth & Margolis	*Between Two Worlds: Choices for Grown Children of Jewish-Christian Intermarriage*	$2.43	
Life Cycle	Maslin	*Gates of Mitzvah: A Guide to the Jewish Life Cycle*	$12.95	X
Marriage	Cowan	*Mixed Blessings: Overcoming the Stumbling Blocks in an Interfaith Marriage*	$3.49	X
Marriage	Diamant	*The New Jewish Wedding*	$11.20	X
Marriage	Friedland & Case	*The Guide to Jewish Interfaith Family Life*	$13.27	X
Marriage	Goodman	*The Jewish Marriage Anthology*	$8.98	
Marriage	Olitzky & Littman	*Making a Successful Interfaith Marriage*	$11.87	X
Marriage	Osherson	*Rekindling the Flame: The Many Paths to a Vibrant Judaism*	$2.00	
Marriage	Petsonk, Judy	*Intermarriage Handbook: A Guide for Jews and Christians*	$11.17	X
Marriage - Childrearing	Reuben	*A Guide to Interfaith Marriage: But How Will You Raise Your Children?*	$6.00	X
Marriage - Childrearing	Gishman	*Double or Nothing? Jewish Families and Mixed Marriage*	$16.47	X
Reform Judaism	Washofsky	*Jewish Living: A Guide to Contemporary Reform Practice*	$14.95	X
Reform Judaism	Bial	*Liberal Judaism at Home: The Practices of Modern Reform Judaism*		
Reform Judaism	CCAR Press	*Questions and Reform Jewish Answers*	$10.00	
Sabbath	Heschel	*The Sabbath: Its Meaning for Modern Man*	$9.60	
Shabbat	Perelson	*Invitation to Shabbat*	$18.00	X
Shabbat	Shapiro	*Gates of Shabbat: A Guide for Observing Shabbat*	$12.95	X
Shabbat	Syme	*The Jewish Home*	$12.95	X

Walking the Interfaith Family Through the Jewish Year

Congregation:	Temple Israel of Hollywood
Address:	7300 Hollywood Blvd.
	Los Angeles, CA 90048
Phone Number:	(323) 876-8330
Contact Name and E-mail:	David Aaronson, daviddca@earthlink.net
Number of Member Units:	850
URJ Region:	Pacific Southwest Council
Rabbis:	John Rosove, Michelle Missaghieh
Outreach Chairperson:	Susan Core
Program Chairperson:	David Aaronson

Brief Description: The program meets approximately once a month during the program year to discuss the cycle of the Jewish year and to provide support for conflicts faced by interfaith couples. Temple Israel of Hollywood is a large temple that offers programs that are focused on the Outreach population. Until the beginning of "Walking the Interfaith Family Through the Jewish Year," the temple did not specifically have a program for this niche. Now this class provides a combination of discussion and learning with time to process all of the issues associated with interfaith parents and raising Jewish children.

Program Goal: To help affiliated interfaith families become more comfortable with Jewish holidays and the Jewish calendar year, making the transition from the schools to the congregations and Jewish life easier.

Target Population: Nursery school, day school, and religious school families with an interfaith background.

Number and Length of Sessions: There were five sessions. They were held on Sunday mornings and on one weeknight to accommodate participants. Each session was approximately ninety minutes.

Staffing Required: Each program was facilitated by David Aaronson, a certified URJ Outreach Fellow. David spent about one hour prior to each session with Rabbi Missaghieh debriefing the previous session and discussing plans for the next session.

Total Cost of Program: The cost of duplicating materials.

Source of Funding: General administrative fund for use of copy machine.

Fee for Attendees: Free.

Logistics:
Sunday Sessions: Arranged a meeting room with chairs in a semicircle. There were no refreshments, but coffee is available on entrance to the temple. All materials were supplied by the facilitator.

Evening Sessions: The evening sessions were held in volunteers' homes. Refreshments varied from homemade cookies to wine and cheese. The refreshments were left to the host. At the meeting when we discussed Passover the host provided a variety of Passover dishes including chopped liver and two kinds of charoset.

Evaluation of Program: A survey was sent to all who participated in any of the sessions. The responses indicated that the programs were very good and informative; however, sometimes people could not attend because of baby-sitting constraints.

Instructions to Facilitators: The program relies on materials found on the URJ Web site (**www.urj.org**) and URJ Press resources, including the *Outreach Idea Book* series. The facilitator should be flexible and adjust the balance between learning and discussion according to the needs of each specific group.

Follow-up: The outreach committee has a subcommittee that is reviewing the program and materials and will be making recommendations for the second year of the program. One recommendation is to run the program for six consecutive weeks. There is a hope that this will create a more cohesive group feeling among the attendees. The extended time between sessions in the inaugural year did not achieve this.

Publicity Used: A letter was sent from two mothers of children in the nursery and day schools about the program inviting those interested to attend. A flyer that contained information about the program was displayed in the temple information desk and was also sent home to all families with children in the nursery, day, and religious schools. There was also an ad in the temple bulletin and on the temple Web site.

Curriculum Summary

1st session: Introduction to program
2nd session: December dilemma
3rd session: Shabbat and the Jewish view of God
4th session: Purim
5th session: Pesach

Each session included information about the topic of the session (except the first session), a discussion, and a teaching from Torah. Sessions 3-5 used the URJ Shabbat Table Talk for the current *parashah* as the basis of the Torah teaching.

Curriculum Detail

Introduction: The first session was an introduction for everyone. Participants spoke about their faith background and what brought them to Temple Israel of Hollywood. Each person wrote on a 3x5 card questions that he or she would like discussed through the course of the year. These were collected, typed, and redistributed to all participants. At the end of the session there was a teaching from Genesis on *b'tzelem Elohim* and a section of Talmud about each life being the equivalent of an entire world.

December Dilemma: The second session focused on Chanukah, Christmas, and the "December dilemma." We taught about the history of Chanukah from the book of the Maccabees, from Josephus, and how the history evolved into the miracle of the oil described in the Talmud. We discussed how the holiday had changed through Jewish history and that it was not a Torah or agricultural-based holiday like Pesach, Shavuot, and Sukkot. We used "The Tree Scenario" (see next page) from *Working with Interfaith Couples* (URJ Press) and separated into groups of Jewish and non-Jewish participants to discuss privately and then return to report.

Shabbat and Jewish View of God: The third session focused on Shabbat rituals and Jewish views of God. We taught the current *parashah* based on URJ Shabbat Table Talk (**www.urj.org/shabbat/**) for that portion. We then reviewed the 7-minute Shabbat handbook that was created from one of our temple's Synagogue 2000 working groups. We read the following children's story books: *Where Is God?* by Kushner, Kushner, and Majewski, and *What Is God's Name?* by Sasso. This was followed by a discussion that included the distribution of the summary pages about the Jewish views of God from *Finding God: Selected Responses* by Sonsino and Syme.

Purim: The fourth session discussed Purim. We again began the session with Torah study using URJ Shabbat Table Talk for the weekly *parashah*. We read chapter 9 of the book of Esther and discussed its impact on the entire story. With an emphasis on "reversals" of all kinds we read, reviewed, and discussed Yitz Greenberg's section about Purim from his book, *The Jewish Way*.

Pesach: The fifth session's focus was Passover. We again used Shabbat Table Talk to start the session with the study of Torah. We then discussed the seder and various ways to enhance the seder experience for children of all ages.

The Tree Scenario

Objective: To enable participants to consider "to tree or not to tree" objectively; to enable participants to gain a perspective on the issues and strong feelings associated with religious symbols and holiday observance.

Materials: None

Time Required: 30-45 minutes

Instructions: Distribute a copy of the brief scenario below and ask participants to divide into groups to discuss the questions. Each group should choose a "reporter" to describe what took place in the group when everyone reconvenes.

To Tree or Not To Tree?

Dick and Hannah Johnson have been married for nearly ten months when the holiday season begins. They were married in a civil ceremony and have not discussed religion or participated in any religious celebrations or activities since their marriage. Dick unexpectedly tells Hannah that he plans to buy a Christmas tree for their apartment, and he'd like her to help in choosing and decorating it, since in his family cutting the tree and decorating it were always warm family times. Hannah responds that she couldn't possible consider having a tree in her home, and she is appalled at Dick's insensitivity.

Discussion Questions

1. What are the feelings of each partner?
2. Are the reactions of each partner expected? Unexpected? Overreactions? Justifiable?
3. As a friend, what suggestions would you give them for solving their dilemma?
4. How could this confrontation have been avoided?
5. Is there a "right" and "wrong" in this scenario? Explain.

Walking the Family Through the Jewish Year

Purim: Tuesday, Feb. 22 and Sunday, Feb. 27

Families who choose to send their children to Temple Israel's schools are bound to face common issues:

- How to introduce Jewish traditions into home rituals?
- How to teach children that some relatives practice other religions and traditions?
- How to talk about God?

Come and share experiences, feelings and perspectives common to all families. David Aaronson, a TIOH member and Outreach Fellow will facilitate this six-session workshop which will also provide an overview of Jewish holiday practices.

RSVP to Monica Villa, Rabbinic Assistant at Monica@tioh.org, OR 323-876-8330 x225.

SUNDAY MORNINGS 9:15 - 10:30 a.m.

- October 10
- November 21
- January 30
- February 27
- March 13
- May 1

These sessions will be at TIOH

TUESDAY EVENINGS 7:15 - 8:30 p.m.

- October 12
- November 16
- January 18
- February 22
- March 15
- May 3

These sessions will be at the homes of TIOH members

No Fee

Temple Israel Hollywood
7300 Hollywood Blvd.
Los Angeles, CA 90046

FAMILIES @ TIOH
INTERFAITH

God Loves The Stranger,
Providing Food And Clothing For
Each One. You Too Must Love The
Stranger, For You Were Strangers
In The Land Of Egypt.

(DEUT. 10:18-19)

TEMPLE ISRAEL OF HOLLYWOOD
7300 HOLLYWOOD BOULEVARD
LOS ANGELES, CA 90046
323-876-8330,
WWW.TIOH.ORG

- **CHAT WITH THE RABBI: RAISING A MENSCH**
  Friday Mornings, 9:00-9:45 am (immediately before Nursery School Shabbat Services). Facilitated by: Rabbis John Rosove, Michelle Missaghieh and Sherry Fredman Nursery School Principal

  October 29 – Transition, parents of 2-year-olds
  December 10 – The "December Dilemma"
  January 28 – Sibling Rivalry, parents of 3-year-olds
  March 25 – Using the Torah as a Teaching Tool, parents of 4-year-olds
  May 20 – Struggling with Challenging Issues Relating to God, parents of 5- year-olds
  Please contact Sherry Fredman, Nursery School Principal at Sherry@tioh.org if you plan to attend these workshops. No Fee

- **HOLIDAY WORKSHOPS FOR PARENTS**
  Facilitated by: Eileen Horowitz, Day School Principal, and TIOH Clergy

  CHANUKAH: BEYOND CANDLES AND DREIDELS
  Wednesday Morning, November 10, 8:15 am

  PASSOVER: CREATING LIVELY PASSOVER SEDERS
  Thursday Morning, March 17, 8:15 am
  Please contact Eileen Horowitz, Day School Principal at Eileen@tioh.org if you plan to attend these workshops. No Fee

- **JUDAISM/ISLAM: CRUEL OR COMPASSIONATE?**
  DR. REUVEN FIRESTONE & DR. MEHNAZ MONA AFRIDI
  Sunday, December 5, 930—1130 am– No Fee

  Dr. Firestone and Dr. Afridi are the academic co-directors of the Institute for the Study of Muslim-Jewish Interrelations (ISMJI), a joint project of Hebrew Union College, the Omar Ibn Al-Khattab Foundation and the University of Southern California. The goals of the ISMJI and Drs. Firestone and Afridi are to deepen the research n the most difficult issues separating Jews and Muslims, to re-evaluate Islamic and Jewish stereotypes about one another, and to teach its findings and methods in an authoritative academic institution that speaks accurately and confidently about and in the name of Judaism and Islam.

- **THEOLOGICAL BULIMIA AND GIBSON'S "PASSION": CHRISTIAN-JEWISH RELATIONS TODAY**
  NUSSBAUM 2005 SCHOLAR- DR. SUSANNAH HESCHEL
  Sunday, January 9, 10:00 – 11:30 am– No Fee

  Dr. Susannah Heschel is the Eli Black Associate Professor of Jewish Studies in the Department of Religion at Dartmouth College, where she chairs the Jewish Studies Program. She is the author of numerous studies of modern Jewish thought, including Abraham Geiger and the Jewish Jesus, which won a National Jewish Book Award. She is also co-editor of Insider/Outsider: Multiculturalism and American Jews. She has recently completed a book entitled When Jesus was an Aryan: Theologians in Nazi Germany, and has a forthcoming article studying the women of Hitler's SS entitled "Does Atrocity Have a Gender?"

2004-2005 Learning Opportunities

- **WHEN JUDAISM AND CHRISTIANITY MEET: COMPARING OUR RELIGIOUS TRADITIONS**
  Sunday Mornings, 10:00 – 11:00 am, October 3 – June 5
  Instructor: Rabbi John L. Rosove

  Consider the historical development, sacred texts and theological differences on themes such as sin, the Messiah, good and evil, afterlife, redemption and revelation in Judaism and Christianity.

- **NON-JEWISH SPOUSES: SHARING OUR PERSPECTIVES**
  November 14, 11:15–12:15 pm
  Facilitator: Rabbi John Rosove

  Get together on a monthly basis with non-Jewish TIOH parents. Examine issues around choosing to raise one's children in a Jewish environment, non-Jewish grandparents, participation in synagogue rituals and much more.

- **WALKING THE INTERFAITH FAMILY THROUGH THE JEWISH YEAR**
  Sunday Mornings, 9:15 – 10:30 am, October 10, November 21, January 30, February 27, March 13, May 1 and a closing dinner
  Tuesday Evenings, 7:15 – 8:30 pm, October 12, November 16, January 18, February 22, March 15, May 3 and a closing dinner.

  Facilitator: David Aaronson

  Interfaith families who choose to send their children to Temple Israel's schools are bound to face common issues:
  · How to introduce Jewish traditions into home rituals?
  · How to teach children that Daddy or Mommy practices another religion?
  · How to talk about God?

  Come and share experiences, feelings and perspectives common to interfaith Families. David Aaronson, a TIOH member and Outreach Fellow will facilitate this six-session workshop which will also provide an overview of Jewish holiday practices.

  Please contact TIOH Rabbinic Assistant, Monica Villa at Monica@tioh.org, or call 323-876-8330 x225 if you plan to attend any of the above classes. No Fee

  More learning opportunities on the back...

Shalom and Welcome to Temple Israel of Hollywood.

Interfaith couples often experience a unique challenge in creating a spiritual partnership and shared identity. If you or your partner are not Jewish, you may find the programs highlighted here of particular interest.

As always, all members of our interfaith families are welcome to join any of our programs, which include but are not limited to social action, adult education, Torah studies and family programs.

If you are an interfaith family and new to the congregation, or if you're an interfaith family considering membership, Temple Israel can match you with another interfaith family already integrated into our community who may be able to answer questions you may have.

We look forward to seeing you,
The Temple Israel of Hollywood Community.

References

"7-Minute Shabbat." TIOH Synagogue 2000, Shabbat 101 Workshop.

Bogot, Howard. *Becky and Benny Thank God.* New York: CCAR Press, 1996.

Carlstrom, Nancy White. *Does God Know How to Tie Shoes?* Grand Rapids, MI: William B. Eerdmans Publishing, 1993.

Fitch, Florence Mary. *A Book about God.* New York: HarperCollins, 1999.

Grishaver, Joel Lurie, ed. *I Have Some Questions about God.* Los Angeles: Alef Design Group, 2003.

Heschel, Abraham Joshua. *The Sabbath: Its Meaning for Modern Man.* New York: Farrar, Straus & Giroux, 1953.

Kushner, Harold. *When Children Ask about God.* New York: Schocken Books, 1995.

Kushner, Karen, and Laurence Kushner. *Because Nothing Looks Like God.* Woodstock, VT: Jewish Lights Publishing, 2000.

—. *How Does God Make Things Happen?* Woodstock, VT: Skylight Paths Publishing, 2001.

—. *What Does God Look Like?* Woodstock, VT: Skylight Paths Publishing, 2001.

—. *Where Is God?* Woodstock, VT: Skylight Paths Publishing, 2000.

Sasso, Sandy Eisenberg. *In God's Name.* Woodstock, VT: Jewish Lights Publishing, 1994.

—. *God's Paintbrush.* Woodstock, VT: Jewish Lights Publishing, 1992.

Sonsino, Rifat, and Daniel B. Syme. *Finding God: Selected Responses.* New York: UAHC Press, 2002.

Wolpe, David. *Teaching Your Children about God.* New York: HarperPerennial, 1995.

Questions from First Session

- We celebrate Christmas, but we have no Christian faith. How do we explain this to our children if we raise them as Jews and have a Jewish home?
- Can Christmas be just a secular holiday?
- Are my kids going to be confused if I take them to church on Christmas Eve and Easter?
- We do not celebrate Christmas as the birth of Jesus—never have—but as a time for family to be together. How do I explain this to my kids—who love Santa Claus—and to their friends who come to the house and see the tree?
- If we don't do a tree . . . can Santa still come and fill the stockings?
- Is it confusing for my kids to celebrate Christmas and Easter with their dad and his family?
- Is it unfair to my non-Jewish spouse *not* to have a Christmas tree?
- Do you think it is confusing to children who are being raised in the Jewish faith to also celebrate Christian holidays (Christmas), especially if the non-Jewish spouse is not religious?
- What is the value of Jewish education at the Temple Israel Day School in comparison with the education that occurs in a fine purely secular program?
- What is the benefit of instilling a Jewish identity in a young person?
- What is the importance of cultivating a belief in God in a Reform Jewish education?
- Is cultivating a belief in God a goal of a Reform Jewish education?
- If my husband is Jewish and I am not and we raise our daughter Jewish, will she be accepted as Jewish? By Reform? By Conservative? By Reconstructionist? By Orthodox?
- Is it possible for someone who was raised strictly Catholic to ever feel truly comfortable and connected in a Jewish setting and community?
- Do rabbis feel nonjudgmental about intermarriage?
- How do I explain that I am not Jewish when I do not know myself? (I am a lapsed Catholic who does not practice. I go to temple. I do not go to church.)
- As a mother of a girl, age three, who is being raised as a Jew, how do I act as a role model in raising a Jewish woman?
- I love this temple, the community, the religion. How do I show it due respect and yet not convert?
- How do I feel less of an outsider at Temple Israel of Hollywood?
- How do I find my way into the community at Temple Israel of Hollywood?
- Why are there no non-Jews on the board and other key Temple Israel of Hollywood committees? If we make up 20% of families, don't we have a stake?
- Will our converted children be accepted as "real" Jews by the larger Jewish community?
- What do we all have in common religiously?
- Why are there so many Jews who are ambivalent about Judaism?
- Why do so many Jews practice cultural traditions, but not spiritual ones?
- What is a good way to inspire the non-Jewish spouse to participate in services?
- How do you deal with anti-Semitism in your extended family?

- What are good ways to discuss/involve a non-Jewish partner's spiritual belief, which may contradict Jewish teaching, with the whole family?
- Is it difficult or confusing for kids when one parent doesn't participate regularly in religious services?
- Is it difficult or confusing for kids when a non-Jewish parent does participate in all religious activities?
- How do I explain to my son, age six, who identifies himself as Jewish, why I am not?
- How can I come to feel a greater life affinity to my partner's religion?
- I don't want to convert, but as the mom, I'm afraid my kids won't be considered "really Jewish" and that will hurt/confuse them. How can I deal with that?
- How do we integrate the non-Jewish extended family into our religious lives … and not alienate their faith?
- How do we create a strong Jewish identity in our children who were converted?
- Is it disrespectful or unfair to send my kids to Temple Israel of Hollywood, where they will inevitably be exposed to Judaism in a significant way, given that my partner has no interest in religion?
- How do I talk to my kids about why their dad isn't interested in participating in a culture and community that will become increasingly more significant in our lives?
- Is the decision to convert an individual one (solely) or one to be made by the family?
- What are the real issues behind maintaining a separate faith (parents, true belief)?
- How do we explain my in-laws' celebration of Christmas and Easter to the children?
- How do we explain why daddy isn't Jewish?
- What have other people done about guardianship?
- Our non-Jewish family members make more suitable guardians. What should we do to prepare those guardians in case they have to raise our children?
- I have agreed to raise our children Jewish and I like the religion but I have no interest in converting. I am slightly concerned that as time goes on, I will feel somewhat alienated from my children as Judaism becomes more a part of their lives and their experience. Is this a legitimate concern and what can I do to prevent this from happening without converting?
- How can I make my non-Jewish parents more comfortable with Judaism?
- How do my partner and I open discussions about God (in general terms) without it becoming a debate or difficult conversation?
- Is it possible to engender a spiritual base in an "interfaith" home when there is really only one faith and the other is a culture? How can we reach a middle ground?
- My partner is Jewish and his family is unwelcoming of my spiritual beliefs (despite the fact that I am raising our child in a Jewish environment). How can I help them understand and be more comfortable with me and my decisions?
- How should we conduct an interfaith bar mitzvah? What role can my non-Jewish family play?
- How can we set a better example for children to participate in and enjoy services?
- What are the rules and regulations of officiating?
- How, as the woman of the home, do I lead Shabbat and other Jewish rituals?
- Do I have to learn Hebrew? I am not Jewish and feel awkward speaking Hebrew.

Chapter Two Honoring Our Interfaith Families and Inviting Conversion

- Why do so many rabbis refuse to marry interfaith couples even when they plan to raise their children as Jews?
- Why can't non-Jewish parents participate in bar/bat mitzvah more fully, especially if they've supported the Jewish education of their children for so many years?
- What does the conversion process entail?
- What part of the temple rituals and services can a non-Jew participate in?
- What happens when a non-Jew wants to be buried in a Jewish cemetery?
- Where do the two rabbis draw the line on non-Jewish participation vis-a-vis rituals, holiday, bar mitzvah, etc.?
- How do you talk to children about the larger concept of God—that beyond God as Jewish, when their world is rooted in Judaism?
- I want to learn more about how the rhythm of the holidays comes about.
- Could you explain how you feel God lives within each of us?
- How can meditation be included more in temple?
- Is there a way to go through the symbols that are throughout Temple Israel of Hollywood?
- How do we as parents deal with or relate to having children who are being raised (schooled) much more religiously than we were?
- What are some ways to keep up with or in time with our kids' religious education?
- Kosher—to be or not to be?
- How to connect more to services? Or stick with the joy I find in school?
- Since our children have a non-Jewish mother, are they technically not Jews? Is there something we should consider doing to rectify the situation?

(Have available during the sessions)
URJ-CCAR Commission on Outreach and Synagogue Community Mission Statement

God loves the stranger, providing food and clothing for each one. You too must love the stranger, for you were strangers in the land of Egypt.

Deuteronomy 10: 18–19

As Reform Jews, we are committed to actively welcoming all and building vibrant, inclusive congregational communities. We seek to perform the mitzvot of *ahavat hager* (loving the stranger) and *keruv* (drawing near all who are far). Ultimately, the URJ-CCAR Commission on Outreach and Synagogue Community works to strengthen Reform Judaism and the Jewish people in two ways:

- By inviting individuals and families to deepen their personal Jewish choices in the context of membership in a Reform congregation.

- By assisting and providing resources to Reform synagogues in their efforts to become sacred communities that welcome the full diversity of Jews and their families, as well as those seeking to join the Jewish people.

The Commission on Outreach and Synagogue Community will provide Reform congregations with resources and support as they seek to:

- Welcome and educate new Jews-by-choice and those investigating Judaism.

- Welcome interfaith families to take part in synagogue life, to learn more about Judaism and to raise their children as Jews.

- Assist young adults in strengthening their Jewish connection and identity.

- Inspire Jews, especially those who feel disconnected or distant from Judaism, to engage more fully in the synagogue community.

- Educate and sensitize the congregational community to be accepting of all who seek a place in our congregations.

- Enhance the sensitivity of Reform leaders and institutions to the needs of all seeking an entry or a deeper connection to Judaism.

Israel lives in its congregations.
Isaac Mayer Wise, *The American Israelite,* 1887

Everything You Wanted to Know about Judaism: Passover Primer and Practice

Congregation:	Congregation Beth Israel
Address:	9001 Towne Centre Drive San Diego, CA 92122-1222
Phone Number:	(858) 535-1111
Contact's Name and E-mail:	Bonnie Graff, Program Director, bgraff@cbisd.org
Number of member units:	1,350
URJ Region:	Pacific Southwest Council
Rabbis:	Paul Citrin, Sheila Goloboy
Program Director:	Bonnie Graff
Outreach Chairpersons:	Debbie Weiner, Melissa Powers

Brief Description: This event was the highlight of our 2004-2005 programming year. "Passover Primer and Practice" was a very basic, hands-on workshop that gave step-by-step instructions on how to design and lead a Passover seder. Our instructor, CBI Director of Education Emeritus Helene Schlafman, first gave a history of Passover, explaining the many rituals involved. Next, she led the class through the Haggadah, teaching Passover songs and explaining the significance of the symbolic foods. The participants received Passover handouts containing a Passover seder checklist, songs, and recipes. The workshop concluded with a sampling of traditional foods made by outreach committee members. Participants were very pleased with the informality of the program, which enabled them to participate in the seder and ask questions as they came up.

Program Goal: Pesach is perhaps the most beloved of all Jewish festivals and certainly possesses a wider variety of home rituals than any other Jewish holiday. While Passover is one of the most beautiful holidays, it can also be intimidating for those who have never led a seder, making it seem out of reach for those who did not grow up in a Jewish home or those who grew up in a home where they did not have an opportunity to lead a seder. The goal of this program is to give participants the tools to be able to comfortably design and lead their own seder.

Target Population: Our target population for this program is everyone in the Outreach to Interfaith community. We want to meet the needs of those who wish to conduct their own Passover seder, but who do not have the experience or knowledge to do so. This is a diverse population, including those who are considering conversion or intermarriage, interfaith couples and families, Jews-by-choice, and Jews who wish to strengthen their religious identity.

Number of Participants: This program had forty-five participants this year, from young adults to seniors.

Number and Length of Sessions: This was a one-session program, which was scheduled from 7:00 to 9:00 P.M., although many participants stayed and talked with each other until nearly 10:00 P.M.

Staffing Required: This program required one instructor, one event chair from the outreach committee, and six committee members to act as greeters and registrars and help with set-up and clean-up.

Total Cost of Program: The cost of this program was approximately $350 for publicity (photocopying flyers, temple bulletin announcements) and food.

Source of Funding: United Jewish Federation underwrote the cost of this program through an outreach grant.

Fee for Attendees: Free.

Logistics: Logistics for this program were arranged through the CBI facilities coordinator. The room, table and chair set-up, and food service were arranged well in advance by the event chair. Flyers and temple bulletin announcements were written and distributed by the program director and professional staff. UJF's Outreach Program Coordinator Rachel Zagursky handled all outside publicity including press releases to the Jewish and secular press, UJF Chai Times newsletter, UJF Web site, the local NBC affiliate's online calendar, and distribution of flyers through Pathways to Judaism, day schools, preschools, religious schools, the JCC, Jewish restaurants, and stores. The outreach committee members supplied seder plates, candlesticks, charoset, gefilte fish, eggs, matzah, fruit, kugel, cookies, wine, and grape juice. The event chair and instructor worked closely with Program Director Bonnie Graff to design handouts and materials. Seating was around a large table with participants facing each other to allow for interaction. Nametags and "icebreaker" activities were used to encourage participants to get to know one another.

Instructions to Facilitator: Our committee event chair and program director worked with the instructor to review the goals of this program, and to advise her of the very basic needs of this target population. Many of the participants had very little knowledge of Passover, and the instructor structured the class accordingly. The instructor was made aware of the issues that are of special concern to interfaith families, those new to Judaism, and those returning after a long absence.

Evaluation of Programs: Feedback was requested from this program's participants, which was overwhelmingly positive. Evaluation and follow-up was accomplished at the following outreach committee meeting.

Follow-up: Participants in "Passover Primer and Practice" were added to our Outreach to Interfaith mailing list, so they will receive invitations to future events.

Note: "Passover Primer and Practice" is part of "Everything You Wanted to Know about Judaism," a full spectrum of educational and experiential programs that take place over the course of the year. Press releases and flyers for these other programs are included on pages 135–62.

Congregation Beth Israel

**Outreach Committee
and United Jewish Federation
present:**

Passover Primer

Wednesday April 13th
7 pm to 9 pm
Feuerstein Family Activity Center

Did you ever want to have your own Seder but didn't know how?

Come learn all the rituals, music and recipes With Helene Schlafman, CBI Director of Education Emeritus.

Participate in a mock Seder, complete with "Tastes" of Passover, and leave ready to lead your own Seder.

No fee for this educational and informative event
RSVP to Bonnie Graff at (858) 535-1111 ext. 3800 or email bgraff@cbisd.org

For more information on all CBI programs and events, visit www.cbisd.org

Congregation Beth Israel's
OUTREACH COMMITTEE
Presents

PASSOVER PRIMER & PRACTICE

You Can and Should Conduct a Seder

Don't say you can't conduct a seder. You can!

Conducting a seder is neither as hard nor as complicated as you think. It is a source of great satisfaction.

It would be a pity if Passover were to pass over your home without the home observance that enables you to relive the fight for liberty experienced by our ancestors and without the ceremony that strengthens the bond between all Jews.

Here are some tips that will help you make your seder a success:

1. Make sure everyone has the same Haggadah. It is fine for two people to share a Haggadah. There are many beautiful haggadot now on the market, and you have a wide choice.

2. Don't feel that your seder must be too formal. You may interpolate into the various parts of the service your own comments. You may ask others to do the same. Keep the service moving along. The seder does not have the same formality as a synagogue service. Instead it is a unique mixture of the solemn and the joyful.

3. Study the Haggadah before the night of the seder. Decide in advance which parts you can do in Hebrew and which in English. Be familiar with the text before you sit down for the ceremony.

4. Rotate the reading of the parts of the Haggadah among those at the table. Some will read in English; others in Hebrew. Some will sing the songs in one style; others will use another melody. The very mélange of Hebrew dialects and the variations in the manner of reading portions of the service will illustrate the diversity of Jewish life and add a special flavor to the proceedings.

5. Have the guests recite as many of the blessings as possible in unison. Some segments can be read in unison so as to encourage the participation of everyone.

Traditionally, Passover is a time when you can derive both merriment and inspiration from the great saga of the Exodus. Don't lose the opportunity of introducing the Passover spirit into your own home. You will feel amply rewarded for the little effort entailed.

From Introduction to Judaism by Rabbi S. Einstein and L. Kukoff

The Seder Table

- Haggadah for each participant
- Festival candles and candlesticks
- A kiddush cup and wine for the festival kiddush
- Elijah's cup
- Three whole matzot, covered
- Cup, basin, towel for washing
- Seder plate

    a. A roasted shankbone
    b. Maror or bitter herbs
    c. Karpas
    d. A roasted egg
    e. Charoset
    f. A dish of salt water

- Symbolic foods for each participant

    Because the seder actively involves every member of the family, certain foods should be at each place setting.

    a. A wine cup
    b. Matzah
    c. Maror (usually horseradish)
    d. Charoset
    e. Salt water
    f. Karpas (usually parsley)
    g. A hard-boiled egg

The following items are optional:

- Pillows for reclining
- Matzah of Hope
- Afikomen bag
- Empty chair to symbolize those not free to celebrate
- An orange
- Flowers

The Seder Order

1. Light the holiday candles
2. Fill the first cup of wine
   a) *Kadesh* (sanctification); *Borei peri hagafen* and *Shehecheyanu*
   b) Drink the first cup of wine
3. *Urechatz* (ceremonial washing of hands, without a blessing)
4. *Karpas* (greens)
   a) Say *Borei peri ha'adamah*
   b) Eat greens
5. *Yachatz* (breaking of the *matzah*)
   a) Break middle *matzah*, hiding half as the *afikoman* to be eaten after meal
   b) Say *Ha lachma anya*
6. *Magid* (recitation of the service)
   a) The Four Questions
   b) *Avadim Hayinu*
   c) The Four Children
   d) The Ten Plagues
   e) *Dayenu*
   f) Point out the Pesach symbols
   g) *Hallel* (Psalms of praise)
   h) Drink second cup of wine and say *Borei peri hagafen*
7. *Rachtzah* (washing of hands)
   a) Recite the blessing *Al netilat yadayim*
8. *Motzi, matzah*
   a) Say *Hamotzi* and *Al achilat matzah*
   b) Eat the *matzah*
9. Maror
   a) Say *Al achilat maror*
   b) Eat the bitter herb dipped in *charoset*
10. *Korech* (reminder of the Temple)
    a) Break the bottom *matzah* and eat it with horseradish (and *charoset*)
11. *Shulchan Orech* (the Pesach meal)
12. *Tzafun* (eating the *afikoman*)
13. *Barech* (grace after meal)
    a) Fill the cups for the third time and say the *Birkat Hamazon*
    b) Say *Borei peri hagafen* and drink the third cup of wine
    c) Open door and sing *Eliyahu Hanavi*
14. *Hallel*
    a) Say the final benedictions
    b) Say *Borei peri hagafen* and drink the fourth cup of wine
15. *Nirtzah* (conclusion)
16. Sing, sing, sing
    a) *Echad Mi Yodea?* (Who Knows One?)
    b) Others

Passover Terms to Know

Afikomen: From the Greek for 'dessert', afikomen is a piece of unleavened bread which is the last thing eaten at the Seder meal. Taken from the middle of the three portions of matzah on the seder plate, the afikomen symbolizes the Pascal lamb which was eaten at the end of the meal in ancient times. It has become customary for the head of the household to hide it and for the children to try and 'steal' it. The afikomen is usually only returned if a gift has been offered in its place.

Arba Kosot: Hebrew for the four cups or glasses. During the Passover Seder four cups of sweet red wine are drunk to symbolize four characteristics of God's redemption from Egypt mentioned in the Bible (Exodus 6:6-7). The cups are also thought to represent the four cups of punishment which God will pour out on the nations of the world in future times. Red wine is used to remember the blood of the Pascal lamb which the Israelites smeared on their doorposts in Egypt. When Jews suffered from Blood Libel accusations that they used Christian blood at Passover time, white wine was drunk instead of red.

Arba Kushiyot: Hebrew for the 'four questions'. The original Mishnaic account of the four questions (200 C.E.) lists only three of those we use today. One of the original four was dropped, since it referred to the Temple paschal sacrifice, and another question was substituted. The questions are the formalized expression of an underlying theme of the Seder that the rituals should lead the children to ask questions.

1. On all other nights we eat all kinds of bread and crackers. Why do we eat only matzah on Passover?
2. On all other nights we eat many kinds of vegetables and herbs. Why do we eat bitter herbs, maror, at our Seder?
3. On all other nights we don't usually dip one food into another. At our Seder we dip the parsley in slat water and the bitter herbs in Charoset. Why do we dip foods twice tonight?
4. On all other nights we eat sitting up straight. Why do we lean on a pillow tonight?

Arba'at Habanim: Hebrew for the 'four children' (male).

Bedikat Chametz: Since all leavened bread must be removed for Passover, a special search for any hidden crumbs takes place the night before. It is customary to search by the light of a candle so that nooks and crannies can be investigated, to use a feather to clean the chametz away, and to renounce ownership of whatever leaven has not been found. In order that the blessing pronounced before the search should not be entirely in vain, ten carefully wrapped breadcrumbs are hidden in different rooms to be found during the search. All the leaven is burnt the next morning.

Beitzah: A roasted egg symbolizing the festival offering in the Temple and the mourning of the destruction of the Temple. The egg can also be thought of as a symbol of fertility and renewal. Just as an egg becomes harder the longer it cooks, so the Jewish people have emerged from the crucible of persecution as a strong and living people.

Chametz: During the festival of Passover it is forbidden to eat or even possess any leaven. This is defined as anything with yeast in it, as well as dough that has been allowed to rise. All leaven is removed from the home (see bedikat chametz). Chametz may also be locked away and sold to a Gentile before the festival begins to be bought back afterwards. While leavened bread is the food of the rich and powerful, unleavened bread is the 'bread of affliction' which was eaten by the Israelite slaves in Egypt.

Charoset: A sweet paste eaten during the Passover Seder meal symbolizing the mortar used by the Israelite slaves in Egypt or the clay they had to form into bricks. It usually includes chopped fruit and nuts and is sweetened with wine, dates, or honey.

Dayenu: A song typically sung at a Passover Seder.

Haggadah: The text which contains the liturgy recited in the course of the Passover Seder. Its purpose is to enable each family to tell the story of the redemption from Egypt as commanded in the Pentateuch (Exodus 13:8). The Haggadah is made up in the main of biblical selections about the Exodus, Psalms of praise, Rabbinic homilies, hymns and children's songs which are sung at the end of the meal. It has instructions about the ritual eating of matzah and maror, and about the drinking of the Four Cups of wine. Among its contents are some of the best-known and best-loved images and themes of Jewish literature: the Four Questions asked by the youngest member of the family; the typology of the four sons (wise, wicked, simple and unquestioning); the list of the ten Plagues during the chanting of which a drop of wine is spilled for each plague; the request to God to punish the Gentile nations who have oppressed the Jews, which is recited after the cup of Elijah has been poured out and the door opened; the wish to meet 'next year in Jerusalem'; and the song about the young goat (Chad Gadya) bought by the father for two coins whose death is avenged by God.

Karpas: A sprig of parsley or celery representing spring, life, and hope. The Karpas is dipped in salt water, which represents the tears of slavery.

Kos Eliyahu: The cup of Elijah. At the Passover Seder a special cup of wine is poured out for the prophet Elijah, the door of the house is opened and he is invited in. While the door remains open, the family ask God to punish those nations who do not recognize God and who persecute the Jewish People. It is believed that Elijah visits every Jewish home on this night and offers his protection to the household. As the children look towards the door one of the adults spills a little wine from the cup to convince them Elijah has indeed called and drunk his wine, although he cannot be seen.

Makot: Hebrew for the plagues.

Maror: Bitter herbs, usually horseradish or lettuce, eaten during the Passover Seder to remind Jews of the bitter enslavement of the Israelites in Egypt. Maror is dipped in the sweet Charoset paste before being eaten, to mask the bitter taste. Since the Charoset has the consistency of mortar, it also serves as a reminder that the bitterness of slavery was related to the building work undertaken by the Israelites while they labored in bondage to the Pharaohs.

Matzah: The flat bread made out of plain four and water that is eaten on Passover. Matzah is described as 'bread of affliction' (Deuteronomy 16:3), i.e. the bread eaten by the poor and by slaves. It is a reminder of the slavery of the Israelites in Egypt and of the hurried manner of their Exodus, during which the bread they had prepared did not have time to rise (Exodus 12:39). An adult must bake Matzah within eighteen minutes from the time the flour and water are mixed; otherwise the baked product is regarded as leavened bread.

Pesach (Passover): One of the three pilgrim festivals or harvest festivals. Pesach is the festival of freedom, commemorating the redemption of the Israelite slaves from Egypt and pointing ahead to the final redemption of the world in the age of the Messiah. It is also the time of the barley harvest and the end of the rainy season. The lunar calendar must be adjusted by the addition of an extra month, where necessary, so that Pesach always falls in the spring. No leavened bread may be eaten for the whole festival, and a day before Pesach begins, all leaven is cleared out of the house after a search (bedikat chametz). The festival lasts for seven days (eight days in the Diaspora) beginning on the evening before the fifteenth of Nisan, the night of the Exodus, with a ritual family Seder meal. Matzah is eaten at the seder to remind the participants of the bread of slavery, and Pesach is also known as 'chag ha-matzot', the 'festival of unleavened bread'. The end of Pesach is the time when the Israelites crossed over the Red Sea, and because their rescue involved the drowning of the Egyptians, only the shortened form of the Hallel Psalms (psalms praising God) is recited. The Song of Songs is also read. The name of the festival originates in the last of the ten Plagues, when the Egyptian firstborn children were slain by God, who 'passed over' the houses of the Israelites, which had the blood of the Pascal lamb smeared on their doorposts, and spared their firstborn (Exodus 12:27).

Seder: 'Seder' is Hebrew for 'order'. The Seder is the liturgical meal observed at home on the first (and often second) nights of Passover. The family meal is accompanied by the retelling of the story of the Exodus from a Haggadah text, during which the youngest child asks Four Questions of the head of the household. Each person is encouraged to think of himself or herself as having been personally redeemed from Egypt, and the Seder has a number of features to educate children in understanding the message of the Exodus. Special types of food and drink are arranged on the table and included in this Passover meal. It is customary to recline on one's left side during the Seder, since this was once the manner in which free men ate. The seder night is regarded as a time of divine protection for Israel, and the demonic forces at work in the world need not be feared.

Shabbat Hagadol: Hebrew for the 'Great Sabbath'. This is the name given to the Shabbat immediately preceding Passover.

Zeroa: A scorched portion of the leg bone of a lamb representing the Paschal lamb offering.

Thinking Freely About Passover

Use any one of these to start your seder. Talking freely about your feelings is a freedom we can share at the Passover Seder.

1. To me, freedom is _____
2. When I think of Slavery, I _____
3. When I eat matzah, I _____
4. Passover makes me think of _____
5. On Passover I am proud that _____
6. On Passover I am proud that _____
7. If I could change Passover _____
8. Today, Moses would _____
9. I wish the Jews in the wilderness had _____
10. One place I would really like to celebrate Passover is _____
11. At my seder, I _____
12. Freedom sounds like _____
13. Freedom tastes like _____
14. Freedom smells like _____
15. On this Passover, I am most happy for _____

CONGREGATION BETH ISRAEL

<u>FOR IMMEDIATE RELEASE</u>
Contact: Bonnie Graff, Program Director
(858) 535-1111, ext. 3128

FIND OUT HOW TO BUILD A SUKKAH

On Sunday, September 12 at 10:30 a.m., the Outreach Jewish Enrichment Program of Congregation Beth Israel will offer a workshop on how to build a *sukkah*. The class will be held at Home Depot, located at 4255 Genesee, in the Balboa Plaza Shopping Center, at Balboa and Genesee. This class is open to the entire Jewish community.

For everyone who always wished they could build a sukkah, *but never knew how, this class is a simple, hands-on workshop that will give you the expertise to create a* sukkah *for your family. There is no fee for the workshop. Materials will be available for purchase to complete your own* sukkah.

Sukkot is a time to celebrate the fall harvest season, an important part of the agricultural history of the Jewish people. It is the festival where eating, sleeping or living in huts made out of boughs is the custom, and gives the festival its name.

The sukkah *is a very important element in the celebration of the* Sukkot *festival. These huts were made of branches and were easy to assemble, take apart, and carry. The reason for living in huts is that this resembles the way the Jewish people were living during the 40 years of wandering in the desert.*

The Outreach Committee Jewish Enrichment Series of Congregation Beth Israel is a special program for interfaith families, those contemplating conversion or intermarriage, and Jews by Choice and their families. In the upcoming year there will be other informative programs such as "How To" Chanukah, *"How To" Passover and "TGIS" Shabbat and* Havdalah.

To register for the sukkah-building class, RSVP to Bonnie Graff, Program Director, at (858) 535-1111, ext. 3800 or email <u>mbressel@cbisd.org</u>. *For information on other CBI programs and events, go to* <u>www.cbisd.org</u>.

CONGREGATION BETH ISRAEL

<u>FOR IMMEDIATE RELEASE</u>
Contact: Bonnie Graff, Program Director
           (858) 535-1111, ext. 3128

THREE HEBREW LANGUAGE COURSES

Hebrew classes continue at Congregation Beth Israel, beginning in January.

"Hebrew Made Easy" is an 11-session class for those who have never studied Hebrew or who need a good refresher course. Students will be provided with a ten-lesson book and tape or CD series, flash cards and writing guide. By the end of this course, they will be able to read and write all of the Hebrew letters and vowels, read Hebrew fluently and have some basic Hebrew prayer vocabulary.

"Prayer Book Hebrew Made Easy – Part 2" is also an 11-session class for those who can read Hebrew, know basic prayer book Hebrew vocabulary and grammar, and are able to read Hebrew prayers fluently. It follows "Prayer Book Hebrew Made Easy – Part 1" and uses the same textbook. Those who have not taken "Part 1" may enroll if they can read Hebrew and know some basic prayer vocabulary and grammar.

By the end of this course, students will have advanced their knowledge of grammar and increased their vocabulary by studying basic prayers, including the *Shema* and *V'ahavta, Kedushah, Sim Shalom, Amidah, Mi Chamocha, V'Shamru, Kiddush, Aleinu, and* Torah and candle blessings. The classes are given 11 consecutive Monday mornings, January 24 – April 11 in the Jackie Novak Youth Lounge.

"Hebrew Made Easy" is presented from 9:30 – 10:30. The fee for members is $95; nonmembers fee is $145. "Prayer Book Hebrew Made Easy – Part 2" is presented at 11:00 – Noon. The fee for members is $105 for new students, $60 for members who took Part 1. The fee for nonmembers is $155 for new students; $110 for nonmembers who took Part 1 last semester.

The third class to be offered is "Prayer Book Hebrew Made Easy – Part 1," meeting on Friday mornings, for 11 sessions, January 21 – April 15, from 9:30 – 10:30 am in the Jackie Novak Youth Lounge. Fee for members: $105, nonmembers: $155. The fee includes textbook, "Prayerbook Hebrew the Easy Way," and audiotapes or CDs.

Designed for women who can read Hebrew and want to learn basic Hebrew vocabulary and grammar to understand prayers and read them fluently, this 11-session course is a follow-on class to "Hebrew Made Easy."

When you complete this class, you'll be able to determine nouns, pronouns, adjectives, and possessive endings for nouns, participles, and prepositions. You'll also have learned grammar and vocabulary from the *Shema*, blessings over bread and wine, *Sim Shalom*, *Shehecheyanu*, *Aleinu*, *Kedushah*, *Avinu Malkeinu*, and *Oseh Shalom*.

All classes are taught by Judy Fisher, who has taught adults and children prayer book, Biblical, and conversational Hebrew for more than twenty years.

For further information and registration, please contact Bonnie Graff, Program Director, at (858) 535-1111 ext. 3800, or email: bgraff@cbisd.org. Registration required by January 14.

Be sure to check Congregation Beth Israel's Web site regularly at http://www.cbisd.org/ for updated information and additional ALEINU classes and programs.

CONGREGATION BETH ISRAEL

<u>FOR IMMEDIATE RELEASE</u>
Contact: Bonnie Graff, Program Director
(858) 535-1111, ext. 3128

20+ WAYS TO ENHANCE SHABBAT

What is so special about Shabbat? How can a liberal Jew observe this day? A special Shabbat workshop will be presented Saturday, November 20 at noon at Congregation Beth Israel. It is part of the congregation's "Destination Shabbat," which encourages participants to spend Shabbat at the synagogue.

Following Shabbat services, the workshop will provide more than twenty ideas for setting aside the workday world and enhancing the Shabbat experience. In keeping with Ahad Ha-am, who said, "More than Israel has kept the Sabbath, the Sabbath has kept Israel" and with Abraham Joshua Heschel's description of the Shabbat as, "an island in time," Congregation Beth Israel provides this enhanced Shabbat experience.

Joe Oppenheimer, a member of the Aleinu Committee, has compiled a meaningful list of ideas to make Shabbat the very special day it should be. His ideas have been acclaimed by the many students who were introduced to innovative ways to enhance Shabbat.

The one-session class will be held in the Daniel J. Epstein Family Conference Room at Congregation Beth Israel from noon to 2:00 p.m. Participants may bring a brown bag lunch and drinks will be supplied. There is no fee for this course.

For information, please contact Bonnie Graff, Program Director, (858) 535-1111, ext. 3128.

CONGREGATION BETH ISRAEL

<u>FOR IMMEDIATE RELEASE</u>
Contact: Bonnie Graff, Program Director
(858) 535-1111, ext. 3128

LIGHT UP YOUR CHANUKAH

Chanukah is one of the most joyful family celebrations of Judaism, a wonderful opportunity for families and friends to gather for traditional foods, singing, and gift giving. On Wednesday, December 1 at 7:00 p.m., Congregation Beth Israel's Outreach Committee offers a complete "how to" Chanukah workshop.

This hands-on class will cover the history and significance of Chanukah and introduce the sights, sounds, and smells of this special holiday. Participants will make latkes (potato pancakes) and sufganyot (jelly doughnuts), the traditional foods of Chanukah. In addition, they will create their own chanukiah (menorah), and learn to play the dreidel game while enjoying Chanukah music. Participants will come away with the knowledge to help them make a memorable family Chanukah celebration of their own.

Helene Schlafman, Director of Education Emeritus at CBI, will teach the class. Helene is celebrating her 48th year in Jewish education, 38 of them at CBI. She is nationally known for her innovative programming.

CBI's Outreach Committee offers enjoyable, educational programming that is open to anyone who wants to learn more about Judaism and is designed to give an introduction to the warm celebration of Jewish life. Classes are often free and open to the public.

This one-session class will be held in the Feuerstein Activity Center at Congregation Beth Israel from 7:00 p.m. to 9:00 p.m. There is no fee. For more information, please contact Bonnie Graff, Program Director, at (858) 535-1111 ext. 3128, or email: bgraff@cbisd.org. Be sure to check Congregation Beth Israel's Web site regularly at www.cbisd.org for updated information and additional Outreach classes and programs.

CONGREGATION BETH ISRAEL

FOR IMMEDIATE RELEASE
Contact: Bonnie Graff, Program Director
           (858) 535-1111, ext. 3128

OUTREACH TO INTERFAITH SHABBAT SERVICE AND DINNER

You are invited to Congregation Beth Israel on Friday, April 15, 2005 as they honor their interfaith families.

There will be a 6:00 service in the Glickman-Galinson Sanctuary. Dinner will follow in the Feuerstein Family Activity Center. Rabbi Paul Citrin will discuss "Everything You Ever Wanted to Know about Judaism" at dinner.

Dinner participants will include Outreach to Interfaith Committee, Basic Judaism students (dinner included in class fee), and anyone interested in interfaith programming.

Costs: $20 for adults, $9.00 for children ages 2-12. RSVP to Bonnie Graff, Program Director, at (858) 535-1111, ext. 3800 or email bgraff@cbisd.org no later than Monday, April 11.

CONGREGATION BETH ISRAEL

FOR IMMEDIATE RELEASE
Contact: Bonnie Graff, Program Director
              (858) 535-1111, ext. 3128

JUST IN TIME FOR PASSOVER!

On Wednesday, April 13, at 7:00 p.m. in the Feuerstein Family Activity Center, Congregation Beth Israel will hold a "Passover Primer and Practice."

CBI Director of Education Emeritus Helene Schlafman will lead a discussion of the *Haggadah,* and the various rituals observed with wine and symbolic foods.

After this full evening of instruction, ideas, music, and recipes, you will be able to comfortably design and lead your own *seder*. This "how to" workshop concludes with a sampling of traditional foods made by Outreach Committee members. It is co-sponsored by the United Jewish Federation Outreach Program.

There is no fee but reservations are requested. Call Bonnie Graff, Program Director at (858) 535-1111, ext. 3800 or email bgraff@cbisd.org.

CONGREGATION BETH ISRAEL

<u>FOR IMMEDIATE RELEASE</u>
Contact: Bonnie Graff, Program Director
(858) 535-1111, ext. 3128

HOW TO RAISE A JEWISH MENSCH

Congregation Beth Israel presents a new four-week course, "How to Raise a Jewish Mensch," beginning Thursday evening, April 14, at 7:30 p.m.

Parents want to raise a *mensch*. Participants will learn how the Jewish community, with its four thousand years of experience and wisdom, can help that to happen. They will examine what Judaism says about when to say yes and when to say no, how to respect the needs of parents and children, the importance of the individual and his/her place in the Jewish community, creating Jewish family memories, and much more.

The class is designed for parents of children of all ages.

This very interesting and constructive course will be taught by Dr. Harvey Raben, Director of Education at Congregation Beth Israel, and is co-sponsored by the Outreach Committee.

The class meets April 14, and 21, May 5 and 12 at 7:30 p.m. There is no fee for members or non-members.

For further information and registration, please contact Bonnie Graff, Program Director, at (858) 535-1111 ext. 3800, or email: bgraff@cbisd.org. Be sure to check Congregation Beth Israel's Web site regularly at www.cbisd.org for updated information and additional ALEINU classes and programs.

CONGREGATION BETH ISRAEL

<u>FOR IMMEDIATE RELEASE</u>
Contact: Bonnie Graff, Program Director
(858) 535-1111, ext. 3128

GOT SHABBAT (and HAVDALAH)?

As part of Congregation Beth Israel's Outreach Jewish Enrichment Series, there will be an informative *Shabbat* workshop on May 14 at 5:30 p.m. in the Feuerstein Family Activity Center.

Taught by Dr. Al Ray and Cantor Arlene Bernstein, this workshop will focus on the blessings, rituals, food, music, and other creative ideas for celebrating *Shabbat and Havdalah* in your home.

There will be separate "kid friendly" activities for children, instruction and discussion for adults, and all ages will come together for an interactive Havdalah service.

This program is co-sponsored by the United Jewish Federation Outreach Program, Rachel Zagursky, Coordinator.

To RSVP, contact Bonnie Graff, Program Director, at (858) 535-1111, extension 3800. Congregation Beth Israel is located at 9001 Towne Centre Drive.

Congregation Beth Israel
Outreach Jewish Enrichment Series

How to Build a Sukkah

Sunday, September 12th
10:30 AM

Held at   Home Depot
- 4255 Genesee
In The Balboa Plaza Shopping Center
At Balboa & Genesee

Sukkot is a time to celebrate the fall harvest season, an important part of the agricultural history of our people. For everyone who always wished they could build a *sukkah*, but never knew how, this class is a simple, hands-on workshop that will give you the expertise to create a *sukkah* for your family.

No fee for workshop; building materials available for sale. RSVP to Bonnie Graff, Program Director, at (858) 535-1111, ext. 3800 or email mbressel@cbisd.org

For more information on all CBI programs go to www.cbisd.org

CONGREGATION BETH ISRAEL
ALEINU/Adult Learners Network

Aleph Bet 101: Beginning Hebrew... and So Much More

Sunday Mornings
Starting September 12, 2004
(an eight week course)

9 am – 11:30 am
Daniel J. Epstein Family Conference Room

With instructor Dr. Al Ray

Half of the content focuses on learning the Hebrew letters, starting with their stand-alone sound and gradually evolving into words used in our prayers.

A smorgasbord of Judaic knowledge awaits in the rest of each session:
- Tastes of *Kabbala* (Jewish mysticism)
- *Gematria* (analysis of the numeric equivalents of Hebrew letters)
- Jewish history
- Explanation of Jewish rituals and liturgy

Presented in an informal "ask your teacher" ambience.

This course continues in the Spring Semester as
"Aleph Bet 102: Prayer Book Hebrew... and So Much More".
Students who enroll in both courses get discounted fees.

Fees for first semester: members $60, for nonmembers: $80 (fee includes textbook)
Discounted fees (for both semesters): members $90, nonmembers $130

For further information or to RSVP, call Bonnie Graff, Program Director, on the Reservation Line at (858) 535-1111, ext. 3800 or email mbressel@cbisd.org.

For more information on all CBI programs go to www.cbisd.org

Chapter Two Honoring Our Interfaith Families and Inviting Conversion   155

CONGREGATION BETH ISRAEL
ALEINU/Adult Learners Network

Hebrew Made Easy
א ✡ ב ✡ ג ✡ ד ✡ ה

(If you can't read this – call us immediately)

Mondays, September 27 – December 13, 2004

9:30 – 10:30 A.M.

Jackie Novak Youth Lounge

Instructor: Judy Fisher

If you're a woman who has never studied Hebrew or who needs a good refresher course, this 11-session class is for you. You'll be provided with a ten-lesson book and tape series, flash cards and writing guide. Each lesson is accompanied by its own cassette tape, useful for reviewing weekly classes.

By the end of this course, you'll be able to read and write all the Hebrew letters and vowels, read Hebrew fluently and have some basic Hebrew prayer vocabulary.

Fee for Members: $95
Fee for nonmembers: $145
Fee includes textbook and cassette tapes

Your check is your reservation.
Mail to Congregation Beth Israel 9001 Towne Center Drive
San Diego, CA 92122
For further information call Bonnie Graff, Program Director, at (858) 535-1111, ext. 3128

Please RSVP by Monday, September 13, 2004 so materials may be ordered for you.

For more information on all CBI programs go to www.cbisd.org

Outreach Shabbat Service & Dinner

We invite you to join us as we honor our interfaith families.

Friday, April 15th
6:00 p.m.

service in the
Glickman-Galinson Sanctuary

Dinner to follow in the
Feuerstein Family Activity Center

Rabbi Citrin will discuss
"Everything You Ever Wanted to Know about Judaism......."
at dinner.

Dinner is open to Basic Judaism students
and anyone interested in interfaith outreach programming.

Cost of Dinner: $25 for adults, $9.00 for children ages 2-12
No charge for individuals enrolled in Basic Judaism.
$25 fee for Couples sharing a Basic Judaism enrollment.

RSVP to Bonnie Graff, Program Director, at (858) 535-1111, ext. 3800
or email bgraff@cbisd.org no later than Monday, April 11.

Congregation Beth Israel
ALEINU-Adult Learners Network

How to Raise a Jewish Mensch

Thursday evenings,
April 14th & 21st, May 5th & 12th
7:30 p.m. to 9:00 p.m.
Education Building, Room 203
With Dr. Harvey Raben,
CBI's Director of Education

New parents want their child to sleep through the night. That accomplished, fast forward to more complex goals. Parents want their child to grow into a well-behaved youngster... confident teen. successful adult. Overall, parents want to raise a *mensch*, a person with a sense of meaning, purpose and values.

- Look beyond secular society's parenting "how-to's".
- Learn how the Jewish community, with its four thousand years of experience and wisdom, can help you raise a *mensch*.
- Learn what Judaism says about:

  When to say yes and when to say no
  How to respect the needs of parents and children
  The importance of the individual and his/her place in the Jewish community
  Creating Jewish family memories

This course is designed for parents of children of all ages.

No fee for members and non-members. RSVP to Bonnie Graff, Program Director, at (858) 535-1111 ext. 3800, or email: bgraff@cbisd.org.

Visit Congregation Beth Israel's web site regularly at http://www.cbisd.org/ for updated information and additional ALEINU classes and programs.

Congregation Beth Israel

OUTREACH JEWISH ENRICHMENT SERIES
CO-SPONSORED BY THE UJF
OUTREACH PROGRAM

GOT SHABBAT (and HAVDALAH)?

Saturday, May 14
5:30 P.M.
Foster Family Chapel

Taught by Dr. Al Ray and Cantor Arlene Bernstein, this Shabbat workshop will focus on the blessing, rituals, food, music and other creative ideas for celebrating Shabbat and Havdalah in your home.

- Separate "kid friendly" activities for children
- Instruction and discussion for adults
- All ages will come together for an interactive Havdalah service

There is no fee for this program, but reservations are requested for planning purposes. Please RSVP to Bonnie Graff, Program Director at (858) 535-1111, ext. 3800.

For information on all CBI programming, go to www.cbisd.org

Congregation Beth Israel
Course Evaluation

Your response to this survey helps us plan classes and programs that best meet the needs of our community. Please take a few moments to give us your feedback.

Title of Course/Class/Event_____

Instructor_____ Today's Date_____

I learned about this course/class/event from:

☐ Brochure ☐ Mailer ☐ Flyer ☐ CBI Website ☐ Tidings ☐ Friend

☐ Other_____

| 5 Excellent | 4 Good | 3 Average | 2 Fair | 1 Poor |

	5	4	3	2	1
The course was accurately described	5	4	3	2	1
The instructor demonstrated knowledge of the subject	5	4	3	2	1
The instructor was able to convey this information	5	4	3	2	1
There was active class participation	5	4	3	2	1

What might you like to see changed?
_____

Best time for you to participate in a CBI course:
_____

☐ Sundays ☐ Weekday Evenings ☐ Weekday Mornings ☐ Weekday Afternoons

What other courses or topics would you like to see offered?
_____

AdditionalComments_____
_____
_____

Name (optional)_____

The Many Voices of Conversion

Congregation:	Temple Jeremiah
Address:	937 Happ Road Northfield, IL 60093
Phone number:	(847) 441-5670
Contact's Name and E-mail:	Susan Ardell, outreach@templejeremiah.org
Number of Member Units:	785
URJ Region:	Great Lakes Council
Rabbis:	Paul Cohen, Michelle Greenberg
Outreach Chairperson:	Susan Ardell
Program Cochairpersons:	Anne Richards, Greg Richards

Brief Description: A panel representing four perspectives on Reform Jewish conversion, the rabbi's explanation of the history and essentials of conversion, audience Q&A, and *Havdalah*.

Program Goals: To debunk conversion myths, to present real-life stories from varied perspectives, and to open a dialogue on Judaism's most misunderstood life-cycle event.

Target Population: Potential converts and their families or friends.

Number of Participants: Twenty-three.

Number of Sessions: One.

Staffing: Rabbi, program cochairs, and interviewer.

Total Cost: $34 for fruit tray and wine plus an $18 gift certificate for the babysitter.

Fees: Free.

Source of Funding: Outreach budget.

Logistics: Classroom with four eight-foot tables placed in a rectangle and an eight-foot attractively decorated table for the wine and cheese near the door. A committee chair signed people in; we did not do evaluations in order to respect the privacy of the attendees. This was a mistake as our feedback was incomplete and we needed to phone attendees afterward for their comments.

Curriculum: Rabbi Paul Cohen on *keruv*: Rabbi Cohen gave a brief history of Jewish conversion and explained the ritual and requirements expected of a conversion candidate. From the rabbi we learned that a potential convert's sincerity and clarity of conviction, plus an eagerness to study the basics of Judaism are the necessary components to begin the journey. Our panelists echoed the rabbi in reaffirming that conversion (even the steps leading up to the decision to convert or not) is an ongoing process. The born-Jew in a non-Jewish partner's life is urged to be patient and supportive of whatever decision his or her loved one reaches regarding religion.

Panel: The panel consisted of a convert, a congregant who had chosen not to convert, the spouse of a convert, and the child of a convert. We found no parents of converts willing to participate, so we

interviewed converts regarding their parents' reactions (to their converting) and read these comments as part of the panel presentation. Some parental comments were:
- "I felt like I'd been kicked in the gut."
- "I knew you'd finally get religion."
- "I'm afraid you're going to be different now."
- "The paths to God are many; I am glad you found the one that's right for you."
- "I feel so betrayed."
- "You are my child, and I will always love you."

Discussion: A committee member, who happens to be a psychiatrist, led the question and answer segment, urging that queries be respectful and thoughtful.

Instructions to Facilitator: Set the date on the temple calendar, reserve the room, and arrange for an invitation to appear in the temple newsletter. Interview the panelists in order to make informative introductions. Arrange for refreshments. Have a committee member greet guests as they arrive and thank them as they leave. This person is also responsible for the sign-in and evaluation sheets.

Publicity: "An Open Invitation" from Rabbi Cohen and the outreach committee was published in the temple newsletter one month prior to the program.

Program Evaluation: Temple Jeremiah honors those individuals who commit to raising their children in a religion that is not their own (Judaism). Our non-converting panelist is a beloved and active member of our outreach committee. She felt our respect and thus did not hesitate to offer her views. Our program fulfilled its goal both in educating those who attended on the specifics of conversion and assuring participants that Rabbi Cohen welcomes the opportunity to explore Jewish conversion with anyone who is curious. This program provided an opportunity for an open, informed, and ongoing discussion of Jewish conversion.

Follow-up: Rabbi Cohen welcomes new Jews at the Shabbat service following their conversion ceremony. This year the committee invited all Jews-by-choice to gather and discuss issues they would like to see addressed at Temple Jeremiah. Enrichment classes, mentoring of new converts, and sensitivity to those who have no Jewish families with whom to celebrate holidays headed the list. Additionally, Temple Jeremiah has committed to send a lay leader to the Outreach Fellows Program.

An Open Invitation

Your friends on the Outreach Committee and I invite you to attend an informal program on Jewish conversion. There is a lot of confusion and misinformation about conversion to Judaism. Many people have said that they did not know it was possible to convert. Others have said that they did not know where to begin. Some have even said that Jews do not recognize converts as full Jews. This program is meant to address these issues, clear up confusion, set the record straight, and help people who might wish to consider engaging in the process of conversion themselves.

"The Many Voices of Conversion"
Saturday, October 25
3:00–4:30 P.M.
Temple Jeremiah
R.S.V.P. to Jackie @ 847 441-5760, x101

You won't want to miss this innovative program. Rabbi Cohen will explain the ritual and requirements for a Jewish conversion. A panel of experts will offer their diverse perspectives on the subject and answer any questions you may have. All this will take place in a friendly and respectful atmosphere. We will begin promptly at 3:00 with wine and cheese and end by 4:30 with a brief yet beautiful *Havdalah* service, marking the separation between the end of Shabbat and the beginning of the new week.

Rabbi Paul Cohen, D.Min.
Program Chair Persons ~ Anne & Greg Richards
Program Facilitator ~ Sharon Greenburg

Adult Ed Catalogue

"The Many Voices of Conversion"
Saturday, October 25
3:30–4:30 P.M.

Do you know what Reform Jewish conversion entails? Rabbi Cohen and the Outreach Committee welcome interfaith individuals and couples who are curious to learn about the life-cycle event we as Jews tend to overlook. Rabbi will discuss the ritual of Reform Jewish conversion, and a panel representing diverse voices of congregants who have dealt with or chosen *not* to deal with conversion will give you more food for thought. Reform Judaism asks that we make informed choices. The decision to convert or not should be an informed choice as well.

Call Phyllis Z. @ 847 441-5760 for further information.

Chapter Three

Bridging the Membership Gap: Reaching 20s/30s

Members in their 20s and 30s are the next generation of your congregation's leadership. Reaching and engaging them in meaningful programs is the first step to beginning a lifetime of commitment to your congregation. If this generation is missing from your synagogue, try some of the entry programs that follow as well as the educational and leadership development programs that will ensure a deep connection and commitment to the congregation.

Offering a variety of programs has been a key factor in the success that **Young Congregation** has found in reaching and connecting with people in their 20s and 30s in the Los Angeles area. This is a gateway program for younger members to begin to experience the richness of Jewish life through a variety of temple-based educational, spiritual, and social programs.

20s/30s: A Total Approach models successful advertising and programming for singles, couples, and families by offering a number of programs throughout the year. Programs range from "Professional Connections" to "Mitzvah Corps." Ask your 20s/30s members what they're interested in and go for it!

Do young interfaith couples feel welcome in your congregation? **Love Conquers All: The Gift of Dual-Faith Relationships** is an entry program for interfaith couples in your community. This program is for unaffiliated and affiliated couples who may have questions about their relationships or are curious about what their relationship and future can be with a Reform congregation. Send a message of welcome and support to interfaith couples in your community through this one-of-a kind program geared toward people in their 20s and 30s.

Now that they are your members, how can they become your future leaders? The **Young Leadership Initiative** for potential leaders is a comprehensive year-long program that includes sessions focused on the congregation, Reform Judaism, and leadership skills. This program can create a sense of community among the participants, a connection to the greater congregation, and a means of cultivating your future leaders.

Young Congregation

Congregation:	Stephen S. Wise Temple
Address:	15500 Stephen S. Wise Drive Los Angeles, CA 90077
Phone Number:	(310) 476-8561
Contact's Name and E-mail:	Sarah Cohen, scohen@sswt.org
Number of Member Units:	3,200
URJ Region:	Pacific Southwest Council
Rabbis:	Eli Herscher, David Woznica, Alan Rabishaw, Ron Stern, Brett Krichiver
Membership Director and Young Congregation Coordinator:	Sarah Cohen

Brief Description: Young Congregation (YC) offers a wide variety of programs for our 20s and 30s. Our YC board oversees five different committees (Social and Cultural, Social Action, Learning, Sports Leagues, and Holidays) that plan our programming throughout the year.

- *Learning Committee:*
Continuing Jewish learning in a fun and friendly atmosphere, where all questions are welcome and the answers may surprise you. This year we introduced three- to six-session classes where forty students were able to study with Rabbi Rabishaw on the subject of Genesis. We used the book *Self, Struggle and Change* by Norman J. Cohen. We had a total of thirty-one participants and they all want us to continue the classes next year.

- *Social and Cultural Committee:*
The Social and Cultural Committee organizes events that are geared toward the social side of temple life. We plan events that range from horseback rides to theater, amusement park visits to swing dancing classes. These programs have been very helpful in building community. We also have happy hours once a month that bring in an average of sixty people each time.

- *Social Action Committee:*
The Social Action Committee is committed to practicing the mitzvah of *g'milut chasadim*, doing deeds of loving-kindness. We plan and attend philanthropic events that bring us together with our community and those less fortunate. We are driven by the incredible fulfillment that being involved brings. This committee has participated in a variety of events, including Habitat for Humanity, working with children, and cleaning up our beaches.

- *Holiday Committee:*
Our focus is on the major Jewish holidays. We create and implement holiday celebrations that inform and entertain while developing new traditions and memories. Some past events include our annual Rosh Hashanah Apple Soiree, Hanukkah at Guys where we raised money for Beit Issie Shapiro in Israel, and a second night seder for Passover.

- *Sports Leagues:*
This committee has set up a basketball league for men and coordinated a few softball teams for local leagues. It has been very successful. Last year we had more than sixty men and this year our aim is

eighty. It has been an easy way to get men involved. Some have become involved with other temple programs due to the basketball league.

Program Goal: Young Congregation is the gateway for Stephen S. Wise Temple members, single and married, to begin to experience the richness of Jewish life through a variety of temple-based educational, spiritual, and social programs. The YC community establishes connections and builds relationships with each other in a warm, fun, and welcoming environment. Part of our success comes from thinking outside the "Jewish" box. We are able to achieve that through innovative programming ideas and using relevant life issues to discuss and learn from as we use traditional ideas as pretext for personal conversations.

Target Population: Progressive Jews in Los Angeles in their 20s and 30s.

Number of Participants: We have had more than 800 individuals attend at least one of our programs.

Number and Length of Sessions: Each month we have one social and cultural event, one social action opportunity, and one happy hour. We have had three holiday celebrations this past year and three Shabbat dinners. Our basketball league runs every Sunday from the beginning of June to the end of August.

Staffing Required: Our membership director spends half of her time working on Young Congregation. We also have one rabbi who helps with visioning and leadership. He spends about 5 percent of his time directly working with this program.

Total Cost of Program: We have a budget of $26,000 to use on a variety of programs throughout the year.

Source of Funding: Reduced dues for members up to age thirty-two. In 2004-2005 our dues were $85 per individual. We have approximately 550 individual members between the ages of twenty-one and thirty-two.

Fee for Attendees: We charge different fees for different programs.
- Our basketball league is completely self-sufficient. We charged $80 for members and $100 for nonmembers. This cost covers the staff, officials, jerseys, and marketing.
- Fees for our Genesis class were nominal. We served dinner at each class so we charged $50 for members and $75 for nonmembers. We also had a book fee: *Self, Struggle and Change* (required) for $12 and the *JPS Hebrew-English Tanakh* (optional) for $15.
- Happy hours are free. We pay for appetizers and it is a no host bar.
- Social action programs are free.
- Our social and cultural programs vary. For the most part they are also self-sufficient.
- Holiday programming also varies. We don't charge a fee for our Annual Rosh Hashanah Apple Soiree. This is a catered event immediately following our erev Rosh Hashanah service. Chanukah at Guys was a fund-raising event for Beit Issie Shapiro. We asked for a donation of $10 at the door and then we also had a silent auction. It was a no host bar, but we paid for the food that evening. For our Passover seder we charged a discounted rate for the congregational seder and our programming money helped subsidize the meal.

Instructions to Facilitator: The right marketing is an important aspect of a successful 20s and 30s program, but more importantly the leadership needs to understand the importance of knowing the culture of the city and congregation, providing individual attention and encouraging relationships, and most importantly knowing the fundamentals of community building. This age group will try anything once if they trust the leaders and see them as people they can relate to. Those that work with this group must be seen as friends and cohorts at the temple. The most important aspect of successful 20s and 30s programming is meeting them where they are and nurturing them toward involvement in temple life. If we did not have happy hours, we would have never had the attendance we did in our Genesis class. We started the class because of conversations our membership director had with many of the participants during our social events and social action opportunities.

Evaluation of Program: Young Congregation at Stephen S. Wise Temple has been a true success. We have involved more than 800 individuals in our programming over the last two and a half years. We also know our program is a success because we have been able to create a cohesive community and strong leadership. We also use resources such as surveys to find out how programs were received and how we can improve upon them.

Publicity: This age group responds best to virtual information, whether by e-mail or our Web site (**www.sswt.org/yc/calendar.html**). YC sends out e-mail reminders regarding upcoming programs. We have also started using e-vites as a way to publicize all of our social and cultural programs.

COME INSIDE... TO CONNECT
YOUNG CONGREGATION FOR PEOPLE IN THEIR 20'S AND 30'S

We at Stephen S. Wise Temple should be proud! We have an active group of members in their 20s and 30s who, together with Sarah Cohen and Rabbi Alan Rabishaw, are looking to fulfill their spiritual needs by working to create a relevant, uplifting Jewish community. The YC community establishes connections and builds relationships in a warm, fun, and welcoming atmosphere. Part of our success comes from thinking outside the "Jewish" box. And, we are able to achieve that by reading through entertainment magazines and surfing websites to get programming ideas, eating at trendy restaurants to get event locations, and using relevant life issues to discuss at our lunch and learn, where we use traditional ideas as pretext to personal conversations. Most important are the relationships. Getting to know each Young Congregation member helps us understand their needs and tap into their real interests, and nurture them towards involvement in Temple life. For many, our Young Congregation program is what brings them back to Judaism. They know that Stephen S. Wise Temple provides a safe and friendly community where they can live their lives as Jewish adults. And, because of our enormous commitment to this segment of our Temple community, the Young Congregants know that Stephen S. Wise Temple is their Temple.

For a long time I was looking for a place where I could be free to be both a person and a Jew. So many organizations invite you in with flashy marketing or the promise of new friends or spiritual enlightenment, but they often fall short of their promises and left me disappointed. In my search for something more meaningful, I saw that there was a Young Congregation event at Rabbi Alan Rabishaw's home, where Rabbi Mordechai Gafni was lecturing. His inspiring words, the discussion that followed, and the quality people I met that day made me want to become a part of the SSWT community. Since then I've met an intelligent, warm, civic-minded group of people who are equally excited to be a part of this evolving program. I've found a home, a place to channel my energies — and while it's new, I feel that there are so many avenues that I can explore spiritually, emotionally, socially, and philanthropically in a supportive environment. For the first time in a very long time, I'm exploring my Judaism from the inside out and it's been a wonderful experience. All I needed was an opportunity, and thankfully, I was given one.

AIMEE BITTENSON

Aimee Bittenson has been a Young Congregation Board Member since May 2003 and Chairperson of the Social and Cultural Committee.

I have been a member of Stephen S. Wise Temple since I was four years old. My brother, Alex, and I went to day school from kindergarten through eighth grade, my mom was one of its finest teachers, and my family has been a part of the warm family of some ten thousand families for nearly as long as I can remember.

My very first book, Bubble Lubble, was "published" here and can also be checked out at our library. During a Friday Shabbat Service, Cantor Nate Lam taught me the Jewish lesson that embarrassing someone is like killing them. I read Torah for the first time here, heard my first Kol Nidre, and had my first kiss here (on stage, fully supervised). My mom and dad have taught me the values by which I live and Stephen S. Wise Temple has helped to support them.

Because Stephen S. Wise had been a second home to me throughout my childhood and teen years, I was happy to join independently when I turned 26. And, it is important to me now to serve on the Board of the Young Congregation, so that I can be a part of maintaining the community that has done so much for me and help it flourish for future generations.

And, if G-d so wills it, someday I will stand under a chuppah at the Temple I love so much.

NATASHA ZWICK

Natasha Zwick is a current YC Board Member and has been a lifelong member.

"Get yourself to Stephen S. Wise Temple." That is what Rabbi Ron Stern told me five years ago. It was a simple statement, but I didn't realize how it would change my life. I continued to grow as a Jew through the enriching and challenging Shabbat services, studying Torah, and making the Temple community my home away from home. Through different leadership positions, I have been able to give back to my community by planning social and religious events, participating in Mitzvah Day, and co-chairing a major fundraiser for Israeli terrorist victims. My experience with Young Congregation has piqued my enthusiasm to the potential for involvement at Stephen S. Wise Temple. Now, I want to take my experience to the general Temple community. Now I say to you, get yourself to Stephen S. Wise Temple. I did!

LARRY MARKS

Larry Marks joined SSWT in 1998 and has been a YC Board Member and serves on the Community Working Group.

I've been active in the Jewish community since I moved to Los Angeles in 1994 to work for the Anti-Defamation League. Surprisingly, five years later I still hadn't joined a synagogue. I say "surprisingly" because my family had always belonged to a temple for as long as I can remember. Temple was something I had always grown up with-I would attend Shabbat services with my grandfather, High Holy Day services with my extended family, and I became Bar Mitzvah and was confirmed there, as well. So, when I moved to L.A., it was, likewise, important to me to have the support and stability that a synagogue afforded. When I finally went to look for a temple to join in 1999, I knew what I wanted-a synagogue that valued community service and had a large and active membership in their 20s and 30s. That was Stephen S. Wise Temple. Now with the support and stability of this Temple, I belong to a community.

RANDY STEINBERG

Randy Steinberg has been a member since 1999 and serves on the Board of Young Congregation.

Growing up in this community, it was not uncommon to hear the nearby whispers of those fascinated by "the Rabbi's daughter". I felt early on the significance of being associated with Rabbi Eli Herscher, or should I say, honor, but with that brought me a strong desire for leadership and community. I hoped to someday become a leader within the Congregation and had the opportunity when Young Congregation became involved in adopting an Israeli survivor of terrorism. In this role I was able to fulfill the virtues of community, leadership, and love that my parents instilled in me from such a young age, while also touching the lives of others in our global community.

DAWN HERSCHER

Dawn Herscher (pictured above), Chairperson for "From the Heart 2002" — a YC Fundraiser for an Israeli victim of terror.

Are you in your 20s to 30s? For further information about the Young Congregation or to become involved, please contact Sarah Cohen at 310.889.2242 or yc@sswt.org

The Diener and Kadner Families library's

Mother's Day Luncheon

Thursday, May 6
11:00 a.m. - 2:00 p.m.

Special guest and silent auction.

To RSVP, please contact the Library at 310.889.2317

@WISE PROG

YOUNG CONGREGATION
(FOR AGES 21 – 39)

Lunch and Learn with Rabbi Kupetz and Sarah Cohen
Wednesday, March 17
Noon – 1:30 p.m.
Stanley's in Sherman Oaks 12 13817 Ventura Boulevard. A bite to eat, a bit to learn, and a chance to chat. Make reservations by Monday, March 15th to Sarah Cohen at: yc@sswt.org or 310.889.2242.

Happy Hour
Thursday, March 25
6:30 p.m. – 8:30 p.m.
Tengu Sushi Lounge 10853 Lindbrook Drive in Westwood. Let us know if you plan to join us! You can call Sarah Cohen at 310.889.2242 or yc@sswt.org

A Bio-Ethics Discussion
Sunday, March 28
4:00 p.m. – 6:00 p.m.
Is the world ready for stem cell research, cloning, genetic engineering and manipulation? Ready or not, here they come! What does all of it mean? What are the implications of these new technologies, our seeming power over nature? What sort of laws are currently in place to regulate in these fields? What do our ancient Jewish sources and traditions have to offer us for these uniquely modern issues? Join us for a lively discussion of Judaism and medical ethics, facilitated by Rabbi Sharon Gladstone and Biologist Lisa Kivman.
This event is open to the entire congregation

WOMEN'S RETREAT
IN SANTA BARBARA

"Women Who Count"
Friday, April 23 – Sunday, April 25
The momentum continues to build... Over the last couple of years, Stephen S. Wise Temple women have relished over our women's programs... and the participant feedback has been fantastic! Our 3rd Annual Women's Retreat: "Women Who Count", orchestrated by Michelle November, Cantor Linda Kates and Sarah Cohen is a women's weekend for all ages, which balances experiencing the holiness of Shabbat, the exploration of women and Torah and the sharing of ourselves in a nuturing context.

SOCIAL ACTION

Project Chicken Soup
Sunday, March 14 & 28
Hirsh Kosher Kitchen, Fairfax Area. Prepare meals: 8:00 a.m. – 12 Noon. Help with delivery of meals: 11:45 a.m. – 3:00 p.m.

Temple "Pe'ah" Community Garden
Sunday, March 14
10:00 a.m. – 12 Noon
Help with harvesting and planting. All vegetables are donated to The Valley Shelter.

SOVA Food Pantry, Reseda
Sunday, March 14
10:30 a.m. – 12 Noon
Help stock shelves and distribute food to clients. For Shabbat Services, please bring non-perishable food items for the SOVA bin.

Bingo at the Jewish Home for Aging, Reseda
Thursday, March 18 & 25
6:30 p.m. – 7:30 p.m.
Grancell Village (on March 18); Eisenberg Village (on March 25).

JNF Walk for Water 2004
Sunday, March 21
registration starts 9:30 a.m.
Paramount Ranch, Agoura Hills. Walk to help build Israel's reservoirs! The community of Greater Los Angeles has responded to the water crises in Israel by adopting the Livnim Reservoir in the Galilee. For more details, call JNF, 818.704.5454 or 323.964.1400.

FosterHope
Tuesday, March 23
7:00 p.m.
Taub Annex. This new program, generously funded by the Jewish Community Foundation, pairs Jewish foster kids with Jewish foster families. We invite you to join us for an informational meeting, sponsored by Jewish Family services, to learn more about the mitzvah of fostering (see page 6).

Passover Food Drive
Monday thru Friday
March 29 – April 2
Drop-off at Elementary School morning carpool or at Shabbat Services, food can be deposited in the SOVA bin outside the Westwood Sanctuary.

RAMS

MONTHLY SERVICE WITH RABBI ZELDIN

SHABBAT DINNER SPONSORED BY THE ARNON AND CAMILLE ADAR FAMILY. SHORT SERVICE FOLLOWED BY AN EVENING WITH RABBI ZELDIN

Friday, March 26
6:30 – 8:30 p.m.

Join us for dinner at 6:30 p.m., which includes a selection of wine. Service to follow at 8:30 p.m. in Zeldin-Hershenson Hall. Mail your reservations by February 20, attention Ann Terrick. For more information, call Ann at 310.889.2213.

ELI AND NATE

Tuesday, March 2
7:30 p.m.

Please join guest speaker, Donna Rosenthal, author of the nationally acclaimed, The Israelis: Ordinary People in an Extraordinary Land, which has been called the best book about Israel in decades. (see WWW.THEISRAELIS.NET). Despite the barrage of news headlines that come out of Israel each day, many do not know about the current population of Israel and the vast diversity of Modern Israelis. Ms. Rosenthal will discuss who today's Israelis are--what they look like, what they do, and how this unique mix of people find their way in this "extraordinary" country.

Donna Rosenthal earned her Masters degree in International Relations/Middle Eastern studies from The London School of Economics. She was a news producer at Israel Television, a reporter for Israel Radio and The Jerusalem Post, and a lecturer at the Hebrew University of Jerusalem. Ms. Rosenthal's many travels have taken her to over sixty countries, reporting from Iran, Lebanon, Egypt, Jordan, and being the first journalist to travel to the remote mountain villages of Ethiopia. Donna Rosenthal is also a winner of two Lowell Thomas Awards for Best Investigative Reporting and Best Adventure Travel Writing. She is also author of the award-winning book, Passport Israel: Israeli Business, Customs and Etiquette.

Share Your Special Temple Memory in our 40th Anniversary Family Album

STEPHEN S. WISE TEMPLE CELEBRATES ITS 40TH ANNIVERSARY AND HONORS LYNN AND LES BIDER

Join us for a spectacular evening of entertainment at our Gala Concert on Wednesday, May 12, 2004 at Royce Hall, UCLA Campus

You and your family will be able to honor the Biders and have your own personal reflections or memories included as part of the Family Album.

40th Anniversary Family Album

$25,000 includes 10 tickets*

$18,000 includes 8 tickets*

$10,000 includes 6 tickets*

$ 5,000 includes 4 tickets*

$ 2,500 includes 2 tickets*

$ 1,000 full page includes photo and personal reflection

$ 500 half page includes personal reflection

$ 250 quarter page includes personal reflection

$ 100 listing

*All donations of $2,500 or above include a full-page in the Family Album, with a personal photograph of their choosing. Also included is priority reserved concert tickets, dinner reception and complimentary parking.

Those who purchase a ¼ page or larger will be able to include a personal reflection or memory.

For additional information, please contact Corey Slavin, Director of Development at 310.889.2276 or email: development@sswt.org.

THE FORTIETH ANNIVERSARY · 1964-2004

Chapter Three   Bridging the Membership Gap: Reaching 20s/30s   **173**

@WISE PROGRAMS

All kinds of camps

STEPHEN S. WISE TEMPLE
SUMMER CAMPS 2004

All kinds of kids

Register for second session
TODAY!!!

310.889.2345
www.sswt.org/summercamps

SOCIAL ACTION

Stay connected during the lazy days of Summer...

SOVA Food Pantry, Reseda
Sunday, July 11 and August 8
10:30 a.m. – 12 Noon
"Hunger Doesn't Take a Summer Vacation." Help at the pantry or for Shabbat Services, please bring non-perishable food items for the SOVA bin.

Project Chicken Soup
Sunday, July 11 and 25,
August 8 and 22
Hirsh Kosher Kitchen, Fairfax Area
Prepare meals, 8:00 a.m. – 12 Noon
Help with delivery of meals,
11:45 a.m. – 3:00 p.m.

Bingo at the Jewish Home for the Aging, Reseda
Thursday, July 15, 22, and August 26
6:30 p.m. – 7:30 p.m.
Grancell (7/15); Eisenberg (7/22 & 8/26)

Habitat for Humanity
Sunday, July 18 and August 15
8:30 a.m. – 2:30 p.m.
Build at our Pierce Street Project, Pacoima
(No experience necessary. Must be 14 years of age and accompanied by an adult).

Let's Party at Adoption Day
Saturday, July 31
7:00 a.m. – 12:00 Noon
Children's Court in Monterey Park.
We will greet families, serve snacks, and provide entertainment as more than 250 foster children will be adopted by their new families. Sponsored by Public Counsel. Bus transportation will be provided to and from the Temple.

County/USC AIDS Clinic Lunch Program
Tuesday, August 17
6:45 p.m. – 7:30 p.m.
Make lunches for over 150 AIDS patients. We need helpers to deliver meals the next day.

Help plan Mitzvah day 2004
Meeting: Monday, July 19 at 7:30 p.m.
Annual Potluck Dinner: Tuesday, August 17 at 6:00 p.m.
Save the date — Sunday, November 7
For additional summer fun while making the world a better place, join us for our summer meeting.

For information or to register for any of our Social Action activities, please call Diane Kabat at 310.889.2274, visit our website: www.sswt.org/sac, or e-mail: dkabat@sswt.org.

YOUNG CONGREGATION
(FOR PEOPLE IN THEIR 20S AND 30S)

Happy Hours
Let us know if you plan to join us by contacting Sarah Cohen at yc@sswt.org or 310.889.2242.

Thursday, July 22
6:30 until the last person leaves!
Tengu Sushi: 10853 Lindbrook Drive, Westwood, CA 90024

Thursday, August 19
The W Hotel by the pool: 930 Hilgard Avenue, Los Angeles, CA 90024

Shabbat Dinner at Rabbi Rabishaw's
Friday, August 13
Join us for Early Shabbat 6:15 p.m. Services at Stephen S. Wise Temple and then at Rabbi Alan and Laura Rabishaw's home at 8:00 p.m. for dinner. Directions will be sent when we get your reservation. RSVP by August 10 to Sarah Cohen at yc@sswt.org or call 310.889.2242.

YC Joins Habitat for Humanity
Sunday, August 15
8:30 a.m. – 2:30 p.m.
11257 Borden Avenue, Pacoima, CA 91331
If you are interested in joining us, please let Sarah Cohen know by August 11 at yc@sswt.org or call 310.889.2242.

"Under Milk Wood" & Evening at Froggy's
Sunday, July 25
5:00 p.m. – 10:00 p.m.
  Add a little nature, a dash of theatre, sprinkle with some delicious seafood, and you've got a recipe for a fantastic Sunday night! Join us for a sumptuous, seafood dinner at Froggy's Restaurant followed by an evening under the stars at the Will Geer Theatricum Botanicum for a production of "Under Milk Wood," by Dylan Thomas.
  "Under Milk Wood" is a sensitive, often comic examination of Welsh life, in which the people are viewed as being particularly blessed. The fictitious town that Dylan Thomas named "Llareggub" is a town where dysfunctions ranging from alcoholism to xenophobia are a way of life. Even the name of the place is "buggerall" spelled backwards. This production forces members of the audience to interrupt their laughter and ask the chilling question: "What are we laughing at?" And the answer may very well be: "Ourselves."

Poolside Barbecue & Movie
Sunday, August 29
5:30 p.m.
Like, for sure! Gag me with a spoon! Sound familiar? Either that makes you want to cringe or gives you fond memories of big hair, neon clothing, Madonna-bes, and John Hughes movies. Join us as we relive the 1980s in their full glory at a poolside barbecue and movie night! Bring your bathing suit and your appetite for an evening of casual fun by the pool, as we barbecue, swim, and enjoy some of your favorite 80's movies right here at the Freedman Pool of Stephen S. Wise Temple. Like, we'll totally see you there!

174 The Outreach and Membership Idea Book

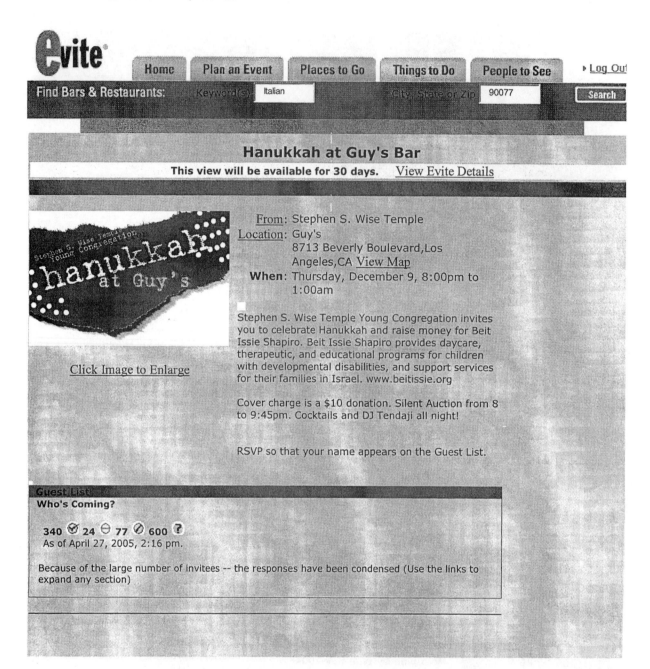

Tuesday, October 14 Sukkot Festival and Concert

In 1964 Stephen S. Wise Temple broke ground and introduced a new era of Jewish life. We are celebrating this time with Grammy Winner Peter Yarrow from Peter Paul and Mary. Come join us as we kick-off our 40th Anniversary with Hayrides, Hoola Hoops, Magicians, Jugglers and a free dinner from our wonderful Casiano Catering. Please RSVP to the Anniversary Hotline: 310.889.2273 or hzolan@sswt.org.

5:30-7:00 - Hayrides, Hoola Hoops, Magicians, Jugglers, Dinner
7:00-8:00 - Peter Yarrow Concert for all Ages
8:15 - More Peter for Adults and Teens

The evening is free of charge, yet reservations are required. RSVP to Anniversary Hotline: 310.889.2273 or hzolan@sswt.org.

Sunday, October 26 Walk for Juvenile Diabetes

On Sunday morning, October 26th, thousands of Angelinos will gather at Santa Monica Beach for the annual Juvenile Diabetes Research Foundation International's "Walk to Cure Diabetes." We at Stephen S. Wise will bring a group of dedicated walkers and supporters to help find a cure for this chronic, debilitating disease. Our effort is being headed by our own Young Congregation Board member, Natasha Zwick. Natasha has been diagnosed with Diabetes for 21 years as of this past July. She is healthy today "but the threat of complications looms forever large over me and over my family, and I, like the other estimated 120 million people worldwide, need a cure now." Register now at: http://walk.jdrf.org/

Sunday, November 2 Mitzvah Day

Through Jewish Big Brothers/Big Sisters, you can change a child's life. Be a "Sports Buddy" for the day at Camp Max Straus in Glendale. Games, Crafts, Hikes. Lunch. 10:00 am - 3:30 pm Dress comfortably! Bring walking shoes and a loving attitude!
If you want to join us contact Sarah at 310-889-2242 or yc@sswt.org by October 27th. Directions to follow

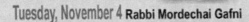

Tuesday, November 4 Rabbi Mordechai Gafni

7:30 p.m. Westwood Sanctuary: Love or Die: The Way of the Kabbalist Although Reb Mordechai will be with us all week Young Congregation is encourage to come for this session especially.

Friday, November 14 Temple and Taquitos!

Join us for 6:15 Services at Stephen S. Wise Temple and then to El Cholo in Santa Monica at 8:00pm for dinner and great times with friends! To make reservations e-mail Sarah at yc@sswt.org or call her at 310-889-2242 no later than November 12th.

Thursday, November 20
A Few Martinis + A Few Friends = Many Good Times!

Join the Young Congregation for Happy Hour on Nov. 20th. Location to be announced. We're getting together for no holiday, no event and no reason; only to catch up with current friends and meet new ones. 6:00pm till whenever! If you are interested e-mail Sarah at yc@sswt.org

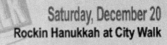

Saturday, December 20
Rockin Hanukkah at City Walk

Save the date and watch for more details.

Holiday Workshop Wednesday Night Classes

7:30pm. The price is very YC friendly $60 and Shelley Fischel, the teacher is very enthusiastic. Shelley really gets into the 'Why' not just the 'What' of holidays, which is a draw for Young Congregation. You can either sign up for one workshop for $60 or the entire series for $275

Shabbat: October 22, 29, and November 5, 12
Hanukkah: November 19 and December 3, 10, 17

Winter '04

Lunch & Learn
with Rabbi Kupetz and Sarah Cohen
A bite to eat, a bit to learn, and a chance to chat. Make reservations the Monday before to Sarah Cohen at 310.889.2242 or yc@sswt.org

❋ Wednesday, February 11, 2004 - 12:00 Noon - 1:30 p.m.
The Cheesecake Factory in Brentwood, 11647 San Vicente Boulevard

❋ Wednesday, March 17, 2004 - 12:00 Noon - 1:30 p.m.
Stanley's in Sherman Oaks, 13817 Ventura Boulevard

❋ Wednesday, April 21, 2004 - 12:00 Noon - 1:30 p.m.
P.F. Changs in Santa Monica, 326 Wilshire Boulevard

Happy Hours
6:30 until the last person leaves!
Please RSVP to Sarah Cohen at 310.889.2242 or yc@sswt.org

❋ Thursday, February 26, 2004
Watch the Lakers play the Sacramento Kings. BJ's Brewery, 6424 Canoga Ave, Woodland Hills.

❋ Thursday, March 25, 2004
Happy Hour at Tengu Sushi, 10853 Lindbrook Drive, Westwood.

❋ Thursday, May 20, 2004
Join us for drinks and an unparalleled 360° view of the Pacific Ocean, city skyline, and surrounding mountains with friends! Toppers at the Radisson Huntley Hotel, 1111 Second Street, Santa Monica.

Shabbat!

❋ **Saturday, February 28, 2004**
Join in the celebration for our 40th Anniversary
- 4:30 p.m. Wine and Cheese
- 5:00 p.m. Havdalah
Please RSVP to Sarah Cohen at 310.889.2242 or yc@sswt.org

❋ **Friday, April 23, 2004**
- 6:15 p.m. Join us for services
- 8:30 p.m. Dinner at El Dorado
11777 San Vicente Boulevard, Brentwood
Please RSVP by April 21 to Sarah Cohen at 310.889.2242 or yc@sswt.org

Social Action

❋ Sunday, February 8, 2003 - 9:00 a.m. - 2:00 p.m.
Tu B'Shevat Community
Come establish roots for future generations as we celebrate our 40th Anniversary. Join us for a Picnic and Hike with 20s - 30s members at Malibu Creek State Park.
What to bring: Comfortable walking shoes and a picnic lunch to enjoy in the beautiful Santa Monica Mountains.
Suggested donation: $18 to help environmental projects in Los Angeles and Israel. *If you want to join us please RSVP to Sarah Cohen at 310.889.2242 or yc@sswt.org*

❋ Sunday, May 2, 2003
Sports Buddy with Camp Max Straus
Spend the Sunday bringing happiness to children from single - parent homes! Come to Camp Max Straus in Glendale and bring walking shoes and your big heart because we will be a "Sports Buddy" for a day. We will be hanging out, playing games, and having lunch with kids through Jewish Big Brothers/Big Sisters. *RSVP by April 28 to Sarah Cohen at 310.889.2242 or yc@sswt.org We will then send you directions.*

Learning

❋ Sunday March 28, 2004 - 4:00 p.m. - 6:00 p.m.
Udko Annex
An excellent bio-ethics discussion sponsored by Young Congregation. Is the world ready for stem cell research, cloning, and genetic engineering and manipulation? Ready or not, here they come! What does all of it mean? What are the implications of these new technologies, our seeming power over nature? What sort of laws are currently in place to regulate in these fields? What do our ancient Jewish sources and traditions have to offer us for these uniquely modern issues? Join us for a lively discussion of Judaism and Medical Ethics, facilitated by *Rabbi Sharon Gladstone and Biologist Lisa Kivman.*
RSVP by March 24 to Sarah Cohen at 310.889.2242 or yc@sswt.org

❋ *Rabbi Sharon Gladstone* was ordained from HUC-LA in 2003 after completing her rabbinic theses on stem cell research. Rabbi Gladstone is currently the director of the Jeff Herman Virtual Resource Center for Sexual Orientation Issues in the Jewish Community.
Lisa Kivman has a BS in Environmental Biology and is currently working on her Masters thesis in Genetic/Population Biology. She currently works at Amgen Inc. doing expression profiling using microarray.

Basketball Starts November 29th!

To sign-up, go to www.koshermeetmarket.org/bball.htm
Got questions? Write to alicia@koshermeetmarket.org for all the answers!

Happy Hour at the W Hotel

Thursday, November 20th

We will be meeting at the The Backyard at The W Hotel in Westwood (930 Hilgard Ave) starting at 6:30 and ending when the last person leaves. If you are interested in unwinding after a hard day let me know. Drop me an e-mail so we have enough room for all of us!

New Member Shabbat Dinner

Friday, November 21st

For those who joined starting December 2003 until the present we have invited you to join us for service and dinner.
Let me know if you can come! It is a great way to meet our clergy and our board members.

Chanukah Funky Style

December 20
5-9pm

Tu Tu Tango and Universal Citywalk presents Chanukah like you have never imagined!
Great Food, Good times, Ice Skating, Dancing- a night you don't want to miss!
Members $25 and Non members $40.
Make reservations by Tuesday 16th to Sarah Cohen at 310-889-2242 or YC@sswt.org!

Sarah Cohen MSW, MAJCS
Director of Membership
Young Congregation Coordinator
Stephen S. Wise Temple
www.sswt.org

Manischewitz No More!

Experience an array of distinctive Passover wines

from around the world

Join the Young Congregation (20s and 30s) for a

Wine Tasting and Second Night Passover Seder

at Stephen S. Wise Temple's Zeldin-Hershenson Hall

Sunday, April 24, 2005

Wine Tasting 4:30 p.m. and Seder 6:00 p.m.

For special YC price of

$35/members and $45/non-members

RSVP to

http://www.sswt.org/yc/calendar.html

Inquiries: 310.889.2242
lwarshaw@sswt.org

On February 14, 2001, a Palestinian bus driver deliberately ran over a group of soldiers standing at a bus stop, Monique Goldwasser being one of them. Eight young people were killed that day and Monique was given a less than 1% chance of surviving the night. She miraculously survived that night and has spent the last almost two years continuing to survive through numerous surgeries and painful realities.

(All money raised will help Monique as part of the Adopt-a-Family organization.)

Stephen S. Wise Temple's Young Congregation invites you to
our First Annual Fundraiser

"From the Heart"

Join us and other young Jewish professionals and Monique Goldwasser* for a relaxing soirée with delicious food, cocktails, live music, and an exciting raffle all the while supporting a worthy cause.

Thursday February 27, 2003
7:30pm
Skirball Cultural Center
Ahmanson Hall
$30 per person (includes 2 raffle tickets)
$35 at the door

Additional raffle tickets may be purchased at the event.
Some Raffle prizes include: Four Seasons, ski tickets, restaurant certificates and Disneyland tickets.

For more information or to request an invitation for a friend,
Contact Sarah Cohen at YC@SSWT.ORG or call 310-889-2242.

20s/30s: A TOTAL APPROACH

Congregation:	Congregation Schaarai Zedek
Address:	3303 W. Swann Ave. Tampa, FL 33606
Phone Number:	(813) 876-2377
Contact's Name and E-mail:	Sherry Stein, sstein@zedek.org
Number of Member Units:	950
URJ Region:	Southeast Council
Rabbis:	Richard J. Birnholz, D.D., Shoshanah Conover
Outreach Chairpersons:	Wiatt Bowers, Elise DellaRocca, Lisa Rohatiner

Brief Description: 20s/30s outreach programming is carried out through a variety of programming and special low-fee member dues.

Program Goal: To welcome 20s/30s into the Schaarai Zedek community.

Target Population: Singles and couples in their 20s and 30s.

Number of Participants: Twenty-five to seventy-five individuals, depending on the event. There are seventy-eight membership units for this age group in the congregation.

Number and Length of Sessions: Three minutes to two hours, depending on the event.

Staffing Required: Senior rabbi, assistant rabbi, and program director each oversee parts of the program.

Total Cost of Program: Approximately $2,000 (including $600 advertising, $400 printing and postage).

Source of Funding: Temple budget.

Fee for Attendees: Usually no fee, or event is "Dutch treat."

Evaluation of Program: Participation continues to grow. Board of trustees continues to provide support.

20's/30's: A Total Approach

During this time in Jewish history, when demographers are warning about declining Jewish growth, we at Congregation Schaarai Zedek asked ourselves: How do we reach out to young potential members beyond our geographic area when we are no longer the only synagogue available to them? We believe we have found an answer – in fact, several answers – to that question, and are nurturing a group of members (and potential members) in their 20's and 30's.

Our synagogue is located in a sprawling urban area with a population of over 1,000,000. To attract young professionals, we knew we needed special programs in trendy places close to the synagogue. But, paradoxically, to attract young families we had to reach out to new housing developments 15 to 45 minutes from our synagogue's South Tampa location. The lack of property available and escalating real estate costs were preventing young families from moving to South Tampa. We also knew that five other synagogues are available to young families in outlying areas. Thus, the question arose: How do we remain vital when geographic location becomes a factor in young outreach? We answered this using two concurrent approaches. One is Next *Dor*: The Schaarai Zedek Young Professional Connection. The other is establishing neighborhood-based young family programming in our own vicinity and in four growing suburban Tampa communities, (as designated by *The Tampa Tribune*'s community Web sites). We chose the four other areas because we had young congregants living there who could assist us in our outreach efforts. We saw each community as a potential area of growth. We did not think it prudent to limit ourselves to our immediate vicinity or to just one of the growing Tampa suburban areas.

Our goal is to reach out to this population in a variety of ways. Thus, we talk about **20'S/30's: A Total Approach**.

Next *Dor*: The Schaarai Zedek Young Professional Connection:

As the economic potential of the Tampa Bay area began to be realized in the new millennium, Congregation Schaarai Zedek began to receive an energizing number of phone calls from young Jews being lured here by professional opportunities. In response to these calls, **Next *Dor*: The Schaarai Zedek Young Professional Connection** began in November 2000. "*Dor*," of course, means generation. We recognize that these young people, who seek to make Jewish connections in their lives, are our "next generation" of Jewish leaders. Some are single; some are couples. Synagogue membership is not a requirement for participation in this group. And because we know that we must be creative, planning meetings take place in coffee houses and Torah Study (called "Jew on This") is always relevant to modern life. We are not afraid to ask "Where is a good bar?" in planning Next *Dor* Happy Hours, or to offer discussions on contemporary issues such as Internet dating or the *DaVinci Code*. Members periodically plan their own creative Shabbat experiences, such as special worship services or progressive dinners. We try to offer these young people a plethora of options so that each can find what he or she needs to create a fulfilling Jewish life.

Neighborhood Young Family Programming:

Not all of our 20's and 30's are single or couples without children. Programming for those with young children becomes important to outreach if we want to recruit them before their children reach Religious School age. If we wait until later we are afraid that they might choose synagogues closer to their homes.

Our neighborhood-based young family outreach is a multi-pronged approach. We begin with an advertising campaign in neighborhood newspapers in each of the targeted areas. Every year, we plan concurrent **holiday celebrations** in homes in each of the five targeted communities as well. We build Sukkot in the Fall and celebrate Tu B'Shvat in the winter. **Tot Shabbat Services,** though usually held at Temple, are conducted periodically at a suburban preschool. **Mazel Lights** is a group that began to help "young families without local family" celebrate together. Each holiday, this group rotates the location of its activities, so that home-based events are always in different neighborhoods. We light candles. We shake the lulav. We celebrate Pesach. But most important, we go to young families in their own neighborhoods. Families are encouraged to invite unaffiliated neighbors and friends. Our clergy always participates. And we invite groups like *Achot*, Young Women's Hadassah, to participate with us. We believe that our social groups are often the first avenue that young families use to establish their Jewish identity. As with Next *Dor*, membership is not a prerequisite, and non-member fees are never charged. We want the young Jewish community to feel welcome and embraced at Schaarai Zedek. Because young children usually have young parents, these events are powerful outreach opportunities for those in their 20s and 30's.

Young Adult Member Plan:

For many, participating in a Schaarai Zedek event is the first step toward synagogue membership. Our **Young Adult Member Plan**, begun in July 2001, makes it possible for young singles, young couples and young families to join Schaarai Zedek at a highly manageable rate which rises gradually by age without exceeding their budgets. The dues for the Young Adult Member Plan have not been raised since the plan was established. In 2003, the Capital Improvement Commitment required of new members was changed so that payments begin at age 35 instead of age 30. We hope that the Young Member Plan fosters the sense that Schaarai Zedek is a compassionate Jewish synagogue community that understands the needs of young adults. (Of course, we also have a long-standing Temple policy never to turn anyone away because of inability to pay). We want these younger members to know that Schaarai Zedek will encourage and support them as they establish their lives as Jewish adults.

Reaching the 20's and 30's singles and families also takes some "out of the box" thinking. Of course, we advertise Next *Dor* events via periodic mailings, e-mails, and notices in the Temple bulletin. But we also advertise in alternative media, such as *The Weekly Planet* newspaper, neighborhood newspapers, and on the Web in "News for Tampa Bay Jews," a local 20's and 30's listserv.

Is Schaarai Zedek's outreach to young Jews in their 20's and 30's successful? We hope so. We know that in 2000, we had 74 synagogue members in this age group. Today, we have 78. And, in September 2004, the majority of new students enrolled in our Religious School (whose parents were new Temple members) did not live in our South Tampa area. There is no problem finding people willing to lead our 20's/30's social groups. The cost of this program (advertising, reduced fees) will be more than realized as these young participants become our Jewish future, and as Schaarai Zedek becomes the synagogue that they choose to join, despite its location in an older urban area.

Congregation Schaarai Zedek Young Adult Member Plan
Basic Financial Commitment for Under Age 35 years

Please complete this financial form *instead* of the one in the Membership Application. Then return this form *and the rest of the Membership Application* to the Temple Office.

2004-2005

Name_____Birthdate_____

Name_____Birthdate_____

Welcome to Congregation Schaarai Zedek. We hope you will become an active participant in our activities. If you have any questions, call the Temple office at 876-2377. For all High Holy Day Services your special **Young Adult Member Plan** entitles you to one adult ticket for a **Single Membership** and two Adult tickets for a **Family Membership**. Children's tickets are available if applicable. Admission is free to Schaarai Zedek activities unless there is a member charge for the program. **There may be fees for Life Cycle Events, including Weddings, Brit, Baby Namings and Funerals. Religious School fees also apply.**

The **Basic Financial Commitment** is the minimum level of annual support required for each member. **The first three months' payment of the Basic Financial Commitment must accompany your Membership Application.** The Basic Financial Commitment for a **Family Membership** is based on the age of the oldest applicant. No one is ever denied membership at Schaarai Zedek for financial reasons. Contact the Temple Financial Secretary if you need to make special financial arrangements. Please check below to indicate the age of the oldest applicant and circle to indicate if this is a Family or Single membership.

	Family	Single
____ Age 30 and under	$300	$156
____ Age 31	$432	$252
____ Age 32	$552	$360
____ Age 33	$684	$456
____ Age 34	$804	$552

In addition to the *Basic Financial Commitment*, new members are required to make a pledge of $200 a year for five years to the *Capital Improvement Fund*. Singles and Families with the oldest applicant under 35 years of age may defer payment until they reach age 35.

If you are blessed and able to contribute more, please join our Torah Circle. This is a gift of Tzedakah above the Basic Financial Commitment and Capital Improvement Fund. It allows the Congregation to welcome all Jews regardless of their financial ability.

Beracha (Blessing)	$250	*Ahava* (Love)	$2,500
Shalom (Peace)	$500	*Chesed* (Kindness)	$3,000
Kavod (Honor)	$750	*Tzedek* (Righteous)	$5,000
Simcha (Joy)	$1,000	*Maasim Tovim* (Good Deeds)	$7,500
Chai (Life)	$1,800	*Bet HaKnesset* (Synagogue)	$10,000 or more

Please Indicate Your Preferred Payment Plan:
__ Annual __ Semi-annual
__ Quarterly __ Monthly

First 3 Months Financial Commitment Fee... $_____
Life Cycle Fee... $_____
Torah Circle Pledge................................... $_____
TOTAL.. $_____

Applicant's Signature_____Date_____

Applicant's Signature_____Date_____

Next *Dor:* Schaarai Zedek's Young Professional Connection* (Please note change on Nov. 18 event!)

Next *Dor* Mitzvah Corps
Sunday, November 14
9:00 a.m. – 1:00 p.m.
Schaarai Zedek Mitzvah Day/Big Cat Rescue
12802 Easy Street, 920-4130
November is our "Mitzvah Month." Come out, meet Next *Dor* members while you help others. Our Next *Dor* Mitzvah Day project will take us to Big Cat Rescue (near Citrus Park Mall). Big Cat Rescue is a permanent retirement home for more than 150 exotic cats. It is accredited as an Animal Rescue Facility by the Association of Sanctuaries. Help paint cages for these dignified, aging creatures. Call Wiatt (876-2909) for information.

Next *Dor* Third Thursday Social
Thursday, November 18
7:00 p.m. – 9:00 p.m.
Mangroves Grill and Bar
208 S. Howard Ave.
It's time for another Next *Dor* Social. Meet at Mangroves Grill and Bar for fun, friends and conversation. Call Wiatt (876-2909) for information.

Next *Dor* /Collaborative Council Chanukah Party
Saturday, December 11
Save the Date!!

*A social group for Jewish young adults in their 20s and 30s. To learn more, call Wiatt Bowers, chair (876-2909) or Sherry Stein, Program Director (876-2377).

Next *Dor:* Schaarai Zedek's Young Professional Connection*

Next *Dor* "Third Thursday" Happy Hour Social
Thursday, January 20
7:00 p.m. – 9:00 p.m.
Dubliner Pub
2807 W. Azeele
258-2257
Thirsty? Hungry? Our Third Thursday Happy Hour is back! Come to the Dubliner Pub to greet old friends and meet new ones. Call Wiatt (813-876-2909) for information.

Next *Dor* Shabbat Progressive Dinner
Friday, February 4
7:00 p.m. until...
Locations: Rabbi Conover's, Matt Michaels' & Wiatt Bowers' homes
Plan to attend our first Shabbat Progressive Dinner. Begin at Rabbi Shoshannah and Damien Conover's apartment for appetizers. Move to Matt Michaels' new town house for dinner (dairy/veggie) and finish at Wiatt Bowers' for dessert. A gastronomic feast and fun, too! Call Wiatt (813-876-2909) for information.

*A social group for Jewish young adults in their 20s and 30s. To learn more, call Wiatt Bowers, chair (876-2909) or Rabbi Shoshannah Conover (876-2377).

Next *Dor:* Schaarai Zedek's Young Professional Connection*

Next Dor "Third Thursday" Happy Hour Social
Thursday, May 19
7:00 p.m. - 9:00 p.m.
Dubliner Pub
2807 W. Azeele St., Tampa
(813) 258-2257
Thirsty? Hungry? Come to our Third Thursday Happy Hour/Dinner/Social. Meet at the Dubliner Pub -- greet old friends. Meet new ones, too. Co-sponsored with Rodeph Sholom's 20s/30s Committee.

Next Dor 's "Jew on This"
Wednesday, May 25
7:00 p.m. - 8:30 p.m.
Location: Rabbi Conover's Home
J-Date, Speed-dating, Matchmaker. Do you really have a soul mate out there who is also looking for you? What does our Torah teach us about "B'shert"? For information, call Rachel Cohen (813-416-6219) or Rabbi Conover (813-876-2377, ext. 229).

*A social group for Jewish young adults in their 20s and 30s. To learn more, call Wiatt Bowers, chair (813-876-2909) or Rabbi Conover (813-876-2377, ext. 229).

Build a Sukkah ..... Meet Your Neighbors
Sunday, October 12
4:00 pm – 6:00 pm
New Tampa Sukkah at the home of:
Dawn and Doug Schocken
7225 Warcham Dr (972-5006)
(Directions upon request)

Schaarai Zedek is building a sukkah in your neighborhood. We want you and your family to help. Bring fruit (real or paper) ready to hang. One of our Rabbis or Cantor will visit. Stay for "Pizza in the Hut", a family pizza dinner in the sukkah, provided by the Temple. Our "Build a Sukkah" event is great! Invite your unaffiliated friends and neighbors to come, too.

RSVP to the Temple Office 876-2377 by Wednesday, October 8

Build a Sukkah ..... Meet Your Neighbors
Sunday, October 12
4:00 pm – 6:00 pm
Westchase Northwest Sukkah at the home of:
Sharon and Dan Ravner
11635 Fox Creek Dr. (854-1864)
(Directions upon request)

Schaarai Zedek is building a sukkah in your neighborhood. We want you and your family to help. Bring fruit (real or paper) ready to hang. One of our Rabbis or Cantor will visit. Stay for "Pizza in the Hut", a family pizza dinner in the sukkah, provided by the Temple. Our "Build a Sukkah" event is great! Invite your unaffiliated friends and neighbors to come, too.

RSVP to the Temple Office 876-2377 by Wednesday, October 8

Tot Shabbat...
Bringing our Prayground to Westchase!

Tot Shabbat is a brief service with singing, challah and juice, and a special Jewishly oriented craft, for young children to learn about the traditions of Shabbat. Families with young children are invited to celebrate with us....members, non-members, unaffilitated, parents, grandparents are all welcome!

Friday Nov. 5, 2004, 6:45 to 7:15PM at Kids R' Kids, 9802 Westchase Dr.

To make a reservation call 813-876-2377 or go to www.zedek.org

Celebrate Shabbat in Westchase with Rabbi Birnholz! **CONGREGATION SCHAARAI ZEDEK**

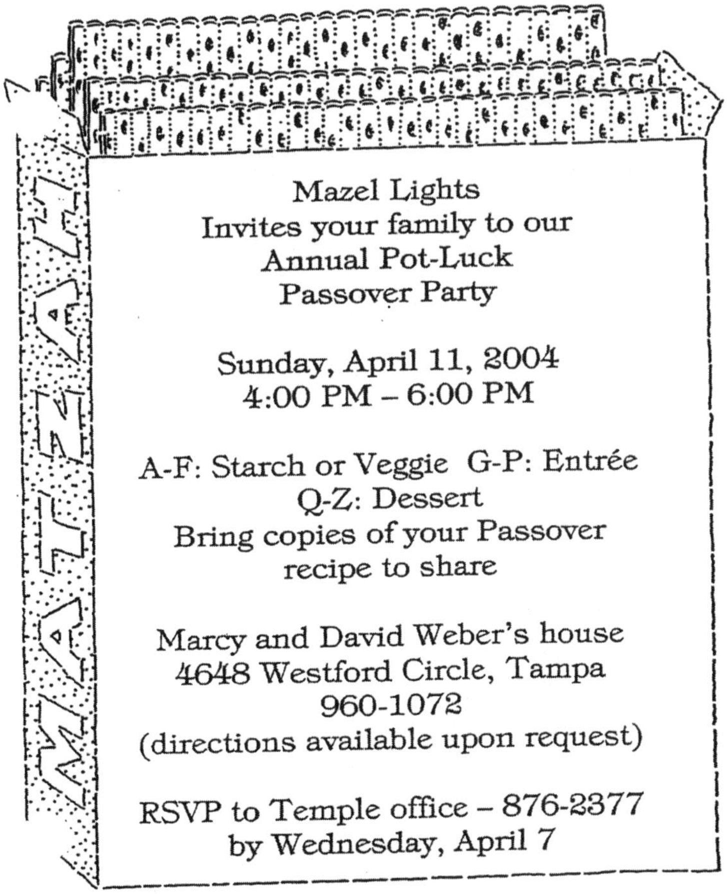

Mazel Lights
Invites your family to our
Annual Pot-Luck
Passover Party

Sunday, April 11, 2004
4:00 PM – 6:00 PM

A-F: Starch or Veggie G-P: Entrée
Q-Z: Dessert
Bring copies of your Passover
recipe to share

Marcy and David Weber's house
4648 Westford Circle, Tampa
960-1072
(directions available upon request)

RSVP to Temple office – 876-2377
by Wednesday, April 7

OCTOBER 24-25, 2003

Congregants introduced to sukkah-building by temple-organized neighborhood parties

By MINDY RUBENSTEIN
Jewish Press

Imagine never having built a sukkah before, the first time being in your backyard with 50 other people and your rabbi helping out. For Sharon and Dan Ravner of Congregation Schaarai Zedek in Tampa, that was their initiation to Sukkot.

On Sunday, Oct. 12, several dozen families gathered for a Sukkot celebration in the backyard of the Ravners' Westchase home in northwest Hillsborough County. Parents and children, led by Rabbi Richard Birnholz, hung tarps for the sukkah walls and strung colorful fruit to adorn the inside.

Part of Schaarai Zedek's second annual community Sukkot event, this was one of four neighborhood parties. The others, held in South Tampa, New Tampa and Carrollwood, were led by other members of Schaarai Zedek's professional staff: Rabbi Eric Lazar, Cantor Riselle Bain, and Educator Ann Rubin.

"We want to introduce more people to the tradition and encourage them to take part in it," Rabbi Birnholz said.

Rabbi Birnholz demonstrates shaking the lulav. Others who attended the sukkah-building party Included (L-R) Randi Mitchell, Sharon Ravner, Chuck Segal, Andrew Bagil, Kate Marcus, Leah Marcus, Kayla Marcus and Randy Marcus.

Children hang fruit in the sukkah.

At the Westchase party, Rabbi Birnholz gave instructions for building the sukkah and explained the meaning behind the various traditions.

Sukkot has a historical and agricultural significance, he said, commemorating the 40 years the children of Israel were wandering in the desert, living in temporary shelters. Sukkot is also a festival that marked the end of a long harvest. To celebrate their hard work, the farmers and their families would go to the temple in Jerusalem to offer thanks. They built sukkot, or booths, to remember how the children of Israel built booths in the desert.

The sukkah should have at least three walls, with a roof made out of something natural such as palm fronds or bamboo that allow those inside to see the stars at night, the rabbi explained.

Another tradition of Sukkot involves the etrog, a citrus fruit native to Israel; a lulav, or palm branch; as well as two willow branches and three myrtle branches. The six branches are bound together and referred to collectively as the lulav. The different shaped leaves represent the eyes, heart, and other parts of human beings, Rabbi Birnholz said.

With the lulav and etrog in hand, the rabbi recited a blessing and waved them in all six directions, east, south, west, north, up and down, symbolizing the fact that God is everywhere. During the light-hearted demonstration, one young girl questioned the rabbi about which direction he started waving the lulav and etrog. It should be east, she pointed out. Acknowledging his mistake, the rabbi noted that he "wouldn't want to interfere with the harvest."

Following tradition, participants ate and socialized inside the sukkah. "Let's enjoy some pizza in the hut," Rabbi Birnholz announced to laughs from the group.

To organize the event at the Ravners and the other homes, invitations were sent to all congregants inviting them to the appropriate sukkah-building party, depending on where they live. In total, about 150 people participated in the four neighborhood events.

"Word had gotten out that this was a fun thing to do with the whole family," said Sherry Stein, Schaarai Zedek's program director. "Our hope is that each person who was there will then go back and (next year) build a sukkah in their own backyard and invite people over, and this will grow exponentially."

PUBLISHED WEEKLY BY THE TAMPA TRIBUNE
IN THE LOOP
WEDNESDAY, OCTOBER 22, 2003 • SERVING NEW TAMPA AND WESLEY CHAPEL

RELIGION SPOTLIGHT

"We care about the synagogue, we care about the community, and it's one of the things we do to give back, by having members of the synagogue to our home..." **DR. DOUGLAS SCHOCKEN**

DAN GURA/Staff photo
Congregation Schaarai Zedek associate cantor Riselle Bain, front row center, leads a prayer inside the just-completed sukkah.

Festival *of the* Harvest
Members Of Congregation Schaarai Zedek Build Hut For Sukkot

By DAN GURA
dgura@mediageneral.com

Friends, neighbors and even complete strangers all gave up a sunny Sunday afternoon to invade the Tampa Palms home of Dr. Douglas Schocken, just to help him add a room to his house.

Actually, the builders were members of Congregation Schaarai Zedek, a reform Jewish synagogue, and what they were really doing was building a temporary hut known as a sukkah in Schocken's backyard in honor of the holiday Sukkot.

In Judaism, Sukkot is the festival of the harvest, when in ancient times, farmers would bring offerings to God and plead to him for a fruitful harvest season so they could sustain themselves.

"Farmers didn't have Kash n' Karry or Publix to go to, so it was important for them to have a good harvest," said Riselle Bain, Congregation Schaarai Zedek's associate cantor.

According to tradition, the sukkah, which means "booth," was built each year as a temporary home for the farmers. From these dwellings, farmers could keep a firsthand watch on their crop, looking out for anything in nature that may try to spoil the goods.

The sukkahs also are meant to remind Jews of the time after the Exodus, when the Israelites wandered the desert, seeking the

See **HARVEST**, Page 13

HARVEST

Continued From Page 1

Promised Land. Since they didn't have homes, they built these temporary dwellings.

The sukkah in the backyard of the Schockens was built to commemorate those events. It was decorated with a variety of fruits to symbolize the harvest.

"We're a very social congregation, and what we do is we bring our congregates together by having sukkah parties," Bain said. "This is the second year having our party here."

So why would anyone want to open their doors to complete strangers? Schocken, a cardiologist, called it an honor.

"We care about the synagogue, we care about the community, and it's one of the things we do to give back, by having members of the synagogue to our home, and opening our home to people we don't even know, but who are members of the synagogue and are part of the community locally," he said.

The event was really his wife's idea. Two years ago, the rabbi at the congregation floated the idea of having multiple sukkahs in the community. When asked if Dawn Schocken would house one, she instantly said, 'Yes.'

"I've been very interested in having community gatherings of congregation members," Dawn said. "We have about 85 families that live in the New Tampa and Wesley Chapel area, and being a board member of the temple I found it extremely interesting to get everyone connected so they feel like they're part of the temple."

About two dozen people came to the Schocken's house to build the sukkah. Doug welcomed them all.

"It's the ultimate in saying that we open our arms to you, to anybody," he said. "We've got a couple of our neighbors here who aren't Jewish but want to learn more about the holiday we are celebrating."

And when the time comes again next year to open his home to the congregation?

"Of course," he said. "It's the kind of thing that allows us to meet and make new friends both in our synagogue community and our neighborhood as well."

Ethan Siver, 14, an eighth-grader at Liberty Middle School, hangs a decorative apple inside the sukkah.

Michael Duncan helps put up the fabric wall of the sukkah.

DAN GURA/Staff photos

Chapter Three   Bridging the Membership Gap: Reaching 20s/30s   **193**

Around Town

Pick Of The Week

DAN GURA/Staff photo

Harvest Carnival
Derek Schoken hangs some grapes in the sukkah being built in his backyard in New Tampa. Sukkahs are built in honor of the holiday Sukkot, the Jewish Festival of the Harvest. Crossroads Community Church in Wesley Chapel will also celebrate the changing of seasons with a Harvest Carnival Oct. 31 from 6 to 8 p.m. The event will be on the church property, 1 mile west of Super Target at Bruce B. Downs Boulevard and County Line Road.

Love Conquers All: The Gift of Dual-Faith Relationships

Congregation: Congregation Emanu-El
Address: Two Lake Street
San Francisco, CA 94118
Phone Number: (415) 751-2535
Number of Member Units: 2,100
URJ Region: Pacific Central West Council
Rabbis: Stephen S. Pearce, Peretz Wolf-Prusan, Helen Cohn, Sydney Mintz
Youth Leadership Chairpersons: Jennifer Baxter, David Coffman
Youth Community Coordinator: Mollie Schneider

Brief Description: Congregation Emanu-El seeks to foster an open and supportive atmosphere for Jewish Bay Area young adults in their 20s and 30s. We are committed to providing for young adults spiritual, educational, and social opportunities that reflect the diversity, talents, and interests of our community. We offer two unique Shabbat services for the young adult community: the Late Shabbat and the Late Shabbat 2 on the second and fourth Fridays of the month. Both Late Shabbat services are lead by Rabbi Sydney Mintz and Marsha Attie, along with three to four folk musicians. The Late Shabbat 2 is a smaller, more intimate experience with a slightly different format: a rabbi, a visiting scholar, or a layperson leads a study session after the service.

The young adult leadership is committed to providing interfaith programming as needs arise. To date, we have had two successful programs. The first interfaith program took place on February 8, 2004 (a Wednesday evening). The second program happened after the Late Shabbat 2 on March 26, 2004, as a continuation of the February 8th program. Karen Kushner, of the Union for Reform Judaism's Project Welcome, presented and facilitated both of these programs. Some focal points and questions brought up by Karen to start discussion during the two programs were: How would you describe yourself in a personal ad? Is "Jewish" here? How would you start a conversation about religion with someone you are dating? When would you have that conversation? Could you imagine a family where your partner practiced another religion? Could you imagine a family where your children practiced your partner's religion? The questions were meant to challenge interfaith daters about the importance of clarifying their religious needs for themselves so they could talk clearly to their partners. Some important issues that arose were extended family issues, being "disowned" by relatives, patrimonial/matrimonial lineage, sharing of cultural rituals, and how religious interfaith families want to be.

Program Goal:
- To uncover the "elephant in the room" for people in our age group, the topic that is on everyone's mind but is not being talked about openly.
- To find out what interfaith questions and concerns were challenging people the most.
- To give people the tools they need to stay within the Jewish faith and community so they can pass their religion and culture along to their children.

Target Population: 20s and 30s who are single, married, or in a committed relationship struggling with these questions.

Number of Participants: Approximately forty-five to fifty people. At least 50 percent to 60 percent were couples.

Number of Sessions: Two sessions, lasting two hours each.

Staffing: Young Adult Community Coordinator Mollie Schneider handled outreach and publicity details; Rabbi Sydney Mintz and Karen Kushner presented and facilitated.

Cost of Program: Free.

Logistics: Sign-up sheets, refreshments.

Evaluation of Program: There was no formal evaluation. The number of participants was more then expected and we felt it was evidence of success. In the end, we wanted to begin a dialogue that tackled the questions people have about being in or thinking about being in an interfaith relationship, and ultimately feel that we succeeded in making the first step in our interfaith programming.

Follow-up: Jennifer Baxter and Mollie Schneider invited two interfaith couples to participate in a discussion about what kind of programs they would like to see at the temple. Neither couple is married, but both are in very committed relationships and interested in participating in upcoming programs. Both agreed that to achieve a healthy and helpful discussion with their partners, they needed to be in a smaller setting, over a longer period of time, to create a safe environment where couples can feel secure about discussing an intimate and private part of their relationship. They all agreed that if couples were serious enough to be there, they were ready to tackle these interfaith questions.

We would like to offer two programs this coming year. One is a series of interfaith Shabbat dinners where couples would have the opportunity to meet with each other, have a rabbi present to explain the significance and observance of Shabbat, and then be given resources about interfaith programs in the San Francisco Bay Area. The couples agreed that if the temple did not offer an interfaith program, they would like resources about other organizations. The second program would be an improved continuation of our current program with Karen Kushner, offering a short film as an added resource. The film would highlight humorous clips from selected TV shows and movies, capturing interfaith couples struggling with Jewish identity. This short clip would be the lead-in segment for discussion on this subject, to help draw people in and begin a dialogue. The film/discussions would continue our series that aims to help "interfaith daters" clarify their religious stance.

Temple Emanu-El's Young Adult Community
February and Beyond

Worship

WHAT: Late Shabbat
WHEN: February 13, 7:30 p.m.
WHERE: Main Sanctuary

As always, Late Shabbat is held at 7:30 on the second Friday of the month. Late Shabbat is a special way to observe Shabbat with other young adults in the Bay Area. Led by Rabbi Sidney Mintz, with Marsha Attie and ensemble, come enjoy the music and prayers that are unique to our Late Shabbat. Stay afterward to meet up with new and old friends, as our Oneg, complete with beer and challah, will immediately follow the service.

WHAT: Late Shabbat 2
WHEN: February 27, 7:30 p.m.
WHERE: Martin Meyer Sanctuary

Late Shabbat 2 was a big success in January! After the usual Late Shabbat 2 service, almost fifty members of the community joined Rabbi Kushner to study, discuss and toast L'Chayim together. This month, please join us in welcoming our guest, Rabbi Henry Schreibman, Head of School at Brandeis Hill Day School, to Late Shabbat 2. Have you ever wondered why we say certain prayers during Friday night Shabbat services? Or why we always end by saying the Kaddish? Come learn about the choreography, the structure, and the meaning behind it all as Rabbi Shreibman leads us in a discussion on the particulars of the Shabbat service.

Young Adult Community

WHAT: Interfaith Program "Love Conquers All: The Gift of Dual-Faith Relationships"
WHEN: Sunday, February 8, 7 p.m.
WHERE: Martin Meyer Sanctuary, Temple Emanu-El
RSVP: Please email yacommunity@emanuelsf.org by February 6, 2004

Have you ever been in an interfaith relationship, or thought about being in one? What does a dual-faith relationship mean for your Jewish heritage and to the Jewish community at large? As Jews today, we are confronted with the question of interfaith relationships more and more, as 50 percent of our community fall in love and have partnerships with people of other faiths. Come join Karen Kushner as she leads us in discussing the issues, the challenges, and ultimately the gifts of dual-faith relationships. Karen Kushner is director of the *Jewish Choice Initiative/Project Welcome* for the Pacific Central West region. This is a grant-funded initiative working to welcome interfaith and unaffiliated Jews into synagogue communities. Karen has worked as a family educator and therapist specializing in the self-healing power of families for twenty-seven years.

WHAT: A February Hike
WHEN: February 15, 10 a.m.
WHERE: Point Reyes, Marin County

This month, Emanu-El will be heading to Point Reyes for what is arguably the BEST hike in the bay area! Mountains, seashore, lakes, and spectacular waterfalls abound. Palomarin trailhead is in Point Reyes

National Seashore near the town of Bolinas. The trail ultimately leads to Alamere Falls, a waterfall that tumbles off a 50-foot bluff into the ocean on the California coast. Reaching this beauty requires over an eight mile round trip hike, so be prepared! Bring warm clothes, hiking boots, water, and your camera. Trailhead elevation is about 250 feet, and the hike's highest point is near 600 feet. Trails are, for the most part, very gently graded.

Getting there:
From Highway 101 in Marin County, exit Highway 1/Mill Valley/Stinson Beach.

Drive on Shoreline Highway to the junction with Almonte, about 1 mile. Turn left and drive about 2.5 miles to the junction with Panoramic. Continue straight on Highway 1 about 13 miles to an undersigned junction with Olema-Bolinas Road (just past Bolinas Marsh). Turn left. At the T intersection, turn left (street sign says Olema-Bolinas Road both ways), drive about 1 mile, and then turn left. Drive to the next stop sign, and then turn right onto Mesa Road. Drive about 4 miles, and then continue the last 1-mile on the dirt road to the trailhead at the end of the road. If you have a high-clearance vehicle, take it. The road isn't terrible, but can be washed out and bumpy.

Please e-mail Aliza at benditsky@hotmail.com if you plan to attend. (Put "hike" in the subject line, please).

WHAT: Hamentaschen Baking with Rebecca Ets-Hokin
WHEN: February 29, 3 p.m.
WHERE: Guild Hall
RSVP: Please email yacommunity@emanuelsf.org by February 27
COST: $5

With the approach of Purim, our troubles are forgotten and the partying begins. Purim is the holiday of letting go and basking in life's physical pleasures. Join Rebecca Ets-Hokin and the Young Adult community in preparing Hamentaschen and goodies for our shalah manot—food gifts. Our instructor, Rebecca Ets-Hokin, writes the Joy of Jewish Cooking feature for *J Magazine*. She is one of the founders of HomeChef Cooking School and Kitchen Store, and is a popular instructor at Temple Emanu-El.

WHAT: Jeff Raz's The Whole Megillah, Abridged
WHEN: Thursday, March 4, 8 p.m.
WHERE: Jewish Community Center of San Francisco
COST: $15

Join the Young Adult Community at one of the first-ever shows at San Francisco's beautiful new Jewish Community Center. On Thursday, March 4 at 8 p.m., Temple Emanu-El has blocked out 200 tickets to Jeff Raz's THE WHOLE MEGILLAH, Abridged, and we're hoping to gather as many young adults as possible to enjoy the show together. There's more to the Purim story than you ever knew: Raz's jazz-tinged, politically incorrect, razor-sharp wit will leave you wanting more. Come early; enjoy drinks from the full cash bar, and be introduced to the new JCC while listening to some excellent comedy. If you are interested in coming along with us, please reserve your place before February 15 by e-mailing yacommunity@emanuelsf.org.

WHAT: AJWS 2nd Annual Salsa Party
WHEN: Saturday, February 21, 8 p.m.

WHERE: Roccapulco, 3140 Mission Street (phone number: 415-648-6611)
COST: $20 (includes VIP room and salsa lesson at 8:30)

Come bust a Latin move and support American Jewish World Service programs in Latin America! American Jewish World Service (AJWS) (www.ajws.org) fights poverty, hunger, and disease by supporting grassroots nongovernmental organizations in developing world countries regardless of race, religion, or gender. The proceeds from the salsa party will go directly to the programs that AJWS supports in Latin America. Bring your friends, boogie down to the live salsa orchestra, and chat with program alums who have worked in Peru, Honduras, El Salvador, and Guyana.

Doors open at 8 p.m., there will be a VIP ALWS line when you arrive. No shoes, and you must be 21+. For more information, email sf@ajws.org or call 510-594-9344. **To get a "leg up" on salsa lessons before the party, check out the schedule of nightly lessons at Bay Area clubs at http://www.salsacrazy.com/ sign up for a multi-week class at http://www.dancesf.com/.Mitzvah.

WHAT: **Volunteer at the Emanu-El Food Pantry**
WHEN: February 22, 9-12 p.m.
WHERE: Temple Emanu-El Food Pantry

The Emanu-El Food Pantry is manned by our Young Adult Community on the fourth Sunday of each month. Come join us in keeping this mitzvah alive—always an excellent way to spend a Sunday morning.

WHAT: **URJ Adult Mitzvah Corps**
WHERE: Orange County
WHEN: August 15-21, 2004

Inspired by these words of wisdom, the Commission on Social Action, the URJ Pacific Southwest Council, and the Striking Sparks & Raising Ruach for 20s/30s program of the URJ-CCAR Commission on Outreach & Synagogue Community have teamed up to create an amazing experience—an intensive week of social action, study, and worship. Together we will build a community of faith and create a Jewish religious living experience. Open to members of Reform congregations, participants will spend the week of August 15–21, 2004 building a home in Orange County, California in partnership with Habitat for Humanity. Each work day will begin with worship and end with study. Local Reform congregations will support the project by providing meals, volunteers, and Shabbat worship. Space will be extremely limited, so please contact us as soon as possible if you are interested in learning more. For more information, check out the program website at http://uahc.org/csa/mitzvahcorps/index.shtml

The Temple Emanu-El's Young Adult Community is generously supported by a grant from the Koret Foundation. For more information, please check out the Temple Emanu-El Web site at www.emanuelsf.org or e-mail YACommunity@emanuelsf.org to join our mailing list. To always keep up-to-date with our Young Adult Community events, go to www.calendar.yahoo.com/emanuelyac.

WHAT: **Interfaith Program "Love Conquers All: The Gift of Dual-Faith Relationships"**
WHEN: Sunday, February 8, 7 p.m.

WHERE: Martin Meyer Sanctuary, Temple Emanu-El
RSVP: Please e-mail yacommunity@emanuelsf.org by February 6, 2004

Are you in an interfaith relationship? What does a dual-faith relationship mean for your Jewish heritage and for the Jewish community at large? As Jews today, we are confronted with the question of interfaith relationships more and more, as 50 percent of our community falls in love and creates partnerships with people of other faiths. Come join Karen Kushner as she leads us in discussing the issues, the challenges, and ultimately the gifts of dual-faith relationships. Karen Kushner is director of *Project Welcome*, a grant-funded initiative working to welcome interfaith and unaffiliated Jews into synagogue communities. Karen has worked as a family educator and therapist specializing in the self-healing power of families for twenty-seven years.

DON'T MISS LATE SHABBAT 2 TONIGHT, FRIDAY, MARCH 26 AT 7:30!

Tonight, help us welcome the wonderful Karen Kushner to Late Shabbat 2. Due to such enthusiastic response to her program "Love Conquers All: The Gift of Dual-Faith Relationships" last month, Karen has kindly agreed to resume our discussion on the issues, the challenges, and the gifts of interfaith relationships. As Jews today, we are confronted with the question of interfaith relationships more and more, as 50% of our community fall in love and have partnerships with people of other faiths. What does a dual-faith relationship mean for your Jewish heritage and to the Jewish community at large? Come find out at this month's Late Shabbat 2.

Held every fourth Friday of the month, Late Shabbat 2 is a smaller and more intimate service than Late Shabbat. Led by Rabbi Sydney Mintz and Marsha Attie, Late Shabbat 2 follows the same musical style and familiar prayers of the second Friday of the month Late Shabbat service. If Late Shabbat appeals to you but you would like to pray with a smaller group of people, this second service may be for you!

The following is a personal e-mail sent to our Young Adult distribution list from Rabbi Sydney Mintz

First, a joke to get you interested....

> A Jewish businessman warned his daughter against marrying a gentile. The daughter replied "But he's converting to Judaism!" "It doesn't matter," the old man said. "A gentile husband will cause problems." After the wedding, the father called his daughter, who was in business with him, and asked her why she was not at work. "It's Shabbos," the daughter replied. The father was surprised: "But we always work on Saturday. It's our busiest day." "I won't work anymore on Saturday," the daughter insisted, "because my husband wants us to go to shul on Shabbos." "See," the father says. "I told you marrying a gentile would cause problems!"

Why this joke? Because, this Sunday, February 8 at 7 P.M., the Young Adult Community is delving into the subject of interdating and intermarriage with a provocative and very relevant program: "Love Conquers All: The Gift of Dual-Faith Relationships." If you have ever considered interdating or intermarriage or are currently in an interfaith relationship, this program is for you. Presenting and helping to facilitate our discussion of the challenges and gifts of interfaith relationships is the fantastic Karen Kushner. Karen is director of the Jewish Choice Initiative/Project Welcome for the Pacific Central West Region, a grant-funded initiative working to welcome interfaith and unaffiliated Jews into synagogue communities.

Bring your partners, bring your friends, bring your potential significant others. Bring questions, scenarios, and concerns. We are very excited about this thought-provoking program at Temple Emanu-El and we hope to see you there!

Emanu-El Interdating: Love Conquers All
Program Outline

> A Jewish businessman warned his daughter against marrying a gentile.
> The daughter replied," But he is converting to Judaism!"
> "It doesn't matter," the old man said." A gentile husband will cause problems."
> After the wedding, the father called his daughter, who was in business with him, and asked her why she was not at work.
> "It's Shabbos," the daughter replied.
> The father was surprised: "But we always work on Saturday. It's our busiest day."
> "I won't work anymore on Saturday," the daughter insisted, "because my husband wants us to go to shul on Shabbos."
> "See," the father says. "I told you marrying a gentile would cause problems!"

Let's dissect this:
What is this joke saying about parents? *Prejudiced, ambivalent about Judaism, assimilated, hypocritical, opinionated, blames others and takes no blame.*

What is this joke saying about gentile partners? Jews-by-choice? *Eager, sincere, unambivalent, consistency in belief and practice, wanting to please.*

> How many people here are casually dating non-Jews?
> How many are pretty seriously involved with people of other faiths?
> How many think they will marry Jews? How many think they won't?
> How many want to share a religion with their life partner?
> How many want that religion to be Judaism?

For small groups (under 20):
- Go around the room for introductions, including dating casually or seriously with person of another faith?
- Adult child of endogamous or dual-faith couple?
- Grandchild of dual-faith couple?
- Mother or father Jewish?
- If parent converted how old were you?
- Unaffiliated, Reform, Reconstructionist, Conservative, Orthodox?
- Do you think you will marry a Jew?
- Do you want to have the same religion as your partner?
- Do you want that religion to be Jewish?

For large groups (over 20):
- Raise your hand if you are the adult child of interfaith grandparents or a grandparent who converted to Judaism.
- Adult child of interfaith parents? Mother Jewish? Father Jewish?
- Adult child of a parent who converted to Judaism?
- Converted before marriage? Before having children? When you were younger than 5? Younger than 10? Converted at your or a sibling's bar or bat mitzvah?
- Raise your hand if both your parents were Jewish.

- Raise your hand if you are here because many of the people you are attracted to are not Jewish.
- How many are in serious or committed relationships with Christians, Hindus, Muslims, Buddhists, Jains, atheists?
- Any as couples?
- To any significant others who are here ... let me say how glad I am that you were interested enough to come, (or maybe accommodating enough or just plain curious enough to come!).
- Raise your hand if you want to share a religion with your life partner. Do you want that religion to be Jewish?

Now, let's talk about what you came to hear.

Love Conquers All: The Gift of Dual-Faith Relationships

I should tell you that more than a few people have been not happy with me for announcing this title. The recently published, controversial, enlightening, and confusing National Jewish Population Study has provided the usual alarming statistics about the increasing number of intermarriages and with lower measures of Jewish connection, affiliation, and practice. And as usual, the Jewish community has reacted with cries of alarm and portents of disaster.

But the study also shows that a good part of the Jewish community is more engaged and more passionate and more knowledgeable and more committed than ever before.

One reason this is so is because of the non-Jewish partners of Jews, who make you their Jewish partner think about the place of religion in a couples' life precisely because they come from a different culture.

Their curiosity challenges you to find the answers to their questions.
They ask practical questions but they also ask philosophical questions.
The why questions.
Because most Jews have stopped their religious education at age 12 or 13, we never got to the philosophical, the deep and rich levels of Judaism.
And now, because of their questions, you will.
THIS IS THE GIFT!

If you were involved with someone who was ambivalent about his or her Jewish identity, or even negative about Judaism, you wouldn't be searching for answers let alone searching your own soul to figure out the place of Judaism in her life.

Keren McGinity says in her essay:

> "Marrying a non-Jew cast my Jewish identity into high relief. Without the luxury of mutual understanding based on a shared heritage, I found myself explaining many aspects of Judaism. More significantly, being intermarried encouraged me to ask and to answer probing questions such as: Who am I? What does being Jewish mean to me? And, how am I Jewish? While I would not argue that being an interfaith couple makes for calm December dinner conversation, I am convinced that being married to a non–

Jew has made me a stronger Jew. Before I married Matt, I took my Jewishness for granted and saw no need to participate in Jewish communal affairs."

One big unspoken secret in the Jewish community is that for some families, **it is the non-Jewish partner who is more clear about the need for religion in their life, for religious education for any children, more committed to spirituality, more comfortable talking about a personal relationship with God than the Jewish partner!**

What is not made explicit in those statistics I mentioned earlier is that a good number of those committed, passionate Jews who are more engaged are Jews-by-choice. **It is another unspoken secrets of the Jewish community.**

Ask any rabbi, cantor, or educator about the regulars, the people who come to every event, who ask for more programs, who study with their kids at home, at the family education programs, and at adult education classes. Who is it that wants to learn every part of the liturgy so that they can sing along with the service? Who is most interested in learning the details about the "low" holidays (as opposed to the High Holy Days) of Sukkot, Tu B'shvat, Purim, Passover, and Shavuot?

The truth is that many of them are new Jews, those who have chosen in adulthood to join the Jewish people, to convert to Judaism.

Some grew up in assimilated Jewish homes and discovered a home in Judaism as adults!

It also includes what I call **common-law Jews**, partners of Jews who want to share the enthusiasm of those they love for Judaism, but who have not made a formal conversion.

As Annie Modesitt wrote in an interfaithfamily.com essay: "When people convert they move into the house, they pass the threshold. However some of us chose to affiliate with Judaism but not to convert... to stay on the porch." She goes on, "I love a good front porch. I love to see the neighbors go by, watch the kids playing, have a glass of tea and a few cookies while I sit and knit through the evening. I have a lot of company out on the porch; good company. But at some point it's nice to go inside—and not just as a guest—but as a treasured member of the household."

What a huge debt of gratitude the Jewish community owes to these people.
Because we have kept these seismic changes a secret we have grossly neglected our hallelujahs, our thanksgiving, and our appreciation.

While intermarriage is growing, the proportion of interfaith households raising their children as Jews is also growing.

The challenge is to use this gift in your relationship.
To be aware of the special needs of having different histories.
To rise to the challenge of accommodating each other.
To create something customized to the two of you and the family you will create.
Not a clone of one family or the other.
This means loss for both of you ... and gain.
It means you will have to push yourself again and again to ask hard questions and avoid the easy answers.

What is essential to your identity?
What values and traditions can be stripped of religious content and passed down in a new way?

I encourage you to avoid doing things that are for your parents. But I encourage you to find ways to maintain the closeness and warmth. Extended families are an important source of support and nurturance to young families.

I encourage you to chose one religion and share it. It would take more time than we have for me to tell you just how I think the philosophical basis and theology of Judaism and Christianity are exclusive to each other.

If you try to do both, you are in real danger of achieving nothing—Judaism lite and Christianity lite. And I think that richness and depth add immeasurably to experience. To children too.

Holiday celebrations for both of you will have shallow rituals because no one has the time or energy or commitment to mine their richness alone, trying to be satisfied with a little of this and a little of that when the meaning of the language of symbols is unknown.

If you try to teach your children both religions in a serious way, the children will be burdened with two religious educations to assimilate and a split identity that leaves them no clear group to identify with. You will be simply avoiding your own pain at having to make a choice by passing it down to the next generation.

But then children are probably not something you are thinking about now. If anything you are trying to imagine a wedding or commitment ceremony that will make everyone happy. Again, I encourage you to avoid that goal—making everyone happy. It will be difficult enough to figure out what is significant to you and why.

But I also don't think you are thinking about the role of religion in life: how sharing a religion gives you ways to celebrate both the miracles that will come your way and the structure of ritual that will sustain you when you are grieving.

I do want to encourage you to try to project yourselves into that distant future.
As Barry Shrage, head of the Federation in Boston once said: The Jewish community will survive because in a time of forgetfulness, we're part of the oldest living chain of learning and literature in the world, inheritors of an ancient and hauntingly beautiful culture.

In a time of loneliness, we carry the secret of community making and caring to provide our children and grandchildren with a sense of community and belonging.

In a time of rootlessness and alienation we're connected to that 3,500-year-old history and an infinite future.

Young Leadership Initiative

Congregation:	Washington Hebrew Congregation
Address:	3935 Macomb Street NW Washington, DC 20016
Phone Number:	(202) 362-7100
Contact's Name and E-mail:	Rabbi Hessel, Jhessel@whctemple.org
Number of Member Units:	2,675
URJ Region:	Mid-Atlantic Council
Rabbis:	M. Bruce Lustig (Senior), Joseph B. Meszler, Joui M. Hessel, and Susan N. Shankman
Outreach Chairperson:	Shelley Singer

Brief Description: Young Leadership Initiative is a program for potential leaders in their 20s, 30s, and early 40s. YLI is a comprehensive year-long program that includes *Mechina*, or Preparation, and *Sheirut*, or Service. The *Mechina* section of the YLI includes monthly sessions comprised of three components: "Reform Judaism," "Washington Hebrew Congregation," and "Leadership Skills." This *Mechina* section of the YLI has been carefully developed to provide a comprehensive overview with specific leadership building skills, each session building on the former. All the sessions take place at Washington Hebrew Congregation on the second Wednesday of every month at 7 P.M., beginning with dinner.

Program Goal: YLI will create a sense of community through a leadership program geared toward younger professionals. YLI will be a program that stresses the value of WHC, and its mission in local, state, federal, and international environs as well as spiritual levels.

Target Population: Jewish adults in their 20s, 30s, and early 40s.

Number of Participants: Forty applicants, twenty-three accepted and participating.

Number and Length of Sessions: *Mechina* sessions are monthly for two hours, including dinner, while the *Sheirut* sessions revolve around the calendar of the particular committee a YLI participant is assigned to.

Staffing Required: Rabbi Hessel prepared an extensive curriculum covering Reform Judaism, Washington Hebrew Congregation, and leadership skills and development. Rabbi Hessel teaches all sessions, with Rabbi Lustig teaching one or two as well.

Total Cost of program: $4,700

Source of Funding: Congregation's worship and music general fund.

Fee for Attendees: Free

Logistics: A room is needed each month with chairs and tables in a square, flip chart and marker, and dinner and dinner supplies. Notebooks for each participant were provided, complete with all reading assignments and materials.

Instructions to Facilitator: The challenge is to create a curriculum that fits with the needs of your target population and synagogue's mission statement. This will vary from place to place.

Evaluation of Program: There is much appreciation from YLI participants for having time to learn with rabbis from the congregation, as well as having an entry point into the synagogue leadership structure. The board of trustees is quite supportive, as they recognize that the graduates of YLI may one day become leaders of the congregation.

Follow-up: There are current discussions about how to integrate the YLI graduates into the synagogue structure once the year-long program concludes in June 2005.

Washington Hebrew Congregation

Young Leadership Initiative
2004-2005
5765

Washington Hebrew Congregation's YLI Program

Goals:

- Creating a sense of community through a leadership program geared towards young professionals.
- Program will begin in September and run throughout the year until June, and will contain two sections: *Mechina* (Preparation), and *Sheirut* (Service).
- The *Mechina* section of the YLI includes monthly sessions on different topics relating to Reform Judaism, WHC, and Leadership Development.
- The *Sheirut* section of the program will include opportunities to work hands-on within the congregation by serving on committees.
- The targeted age group would be between 25-45 years old.
- Curriculum will stress social justice, strengthening of interfaith bonds, community service, and political efficacy. It will not be a "Hebrew School for Young Adults" but rather a program that stresses the value of WHC, and its mission in local, state, federal, and international environs as well as spiritual levels.
- Rabbis and invited guests will teach the YLI sessions. Rabbi Joui Hessel will serve as the coordinator for the overall program.

Application Process:

- Targeted individuals (using specific e-mail lists, letters, and the Journal) received an "Invitation Letter" to apply for the program.
- Each individual completed an application, including a brief personal history, professional activities, Jewish upbringing, and commitment to social justice/community service.
- Interviews were scheduled for those applicants who are accomplished in the field of work and/or social service within the community. Sample questions asked were:
  1. What are some examples of leadership styles you most admire?
  2. Could you tell us about someone who in a leadership position personally influenced you?
  3. Can leadership be taught or is it something that one is born with?
  4. How would you design a program like this one? What elements do you think should be included in the education component and what elements should be included in the hands-on component? Why?

Calendar of YLI:

The YLI sessions will take place at Temple at 7pm, beginning with dinner.
7:00-7:30pm   Dinner with Introduction to Subject Matter/Board Member
7:30-8:00pm   Program on Leadership and Group Building
8:00-9:00pm   Speaker Program

The scheduled dates of the sessions are held on the second Wednesday of every month, beginning in September and ending in June.

March 22, 2004/5764

Dear Young Professional,

Good leaders are the most precious assets of any congregation. Washington Hebrew Congregation's lay leaders are largely responsible for the excellence in all that we do, and that has won us an outstanding national reputation within the Reform movement. We take great pride in our achievements and know that we must continue to develop strong Temple leadership in order to provide for our future.

We are currently looking for good leaders, and we have identified you as an individual who may be interested in our newly developed Young Leadership Initiative (YLI) program that we believe can mutually benefit both you and the congregation. By building upon the leadership experiences and knowledge you may already have, the YLI program will teach you about aspects of Reform Judaism, our congregational structure, and how to become a part of its leadership base.

The program contains a comprehensive year curriculum that includes *Mechina* (Preparation) and *Sheirut* (Service). The *Mechina* section of the YLI includes monthly sessions that will be comprised of three components: "Reform Judaism," "Washington Hebrew Congregation," and "Leadership Skills." This *Mechina* section of the YLI has been carefully developed to provide a comprehensive overview with specific leadership building skills, each session building on the former. All of the sessions will take place at Washington Hebrew Congregation at 7 p.m., beginning with dinner. The scheduled dates of the sessions are held on the second Wednesday of every month, beginning in September and ending in June.

At the beginning of the year, we will offer an opportunity to involve you in a second section of the YLI program, called *Sheirut* (Service), which will include opportunities to work hands-on within the congregation by serving on committees, chairing congregational events and other activities that synthesize the knowledge obtained during the YLI program.

In order to make this a meaningful experience, we will be limiting participants in the first year program to 20-25 people. If you would like to participate, please return the enclosed application by **April 20** to: Rabbi Joui Hessel, Washington Hebrew Congregation, 3935 Macomb Street NW, Washington, DC 20016 or you may e-mail it to her assistant, Britt Fogg, at: bfogg@whctemple.org.

Upon receiving all applications, we may contact you to come to the synagogue for an informal interview. At this time, character references will be requested. Interviews will take place at Washington Hebrew Congregation on the following days: April 21, April 28, and May 19 from 6-9:30p.m. An additional interview date might be added due to the number of applications received. You will have the opportunity to request a specific date and will be notified of your interview time. This interview allows for personal interaction between the applicant and specific synagogue Board Members who may assist in the facilitation of the YLI.

We are very excited about this new program and feel that our future success as a congregation is assured with your commitment to full participation in the program. We hope that in addition to others, you will accept our invitation to apply for this exciting adventure.

B'Shalom,

M. Bruce Lustig, Rabbi   Rabbi Joui Hessel   John Nannes, President

Young Leadership Initiative for Jewish Young Adults

We are looking for good leaders in their 20s, 30s, or 40s who might be interested in our newly developed Young Leadership Initiative (YLI) program. By building on leadership experiences and knowledge you may already have, the YLI program will teach you about aspects of Reform Judaism, our congregational structure, and how to become a part of its leadership base.

The program contains a comprehensive year curriculum that includes *Mechina,* or Preparation, and *Sheirut,* or Service. The *Mechina* section of the YLI includes monthly sessions comprised of three components: "Reform Judaism," "Washington Hebrew Congregation," and "Leadership Skills." All sessions will take place at Washington Hebrew Congregation at 7:00 p.m., beginning with dinner. The scheduled dates of the sessions are held on the second Wednesday of every month beginning September 8, 2004, with the final session taking place June 8, 2005. The second section of the YLI program, called *Sheirut* or Service, will include opportunities to work hands-on within the congregation by serving on committees, chairing congregational events and other activities that synthesize the knowledge obtained during the YLI program.

In order to make this a meaningful experience the first year we are limiting participants to 20-25 people. Applications are due soon, so if you would like to participate, please contact Rabbi Hessel's assistant, Britt Fogg, to receive an application.

We are very excited about this new program and hope those of you who would like to build upon the leadership skills you already have will accept our invitation to apply for this exciting adventure.

Washington Hebrew Congregation

Young Leadership Initiative (YLI) Application

Name _____

Address _____

City, State, and Zip _____

Home Phone _____ Work Phone _____

Cell Phone _____ Age and DOB _____

E-mail _____

Occupation _____

On a separate sheet of paper, please tell us a little bit about yourself, including professional activities, Jewish upbringing, and commitment to social justice/community service. Please be sure to include a description of your leadership activities and experiences to date, along with why you are interested in the Young Leadership Initiative.

Please accept my application for participation in Washington Hebrew Congregation's 2004-2005 Young Leadership Initiative that begins in the Fall. I am willing to make a commitment to participate in the YLI sessions as well as to the committee/congregational program meetings with which I will be assigned to work.

_____   _____
Signature   Date

June 2, 2004/5764

Phyllis West
XXXXXXXX
XXXXX, XX XXXXX

Dear Phyllis,

I want to thank you for taking the time out of your busy schedule to interview the prospective candidates for the Young Leadership Initiative program.

As you probably noticed, we have a number of highly qualified applicants who have the potential to benefit greatly from this program by building on their prior leadership experience. I know Washington Hebrew Congregation will also profit from this program and it could not have been done without your help.

L'shalom,

Rabbi Joui Hessel

June 11, 2004/5764

Dear _____,

Mazel Tov on your acceptance to our congregation's Young Leadership Initiative program. As the Senior Rabbi of Washington Hebrew Congregation, I am proud to sponsor and support such an important program. Our congregation recognizes the need to welcome and integrate young adults into the congregation in order to produce the next generation of synagogue leaders.

The Young Leadership Initiative program will introduce you to our congregation and its committees, teach you about Reform Judaism, and explore ways to develop and improve your own leadership skills. In addition to monthly sessions, some of which I will be teaching, you will have the opportunity to serve on a committee and attend a Board of Directors meeting.

On behalf of the congregation and the Board of Directors, I welcome and congratulate you as we embark upon what will prove to be an intensive and rewarding experience.

Shalom,

M. Bruce Lustig, Senior Rabbi

Young Leadership Initiative Curriculum

September 8, 2004
Introduction to Course

When two sit together and exchange words of Torah, then the Divine Presence dwells with them. (Pirkei Avot 3:2)

October 13, 2004
Introduction to Leadership/Leadership Throughout Jewish History

If one does not plow in the summer, what will one eat in the winter? (Midrash Mishlei 6)

November 10, 2004
Reform Judaism: Beliefs and Practices

If you want the present to be different from the past, study the past. (Baruch Spinoza)

December 8, 2004
Washington Hebrew Congregation: A Closer Look

A community is too heavy for anyone to carry alone. (Deuteronomy Rabbah 1:10)

January 12, 2005
Leadership Styles and Skills

It is not up to you to finish the task, yet you are not free to avoid it. (Pirkei Avot 2:16)

February 9, 2005
Synagogue Transformation and Renewal

Turn it, and turn it, for everything is in it. (Pirkei Avot 5:22)

March 9, 2005
How a Synagogue Lives the Jewish Calendar

The best we can do to achieve holiness is to make a beginning and to persevere in our efforts. (Moses Hayyim Luzzatto)

April 13, 2005
Change in the Synagogue: It's Not a Bad Word!

Know where you came from; know where you are going; and (know) in whose presence you will have to make an accounting. (Pirkei Avot 3:1)

May 11, 2005
Learning About Ourselves and Building Relationships

Don't judge your fellow human being until you have reached that person's place. (Pirkei Avot 2:4)

June 8, 2005
Where Do We Go From Here?

According to the difficulty is the reward. (Pirke Avot 5:23)

Young Leadership Initiative Program Homework:

Due Date	Homework Assignment
Oct 13	Choose two leaders and identify important qualities and behaviors of each.
Nov 10	Read about Reform Judaism (article).
Dec 8	Read Washington Hebrew Congregation's history.
Jan 12	Read Covey's *Seven Habits of Highly Effective People.* Take and print out the DiSC survey. Decide upon a personal learning project.
Feb 9	Attend at least two committee meetings no later than April 1.
March 9	Read through the Jewish Calendar to familiarize yourself with the holidays. Evaluate how many personal learner objectives you have fulfilled thus far in the program.
April 13	Read through the Membership Packets, focusing on the auxiliary groups.
May 11	Read *What Can Lion Tamers Teach Us About the People Around Us, Communicating with Them, and Building Successful Relationships?*
June 8	Prepare a presentation on your committees: what committee you served, what the goals of the committee were, and the evaluation as to whether the committee reached its goals. Also, you will present your personal learning project at this time.

YLI Program Learner's Objectives

Leadership

1. Identify other YLIers and state three things about each person/create a group dynamic (9/8)
2. Identify and describe personal leadership attributes (9/8)
3. Discussion of experiences and perspectives of leadership with others (9/8)
4. Describe the Seven Key Areas of Leadership and the 5 Levels of Leadership (9/8)
5. Identify important qualities and behaviors of effective leaders (9/8)
6. Describe the value of facilitative leadership (5/11)
7. Identify a personal DiSC style (10/13)
8. Describe the differences between DiSC Profile types and how they impact one's ability to lead (10/13)
9. Recognize opportunities to better understand others (10/13)
10. Identify personal influence style preferences and apply a variety of influence strategies (10/13)
11. Describe the value of integrity and trust to an effective leader (6/8)
12. Recognize situations when feedback is necessary (6/8)
13. Identify strategies for soliciting and receiving feedback (6/8)
14. Describe the value of vision to organizations (mission statements) (12/8)
15. Identify a methodology for developing a vision (12/8)
16. Identify Covey's *Seven Habits of Highly Successful People* and how they relate to Judaism (11/10)
17. List some of Judaism's leadership values (10/13)
18. Explore types of people who serve on committees and how to work with them (5/11)

Reform Judaism

1. Identify the three commonplaces of Judaism: God, Torah, Israel (11/10)
2. Describe the various platforms of RJ: Pittsburgh, Columbus, Centenial Perspective, Pittsburgh (11/10)
3. Discuss the history of RJ, starting with the early Reformers: Israel Jacobson, Leopold Zunz, Kaufmann Kohler (11/10)
4. Explore RJ innovations: Confirmation, Female Clergy, Outreach to non-Jews (1/12)

Washington Hebrew Congregation

1. Explore the history of the congregation (12/8)
2. Compare and contrast Mission Statements, past and present (12/8)
3. Identify changes in Worship and Music over time (1/12)
4. Recognize the WHC leadership structure (clergy/board, committees, congregants) (10/13)
5. List the various constituency groups WHC serves as well as the various types of programming (adult ed, youth, auxiliaries) we offer (3/9)
6. Identify how WHC shows its commitment to the community (Mitzvah Day, Abram Simon, Carrie Simon) (4/13)
7. Explore the Jewish Calendar—through the synagogue's eyes (2/9)
8. Compare/contrast the leadership of a congregation verses a business; ethics, people, etc. (12/8)

Chapter Four

Outreach Programming All Year for All

Outreach programming is ongoing and happens on all levels. Whether through advertising, classes, or experiential learning, outreach programming is an opportunity for your members to connect with others, to learn about Judaism, congregational life, and the possibilities of involvement. This chapter contains programs that lower the barriers to synagogue engagement by providing inclusive teaching communities that welcome and educate those who may be new to Judaism or those who are looking to learn more.

Taste II: Jewish in America is a follow-up to the national program "A Taste of Judaism." This three-session course for those who took "Taste" enables participants to spend more time together learning about areas of interest to them. If you offer "Taste" and find participants are eager for more but are not yet ready for "Introduction to Judaism," then this program will be a valuable learning bridge.

Entrée to Judaism is a program for graduates of the "Introduction to Judaism" course and continues where the "Intro" ends. This interactive series offers participants the opportunity to gather throughout the year to learn about holidays while preparing Jewish food and to develop personal connections with the instructor and with each other.

Using **Outreach Brochures** to educate newcomers and members about holidays can also be an easy way for people to learn about Judaism and your synagogue's *minhag*. Brochures were created for the High Holy Days, Sukkot, Chanukah, and Shavuot and are made available outside the sanctuary prior to each holiday. If your synagogue is looking for a model brochure, you've found it.

Open the doors wide and let them in! **Opening Doors to Shabbat** is a creative service to bring people in to the synagogue to learn about the Shabbat service using a projector and screen for everyone to follow together. If you are looking for an innovative way to share Shabbat with newcomers and those who want to learn more about the service, incorporate this service into your Shabbat worship schedule.

Taste II: Jewish in America

Congregation:	Temple Emanu-El
Address:	225 N. Country Club Road Tucson, AZ 85716
Phone Number:	(520) 327-4501
Contact's Name and E-mail:	Mila Anderson, temple@templeemanueltucson.org
Number of Member Units:	800
URJ Region:	Pacific Southwest Council
Rabbis:	Samuel M. Cohon, David Freelund
Membership Director:	Barbara Zaslofsky
Program Coordinator:	Mila Anderson

Brief Description: Taste II: Jewish in America is a follow-up to the national URJ Outreach program Taste of Judaism (which, for its fifth year, is being sponsored by a grant from the Jewish Federation of Southern Arizona). Many people who had attended the Taste of Judaism course requested a follow-up seminar. Topics chosen for Taste II came from the three topics most commonly raised by attendees in post-course surveys. The class is three two-hour sessions with a break, during which "tastes" of Jewish food are provided by the temple's Sisterhood (recipes are provided). Class 1 is Jews in America: Movements, Assimilation, Creativity; Class 2 is From Davening to Rock: A Jewish Way to Pray (two CDs of Friday night and Saturday morning Shabbat music are provided); Class 3 is American-Israeli Relations.

Program Goals:
- Respond to requests from Taste of Judaism attendees for a follow-up seminar, allowing them an additional opportunity to take another three-session class addressing topics and questions that remained after the original Taste series; to keep them engaged in Jewish learning while still exploring Jewish options.
- Give a deeper insight into contemporary Jewish life for unaffiliated Jews who are exploring their personal return to Judaism and for interfaith couples who are considering Jewish possibilities.
- Increase Jewish cultural literacy through learning and discussion, since this class is open to all members of the community, and explain aspects of Judaism not commonly explained in popular media.
- Provide an interim step between Taste of Judaism and the year-long Basic Judaism class, and provide an additional option for those who are interested in continuing their Jewish education and are not ready to commit to a long-term course.
- Pique interest in participants to explore other things Jewish, such as Jewish festivals, food, books, movies, and the Jewish Community Center, as well as synagogues, services, and education, through discussion of contemporary American Jewish topics.

Target Population: Unaffiliated Jews, interfaith couples, Taste of Judaism graduates who want to continue their Jewish education, anyone interested in exploring American Judaism.

Number of Participants: 163 participants in three sessions.

Number and Length of Sessions: Three weekly two-hour sessions.

Staffing Required: Teachers (the course is taught by our rabbis) and an administrator.

Total Cost of Program: Cost of food, two CDs, photocopying reading packets, venue rental (if held outside temple), advertising.

Source of Funding: Registration fees per student, Temple Emanu-El Outreach advertising budget. The Green Valley class was partially underwritten by St. Francis Episcopal Church, which hosted the class series.

Fee for Attendees: $25 per student, $40 for couples ($10 per person for the Green Valley class in collaboration with St. Francis, which paid for the food and provided the facilities for free).

Logistics and Instructions to Facilitator:
The program coordinator needs to:
- Write and distribute press releases, make up flyers, place ads
- Arrange food baked by members of temple's Sisterhood and buy the rest of the snacks; one Sisterhood-provided homemade item and one store-bought item is offered for each class (Sisterhood has provided dishes like fruit compote, blintz soufflés, kugel, hamantashen, Mandelbrot, kasha varnishkes, and apple cake; purchased snacks include bagels and cream cheese, herring on rye bread, rugalach, latkes with applesauce and sour cream, and challah)
- Arrange the venue (if class is held outside of temple)
- Prepare handouts: class reading materials; flyers of temple programming; adult education brochures; information on conversion, interfaith families, and Jewish options in the community
- Create a database and mailing list of participants to facilitate follow-ups and referrals

On the days of the classes, administrator needs to:
- Set up the room for discussion
- Take attendance and hand out class materials
- Prepare food service for the break
- Make herself available to chat with participants, answer questions, and provide materials
- Assist rabbis as needed

Evaluation of Program: When Rabbi Cohon came to Temple Emanu-El in 1999, there was no Basic Judaism class. Now more than fifty people annually take the year-long Basic Judaism; half of these are Taste of Judaism graduates, many of whom have taken Taste II as an interim step. Taste II is also a good introduction to the Jewish Home and Family class, a monthly, year-long series on how to lead a Jewish life. Taste II retains the open, nonthreatening feel of the Taste of Judaism program where everyone is welcome, all questions are addressed, and there is no commitment. Participants have little or no knowledge about Judaism and therefore learn together.

People who attend are born Jews who are attracted to the class topics or looking for a way to come back to temple life and learning, interfaith couples who are interested in pursuing Jewish options, people who want a better understanding of modern American Judaism, and those for whom Taste of Judaism was not enough to satisfy their appetite. The class gives those who are interested but still tentative about their involvement in Judaism three more weeks to explore their options and gain more information. Charging a nominal fee gives people a sense of commitment to continuing their Jewish learning. Essentially, Taste II brings participants in the door of the synagogue for three more weeks.

This year we held a session of Taste of Judaism outside of Tucson—in Green Valley, a small community about thirty miles south of Tucson. The Taste class attracted almost one hundred participants from the general community. The response to the class was tremendous, with many requests for additional classes in Green Valley. The rector of the local Episcopal church offered to host further classes. He also offered to partially underwrite the cost of Taste II to reduce the cost per student. Although some of the one hundred people signed up for this class were members of the church, most were simply members of the community; roughly half were Jewish. Not only did so many people come to learn about Judaism and Jewish life, the spirit of interfaith cooperation created a tremendous amount of goodwill.

Follow-up: Although participants have requested a Taste III, our outreach plan is not to provide another short-term class for this audience, but, instead, to guide them toward other adult education classes and opportunities to participate in temple life. Using the opt-in mailing list created during enrollment and from requests for follow-ups, Taste II alumni are invited to attend temple events, celebrations, and services; invited to Simply Shabbat (an Outreach learning service that provides explanations of the Friday evening service); offered High Holy Day tickets; given information about conversion; and invited to take additional adult education classes that suit their interests.

Resources made available to Taste II participants are the temple calendar, Adult Education Academy brochure and enrollment application, all temple flyers and brochures, our monthly newsletter, and the URJ Outreach brochures "Becoming a Jew" and "Intermarried? Reform Judaism Welcomes You." They are told about the holidays, informed about upcoming events, and given temple event flyers at the classes.

Taste II participants have gone on to take a wide variety of Adult Education classes: Basic and Intermediate Judaism, On Wings of Awe, Sefer Book Club, Yiddish, Hebrew Marathon and Prayerbook Hebrew, joined the Zohar study group, and participated in our Scholar in Residence programming events. For the two most recent sessions alone, three participants have begun the conversion process and a family has joined the membership of Temple Emanu-El.

FOR IMMEDIATE RELEASE

CONTACT: Rabbi Samuel M. Cohon
or Mila Anderson, Taste Administrator, AT 327-4501
Temple Emanu-El, 225 N. Country Club Road,
Tucson, AZ 85716

Taste II Offers Another Bite of Judaism

Following the success of the Taste of Judaism series, Temple Emanu-El is offering Taste II: Another Bite—Jewish in America. Created by Temple Emanu-El's Rabbis Samuel M. Cohon and David Freelund and introduced in 2003, Taste II is the first course of its kind. The topics for the class came out of questions that arose most frequently during the first Taste classes. While Taste of Judaism examines the foundational principles of Judaism and is grounded in Biblical text and historical context, Taste II focuses on contemporary Jewish issues in America. Topics for Taste II include Jews in America—Movements, Assimilation, and Creativity; From Davening to Rock—A Jewish Way to Pray; and American-Israeli Relations. The classes explore in a fun, energetic, and interactive style the modern-day practices and interpretations of American Jews.

Like the Taste of Judaism series, Taste II—Jewish in America is three sessions and is open to the entire community. And, of course, a delicious "taste" of Judaism will be provided. Taste II will be offered at Temple Emanu-El on October 3, 10, and 17, 7-9 pm. Registration for Taste II is $25.00 and includes two CDs of Jewish music and all the snacks. Please call 327-4501 for information and registration.

From the team that brought you the popular series "Taste of Judaism" comes...

TASTE II - ANOTHER BITE: JEWISH IN AMERICA

Continue learning and sampling with our rabbis in this three-part class

Topics for this class include:
  Jews in America – History, Movements, Assimilation and Creativity
  From Davening to Rock – A Jewish Way to Pray and Sing
  American-Israeli Relations

At Temple Emanu-El
Sundays, October 3, 10 and 17, 2004
7:00-9:00 pm

Open to the entire community, Jewish or not

The cost for the class is $25 (members and non-members), includes snacks and two CDs of Jewish music.

To register by mail for Taste II - Another Bite:

Name(s)_____

Address_____

City _____ State _____ Zip _____

Phone _____

Number attending _____ Amount enclosed _____

Visa/MC#_____ exp._____

Please Mail to:
Temple Emanu-El
225 N. Country Club
Tucson, AZ 85716
Telephone (520) 327-4501
Fax (520) 327-4504
www.templeemanueltucson.org

Taste II: Another Bite – Jewish in America

Class 1: Jews in America
Movements, Assimilation, Creativity

January 18, 2005

Rabbi Samuel M. Cohon
Rabbi David Freelund

Class held at St. Francis-in-the-Valley Episcopal Church
600 S. La Canada, Green Valley

Temple Emanu-El
225 N. Country Club Rd.
Tucson, AZ 85713
327-4501
www.templeemanueltucson.org

Resources and materials used for Class I

1. Statement of Principles for Reform Judaism
Adopted at the 1999 Pittsburgh Convention
Central Conference of American Rabbis, May 1999 – Sivan 5759
www.ccarnet.org
http://www.mazornet.com/jewishcl/judaism/reform-1999statement.htm

2. Conservative Judaism
Conservative Judaism: Statement of Beliefs and Principles
For more information on history, mission, and vision of this organization, go to:
http://www.uscj.org/index1.html

3. Orthodox Judaism
Orthodox Judaism: One Torah Many Paths
For more information on history, mission, and vision of this organization, go to: http://www.ou.org/

Additional resources for Class I

The American Jewish Experience through the Nineteenth Century: Immigration and Acculturation.
Jonathan D. Sarna and Jonathan Golden
Brandeis University, National Humanities Center

The American Jewish Experience in the Twentieth Century: Anti-Semitism and Assimilation.
Jonathan D. Sarna and Jonathan Golden
Brandeis University, National Humanities Center

Class 2: New Approaches to Prayer and Prayer Music Resources and References

Prayers and Blessings
http://www.mechon-mamre.org/jewfaq/prayer.htm

Taste II: Another Bite – Jewish in America

Class 2: New Approaches to Prayer And Prayer Music

January 25, 2005

Rabbi Samuel M. Cohon
Rabbi David Freelund

Class held at St. Francis-in-the-Valley Episcopal Church
600 S. La Canada, Green Valley

Temple Emanu-El
225 N. Country Club Rd.
Tucson, AZ 85713
327-4501
www.templeemanueltucson.org

Innovation in Prayer *January 2005*

From the Desk of Rabbi Cohon

One of the most remarkable aspects of our congregation is the truly amazing variety and quality of our religious expression. Every Shabbat we offer the finest of contemporary Jewish prayer and liturgical music - but each Shabbat is also unique. On any given Friday night at Temple Emanu-El you can experience Jewish prayer in at least two different styles while Saturday morning offers another meaningful prayer option. Obviously, we think prayer matters, and we put a lot of attention and effort into our religious offerings.

In a typical non-summer month the first Friday night includes an early Tot Kabbalat Shabbat dinner and service, and a Contemporary Reform service, sometimes with a guest speaker. The second or third Friday includes a Shabbat Dinner and Shabbat Rocks Family services with our Avanim band, with a Reform Classic or Contemporary Reform service, as well as a Northwest Outreach Shabbat dinner and service. Either the third or fourth Friday night will usually be a Kabbalistic Shabbat service or a Simply Shabbat Outreach service. And once every other month we have a Bilgray Living Judaism Series speaker or presentation.

When you add in other special Friday night services - Shabbat Shirah All-Music services, or Wandering Jews Hike Shabbat, Chardonnay Shabbat on a holiday weekend, Sisterhood Shabbat, Board Installation or Social Action Shabbat - we seem to have several special events every Friday night. And when you add in our vibrant Shabbat morning service program, which includes monthly Project Ezra Torah readers and the Rabbi's Tish, and Pray and Play for younger families, it's a truly amazing array of Jewish religious choices. So why do we do so many different kinds of services?

The simple answer is that today's Reform Jews pray in many different ways, and that as a congregation we strive to offer meaningful, engaging, Jewishly authentic and dynamic prayer experiences that reach as many people as possible. Our way of praying at Temple has evolved over the last five years, and I expect it will continue to grow and change, for the development of Jewish prayer and religious practice is itself an organic process. Seeing other congregations repeatedly imitating us makes it clear that there is a need for quality and innovation in reaching towards God in the 21st century-even if that sometimes takes the form of "retro" approaches like Classical Reform services. We will always seek to make Jewish prayer relevant and meaningful, and do so in new ways whenever it seems appropriate. And, to judge by the numbers, it all seems to work. When we have special simchas or speakers, of course, many visitors attend. But what we are most proud of is the vibrance of our "normal" congregational participation in meaningful, and varied, Jewish prayer.

Prayer is a central way that we Jews seek meaning and community, and find both. If you haven't yet tried one of our service styles, do! Until then, I look forward to praying with you.

L'shalom v'rei'ut, in peace and friendship,

Rabbi Samuel M. Cohon

Taste II: Another Bite – Jewish in America

Class 3: American – Israeli Relations

February 1, 2005

Rabbi David Freelund
Rabbi Samuel M. Cohon

Class held at St. Francis-in-the-Valley Episcopal Church
600 S. La Canada, Green Valley

Temple Emanu-El
225 N. Country Club Rd.
Tucson, AZ 85713
327-4501
www.templeemanueltucson.org

Taste II: Another Bite—Jewish in America
Class 3: American-Israeli Relations
Resources and References

Declaration of Principles: 1885 Pittsburgh Conference
http://www.sacred-texts.com/jud/1885.htm

The Columbus Platform: The Guiding Principles of Reform Judaism (1937)
http://www.sacred-texts.com/jud/colplat.htm

Reform Judaism: A Centenary Perspective, Adopted at San Francisco, 1976
http://www.sacred-texts.com/jud/100.htm

A Statement of Principles for Reform Judaism Adopted at the 1999 Pittsburgh Convention Central Conference of American Rabbis, May 1999—Sivan 5759
http://www.gfn.com/archives/story.phtml?sid=1346

The Declaration of the Establishment of the State of Israel
http://www.jewishvirtuallibrary.org/jsource/History/Dec_of_Indep.html

A Definition of Zionism
http://www.us-israel.org/jsource/Zionism/zionism.html

Abba Eban on Zionism
http://www.us-israel.org/jsource/Quote/eban4q.html

Could the Zionists Have Chosen Another Country besides Palestine? by Mitchell Bard
http://www.jewishvirtuallibrary.org/jsource/Zionism/palalt.html

Anti-Zionism Among Jews
http://www.us-israel.org/jsource/Zionism/Anti-Zionism.html
Alfred Dreyfus and "The Affair"
http://www.jewishvirtuallibrary.org/jsource/anti-semitism/Dreyfus.html

Christian Zionists Rally for Jewish State; Christianity Today, April 23, 2001
http://www.christianitytoday.com/ct/2001/006/18.23.html

I Am a Zionist, Because by Gil Troy
http://christianactionforisrael.org/because.html

Entrée to Judaism

Congregation:	University Synagogue
Address:	11960 Sunset Blvd Los Angeles, CA 90049
Phone Number:	(310) 472-1255
Contact's Name and E-mail:	Rabbi Shapiro, zrshapiro@sbcglobal.net
Number of Member Units:	626
URJ Region:	Pacific Southwest Council
Rabbis:	Zachary R. Shapiro, Morley T. Feinstein
Outreach Chairperson:	Ellen Stang

Brief Description: Entrée to Judaism is a community-building program designed to engage graduates of the URJ's Introduction to Judaism course. Participants seeking a continued relationship with each other and with the rabbi/instructor will have joined four times this year to learn about a Holy Day or festival while learning to prepare a Jewish food (challah, latkes, hamantaschen, matzah balls). During the cooking demonstration, the Hebrew instructor from the Intro class taught the Hebrew ingredients. The heart of the program took place over dinner, where we studied and discussed themes related to the festivals. The dinners themselves ranged from a fully catered Shabbat meal to delivered pizza.

Program Goals: Entrée takes over where Intro leaves off. Students during the eighteen-week Intro course often focus their Judaism to one day a week. When the course is over, there is often little in place to guide them through the next steps. This is such a critical transition time, and we wanted to create a niche in our medium/large-sized congregation in which participants can feel both involved and committed. Further, creating a venue for one-on-one time with the rabbi was essential. Entrée is designed to help members relate in a more meaningful way to the synagogue community. One example occurred this year at Purim. We asked participants in Entrée to help volunteer at our Purim carnival. Without hesitation, they rolled up their sleeves and helped out. This program has been the perfect bridge to getting people involved and committed.

Target Population: While we extend personal invitations to all those from Intro, any member of the congregation is welcome.

Number and Length of Sessions: Four sessions, two and a half hours each.

Number of Participants: Fifteen to twenty.

Staffing Required: Host (rabbi or instructor), someone who can lead a cooking demonstration, Hebrew teacher.

Total Cost of Program: $1,300 (covers advertising and food).

Source of Funding: Rabbi's Discretionary Fund and program fee.

Fee for Attendees: $50/series or $15/session.

Logistics: For each session, the facilitator needs study materials, dinner-wear, and food to eat. Whoever is leading the cooking demonstration should have much of the work done in advance. This requires shopping, preparation of ingredients, and printing of recipes.

Instructions to Facilitator: Have fun with this! Participants will ask the questions they never did in class. And if they ask if they can help clean up, say "Yes!"

Evaluation of Program: We have had overwhelmingly positive feedback. Established *chavurot* within the congregation are working to start their own versions of Entrée, and others are looking to the concept to help motivate additional groups to form (singles, empty-nesters, etc.).

Follow-up: After each event, we e-mail all participants "Save the date" notices for upcoming Entrée programs as well as synagogue-wide programs. We include digital photos with each mailing. We also include the photos in our synagogue newsletter so that others who might be interested can learn about it. Most important, because this program has ensured not only retention of our Intro students, but full integration into our synagogue family, we are confident that having it modeled in other congregations will amplify its success.

E-mail from Rabbi Shapiro to Temple members

Subject: Entrée to Judaism

Dear friends,

Hope you all had a great Holy Day experience. It was wonderful seeing so many of you, and Ron joins me in extending a "L'shana Tova."

As you may have seen, we are beginning a new program called "Entrée to Judaism." While the class is open to all members, I am extending a special invitation to those who are recently married and/or have been through our Introduction to Judaism course. Please read below to find out about the course. Love to see you there!

Rabbi Zach Shapiro

Join Rabbi Shapiro and Ron Galperin in their home to further explore the Jewish Holy Days and festivals. Learn about the traditional foods, schmooze with one another, and discuss the history and values of our specials days.

Dates:
Friday   October 20   "Shabbat"
Saturday   December 11   "Hanukkah"
Thursday   March 17   "Purim"
Sunday   April 17   "Passover"

Time: 7:00–9:30 P.M.
Location: Home of Rabbi Shapiro and Ron Galperin
Tuition: $15 per person per session/$50 for the series
RSVP: No later than one week prior to each session to jchernow@unisyn.org

Chapter Four   Outreach Programming All Year for All   233

| Home | Plan an Event | Places to Go | Things to Do | People to See |

Find Bars & Restaurants   Keyword(s) Italian   City, State or Zip 90210

Entree to Judaism Purim Party!

This view will be available for 30 days.   View Evite Details

From: Rabbi Zach Shapiro and Ron Galperin
Location: ZRSG
9316 Beverly Crest Dr., Beverly Hills, CA
View Map
When: Thursday, March 17, 7:00pm
Phone: 310 273 2475

To those of you who attended our Channukah gathering, what a great time we had! To those of you who missed out, what can I say? YOU MISSED OUT!

Don't miss our next Entrée to Judaism. Thursday, March 17 beginning at 7pm. We will bake fresh Hamen-tashen (Purim cookies) while learning about the festival!

Fee is $15 per person (which includes dinner).
Please RSVP no later than March 10.

See you all there!

Rabbi Zach Shapiro and Ron Galperin

E-TORCH: ELECTRONIC NEWSLETTER

Entrée to Judaism!

"Entrée to Judaism" is a new and exciting program at University Synagogue. Members of the congregation gather at the home of Rabbi Shapiro and Ron Galperin to learn to cook a Jewish food associated with a Holy Day or Festival. A fabulous part of the evening comes when Allison Lattman, a member of University Synagogue's Generation Chai, teaches with a hands-on demonstration! Following the instruction, we enjoy a meal and discuss the rituals, history, and modern contexts of the special day. Don't miss our next Entrée to Judaism **Thursday, March 17 beginning at 7pm**. We will bake fresh Hamentashen (Purim cookies) while learning about the festival! Fee is $15 per person which includes dinner. Please RSVP at (310) 472-1255 by March 10th. See you there!

THE TORCH

ENTRÉE TO JUDAISM

Join Rabbi Shapiro and Ron Galperin in their home to further explore the Jewish Holy Days and festivals. Learn about the traditional foods, schmooze with one another, and discuss the history and values of our special days.

Dates:
Friday, October 30   "Shabbat"
Saturday, December 11   "Hanukkah"
Thursday, March 17   "Purim"
Sunday, April 17   "Passover"

Time: 7:00 – 9:30pm
Location: Home of Rabbi Shapiro and Ron Galperin
Tuition: $15 per person per session; $50 for the series.
RSVP: No later than one week prior to each session to jchernow@unisyn.org.

Entrée to Judaism

March 17, 7:00 – 9:30 p.m. Join Rabbi Shapiro and Ron Galperin in their home to explore the joys of Purim. Allison Lattman will teach us to bake Hamentashen, and we will schmooze with one another and discuss the history and values of this special festival. Cost is $15. Please RSVP no later than March 10 to Rabbi Shapiro at zshapiro@unisyn.org. Please hold April 17 for our Passover Entrée event!

Entrée to Judaism Hanukkah Party

Temple Chai Outreach Brochures

Congregation:	Temple Chai
Address:	45 E. Marilyn Road Phoenix, AZ 85032
Phone Number:	(602) 971-1234
Contact's Name and E-mail:	Rabbi Tzur, RabbiTzur@templechai.com Toni Smeltzer, tonismeltzer@cox.net
Number of Member Units:	1,150
URJ Region:	Pacific Southwest Council
Rabbis:	William Berk, Lisa Tzur, Peter Levi, Mari Chernow
Outreach Chairperson:	Toni Smeltzer

Brief Description: In 2003, Temple Chai decided to reintroduce and revitalize the synagogue outreach program. Under the leadership of lay leader Toni Smeltzer and Rabbi Lisa Tzur, a committee formed and began to research and develop a plan of action. Early in the planning, the committee turned to the board of directors and requested an evening with the board to discuss the matter of outreach, its place in the congregation, and to be given an opportunity to solicit suggestions from the board vis-à-vis how the outreach committee could help to make the synagogue a more welcoming place for all congregants.

During the conversation, the board member in charge of High Holy Days suggested that we should create a brochure for Rosh HaShanah providing simple explanations for some of the practices and customs associated with Rosh HaShanah and Yom Kippur. After ascertaining that such a brochure was not available through the URJ or through any other available resource, the chair of the outreach committee, Toni Smeltzer, immediately began to design a booklet. With only a few days left before the High Holy Days, Toni and Rabbi Tzur together edited the booklet and were able to make it available to the congregation. The entire congregation received the brochure during Rosh HaShanah and the response was very positive. Many congregants took the brochures and gave them to relatives and friends who were not in attendance. Following the holiday, so many people asked for copies of the brochure that the committee created a display to be placed in the lobby of the sanctuary, where the brochure was easily accessible. It was also distributed the following year at Temple Chai and equally well received.

When the regional director of outreach saw the brochure, she immediately announced to her local outreach chairs on the URJ Pacific Southwest Council Outreach listserv that Temple Chai had developed a very useful tool—and that the synagogue was pleased to make the brochure available to whoever would like to use it. Despite the fact that there were only five days left before Rosh HaShanah, five congregations used the brochure, modifying it to reflect the practices in their own congregations. The second year, many more synagogues took advantage of the resource.

The brochure was so popular that the outreach committee agreed to produce additional holiday brochures. Currently, there are brochures for Sukkot, Chanukkah, and Shavuot. The Shabbat brochure will be completed and released shortly. Copies of each brochure are available outside of the sanctuary six weeks prior to the start of the respective holiday, and all of the brochures are included in the membership packet that every potential member receives.

Program Goal: To give congregants and visitors basic information about Jewish holidays. To increase synagogue participation from Jews-by-choice, those considering conversion, interfaith couples, and congregants who are born Jewish but who are insecure about Jewish practice.

Target Population: Interfaith couples, Jews-by-choice, parents raising Jewish children, relatives of interfaith couples, relatives of Jews-by-choice, those who just want to learn more.

Number of Participants: At Temple Chai several thousand of the High Holy Day brochures have been distributed and approximately 500 to 600 of the other holiday brochures have been given out.

Staffing Required: There was a partnership between lay and clergy. The first draft was done by Toni Smeltzer and revised by Rabbi Lisa Tzur and formatted by Marcy Burgis, our Chai Lights editor.

Total Cost of Program: Cost of paper.

Source of Funding: Initial cost was from the temple budget.

Evaluation of Program: Our board of directors was overjoyed at the positive response from our congregants. Members continually ask when the next brochure will be available. The response from around the region tells us that congregations are very excited to have them. The synagogue received a call from a congregant's mother who lives in Pennsylvania and belongs to a Conservative synagogue asking for copies of all the brochures so that she can distribute them to her congregation.

Follow-up: At Temple Chai a Shabbat brochure is in production and Purim and Passover brochures will follow. Helen Sabo, a member of the regional outreach committee, has archived them so that congregations in the PSW Council and elsewhere can have access to the brochures. Each year Helen posts a reminder on e-connections about six weeks before each holiday so that outreach and synagogue community chairs can have time to prepare the brochures for their congregations.

The High Holy Days
5765

Questions and Answers to help you more fully experience and enjoy these Holy Days

brought to you by the Outreach Committee

4645 E. Marilyn Road
Phoenix, Arizona 85032

What do the words Rosh Hashanah mean?

Rosh Hashanah is Hebrew for "head of the year" (literally) or "beginning of the year" (figuratively). In the Torah, we read, "In the seventh month, on the first day of the month, there shall be a sacred assembly, a cessation from work, a day of commemoration proclaimed by the sound of the Shofar." Therefore, we celebrate Rosh Hashanah on the first and second days of Tishrei, the seventh month of the Jewish calendar.

Why is the New Year in the fall?
And why do we start the New Year in the seventh month?

Our ancestors had several dates in the calendar marking the beginning of important seasons of the year. The first month of the Hebrew calendar was Nisan, in the spring. The fifteenth day of the month of Shevat was considered the New Year of the Trees. But the first of Tishrei was the beginning of the economic year, when the old harvest year ended and the new one began. Around the month of Tishrei, the first rains came in Palestine, and the soil was plowed for the winter grain. Eventually, the first of Tishrei became not only the beginning of the economic year, but the beginning of the spiritual year as well.

What are the "Days of Awe?"

Rosh Hashanah is the first of the "High Holy Days," and begins the most spiritually intense part of the Jewish year – the *yamin nora'im*, the Days of Awe. The Days of Awe begin on Rosh Hashanah and conclude on Yom Kippur, a total of 10 days. According to the tradition, on Rosh Hashanah the wholly righteous are inscribed in the Book of Life. For the rest of us, judgment is suspended until Yom Kippur, when our good works and acts of repentance during those 10 days can tilt the balance in our favor so that we may live. These 10 days are devoted to a careful examination of who we are in an attempt to become cognizant of the ways we have failed – failed others, failed our own selves, and failed God. This is the time given to ask forgiveness to those you might have failed, hurt, or offended during the past year. During this period, emphasis is placed on the sincerity of one's repentance.

Why is the Challah baked round for this holiday?

The loaves of egg bread, challah, which are normally braided on Shabbat, are baked in round shapes to symbolize the cyclical nature of the year, and of life. It is also customary to celebrate the sweetness of the New Year by baking with raisins.

What Is Outreach?

Outreach is an effort by the Reform Jewish community to welcome and include those seeking a stronger connection to Judaism, as Jews-by-Choice, interfaith couples and families, parents of interfaith married children, or anyone interested in knowing more about Judaism.

Outreach does not seek to convert non-Jewish partners. Rather, it enables them to explore, study, and come to understand Judaism, thereby providing an atmosphere of support in which a comfortable relationship with Judaism can be fostered.

Outreach encourages people to make Jewish choices in their lives through community support and adult education, and by making Jewish resources at Temple Chai readily available.

Outreach educates and sensitizes the Jewish community to be receptive to Jews-by-Choice and intermarried couples.

Outreach enables children and young people to clarify issues, to strengthen their Jewish identity, and to examine the implications of interdating and interfaith marriage.

This brochure is brought to you by the
Temple Chai Outreach Committee

with thanks to:

Celebrationsguide.org
various web sites
and numerous resource books,
and Marcy Burgis for brochure layout and design.

We have tried to address most of your questions in this brochure.

If you have any suggestions or additions for next year or would like to get information about our Outreach programs please contact our Outreach committee.

Toni Smeltzer, Chair
Rabbi Lisa Tzur

Helaine Adler Mickey Greenberg Cynthia Salk
Michelle & Steven Bernstein Marc Hudson Stephanie Schlossmacher
Julie Blades Ginny Keller Doug & Francine Sumner
Brad Gibson Brenda Levin Debbie Popiel White
Penny Goodman Gloria and David Rickerd

Temple Chai

Sukkot 5765

Questions and Answers to help you more fully experience and enjoy this holiday.

brought to you by the Outreach Committee

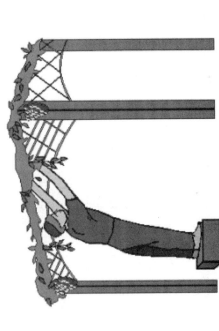

What Is Outreach?

Outreach is an effort by the Reform Jewish community to welcome and include those seeking a stronger connection to Judaism, as Jews-by-Choice, interfaith couples and families, parents of interfaith married children, or anyone interested in knowing more about Judaism.

Outreach does not seek to convert non-Jewish partners. Rather, it enables them to explore, study, and come to understand Judaism, thereby providing an atmosphere of support in which a comfortable relationship with Judaism can be fostered.

Outreach encourages people to make Jewish choices in their lives through community support and adult education, and by making Jewish resources at Temple Chai readily available.

Outreach educates and sensitizes the Jewish community to be receptive to Jews-by-Choice and intermarried couples.

Outreach enables children and young people to clarify issues, to strengthen their Jewish identity, and to examine the implications of interdating and interfaith marriage.

This brochure is brought to you by the
Temple Chai Outreach Committee

with thanks to:

Celebrationsguide.org
various web sites
and numerous resource books,
and Marcy Burgis for brochure layout and design.

We have tried to address most of your questions in this brochure.

All Outreach programs are open to the community.

If you have any suggestions or additions for next year or would like to get information about our Outreach programs, please contact our Outreach committee.

Toni Smeltzer, Chair
Rabbi Lisa Tzur

Helaine Adler
Michelle & Steven Bernstein
Julie Blades
Brad Gibson
Penny Goodman
Mickey Greenberg
Marc Hudson
Ginny Keller
Brenda Levin
Gloria and David Rickerd
Cynthia Salk
Stephanie Schlossmacher
Doug & Francine Sumner
Debbie Popiel White

What does the word Sukkot mean?

The word Sukkot means *booths* or *tabernacle*, and refers to the temporary dwelling in which we are commanded to live during this holiday. The name of the holiday is frequently translated as The Feast of Tabernacles. It is also one of the Three Pilgrimage Festivals (the other two are Passover and Shavuot).

How do you pronounce Sukkot?

The Hebrew pronunciation is *sue-coat*, the Yiddish pronunciation *sook-us* (rhymes with book us). Either pronunciation is acceptable!

Why do we celebrate Sukkot?

Sukkot is celebrated for seven days as both an agricultural festival and an historic reminder of the years that the Israelites wandered in the wilderness of Sinai. Sukkot is a reminder that we should not become excessively attached to material wealth and fame. It is a time to reconnect with the natural state of the world.

Why is Sukkot considered an agricultural/harvest festival?

Autumn was a time when the crops were gathered, so Sukkot became a double celebration. We were grateful that we were no longer wanderers in the desert, and we offered thanks to God for the gathering of the crops.

What is a Sukkah?

The Sukkah is a temporary structure erected for use during the festival of Sukkot. It is a temporary dwelling large enough for a family to eat and live in. In Leviticus 23:42-43 we are taught, "You shall live in booths seven days in order that future generations may know that I made the Israelite people live in booths when I brought them out of the land of Egypt." The sukkah symbolizes the booths or tents in which the Jewish people lived during their forty years of wandering It has three "walls" and a top. The walls are normally made of wood or canvas and the whole structure is covered by *sechach*, a covering that must be made of material that grows in the ground and has been detached from it. Usually separate twigs, palm fronds, bamboo sticks, or the like are used so that the stars may shine through. The Sukkah is decorated with apples, pomegranates, clusters of grapes, Indian corn, gourds, flowers, decorations made by children about nature and harvesting, etc….

When does Sukkot fall?

The Festival of Sukkot begins on the eve of the 15th day of *Tishri*, just five days after Yom Kippur, and lasts for seven days. This year, Sukkot begins on Friday evening, October 10, 2003.

What do you do in a Sukkah?

Some Jews take the words in Leviticus 23, "You shall live in booths…" literally! They eat and sleep in the sukkah. Many just eat their meals in the sukkah. There is also a custom called *ushpizin*, the welcoming of guests into the sukkah. Each and every meal can be an opportunity to invite people into the sukkah for a meal. Traditionally, all food eaten during Sukkot should be eaten inside the sukkah.

What are the etrog and lulav?

The etrog is a citrus fruit that Leviticus 23:40, "And you shall take on the first day (of the holiday) the fruit of goodly trees, branches of palm trees, and boughs of thick trees, (myrtle branches), and willows of the brook, and you shall rejoice before your God seven days." During certain prayers on Sukkot, we wave the lulav and etrog together, up and down, left and right, to symbolize that God is the true owner of the world, and that we are indebted to God for providing us with our material wealth.

Are there any special prayers that are said?

Every time we eat in the Sukkah, we say the following blessing:

Baruch ata Adonai Elohainu Melech ha-olam asher kid'shanu b'mitzvotav v'tzivanu leysheyv basukkah."

Blessed are You the Eternal One who commands us to sit in the sukkah.

The first time that we eat in the Sukkah each year, we say this additional blessing;

Baruch ata Adonai Elohainu Melech ha-olam shehechiyanu v'kiymanu v'higyanu laz-man ha-zeh.

Blessed are You the Eternal One who created us, sustained us, and allowed us to reach this season.

This blessing thanks God for sustaining our lives and enabling us to reach special times. We say this blessing at special times, such as weddings, B'nai Mitzvah, and holidays like Sukkot.

How do I shake a lulav and etrog?

We shake the lulav and etrog every day except for Shabbat. The blessing over the lulav must be said during the day. The lulav is held in the right hand and the blessing is:

Baruch Ata Adonai Eloheinu Melech ha-olam asher kid'shanu b'mitzvotav v'tzivanu al netilat lulav.

Blessed are You the Eternal One who commands us to wave the lulav.

The *first* time we shake the lulav and the etrog, we also say the *Shechiyanu* (see previous prayer for eating in the Sukkah for the first time).

The etrog is then picked up with the left hand, (the lulav is already in the right). They are brought together and touched to the heart. The four should then be waved together in all directions three times: three times to the right, three times to the left, forward, up, down, and to the back. After each direction, touch the etrog and the lulav back to the heart.

Chapter Four Outreach Programming All Year for All

Chanukah
5765

Questions and Answers to help you more fully experience and enjoy this holiday.

brought to you by the Outreach Committee

4645 E. Marilyn Road
Phoenix, Arizona 85032

What does the word Chanukah mean?

The most frequent translation of Chanukah is dedication – that is, we remember the rededication of the temple.

Why is Chanukah celebrated?

Chanukah marks the deliverance of the Jews of Palestine from the oppression of the Syrian-Greeks in the second century B.C.E. (Before the Common Era). The Greeks attempted to impose heathen practices upon the Jewish population, but Judah Maccabee and his four brothers, sons of Mattathias the Priest, all members of the Hasmonean family, led a rebellion against them. The revolt reached its climax when King Antiochus IV of Syria prohibited the observance of sacred Jewish practices, including circumcision, Temple ritual, Sabbath observance, and the study of Torah. The decisive insult was the conversion of the Temple into a pagan shrine. In the year 165 B.C.E., the rebels succeeded in defeating the Syrian armies, after which the Temple was cleansed and rededicated. According to some traditions, the Maccabees built a new altar and/or Menorah (candelabrum) since the old ones were profaned by the Syrians. Thus, Chanukah marks the dedication specifically of these objects in the temple.

Why does the celebration of Chanukah last for eight days?

There are many reasons why we celebrate Chanukah for eight days. Here are some of the most popular.

- The *Talmud* explains that when the Syrian-Greeks captured the Temple, they desecrated all the jugs of oil that the High Priest had prepared for lighting the Temple Menorah. After much searching, only one small undefiled jug still bearing the unbroken seal of the High Priest could be found. This cruse contained only enough oil to burn in the Menorah for one day. Nevertheless, the High Priest kindled the Menorah and a miracle happened – the Menorah flame continued to burn for eight days. To commemorate the event, it was decided that the holiday would be observed annually by kindling lights for eight days and Chanukah became known as the Feast (or Festival) of Lights.

- The Maccabees divided one night's oil into eight portions, and miraculously, each portion lasted an entire night.

- Seven days commemorate the miracle of the oil, and one day commemorates the miracle that a few weak Jewish soldiers defeated the mighty Greek legions.

What Is Outreach?

Outreach is an effort by the Reform Jewish community to welcome and include those seeking a stronger connection to Judaism, as Jews-by-Choice, interfaith couples and families, parents of interfaith married children, or anyone interested in knowing more about Judaism.

Outreach does not seek to convert non-Jewish partners. Rather, it enables them to explore, study, and come to understand Judaism, thereby providing an atmosphere of support in which a comfortable relationship with Judaism can be fostered.

Outreach encourages people to make Jewish choices in their lives through community support and adult education, and by making Jewish resources at Temple Chai readily available.

Outreach educates and sensitizes the Jewish community to be receptive to Jews-by-Choice and interfaith couples.

Outreach enables children and young people to clarify issues, to strengthen their Jewish identity, and to examine the implications of interdating and interfaith marriage.

This brochure is brought to you by the Temple Chai Outreach Committee

with thanks to:

Celebrationsguide.org
The Book of Why by Alfred J. Kolatch
The Book of Jewish Literacy by Joseph Telushkin
various other web sites and resource books,
and Marcy Burgis for brochure layout and design.

If you would like to get information about our Outreach programs, please contact our Outreach committee chair.

Toni Smeltzer, Chair
Rabbi Lisa Tzur

Helaine Adler
Michelle & Steven Bernstein
Julie Blades
Brad Gibson
Penny Goodman

Mickey Greenberg
Marc Hudson
Ginny Keller
Brenda Levin
Bonnie Moyer

Gloria & David Rickerd
Cynthia Salk
Stephanie Schlossmacher
Doug & Francine Sumner
Debbie Popiel White

Chapter Four   Outreach Programming All Year for All   **243**

- The world was created in seven days. There are seven notes in the musical scale, seven days of the week. Therefore, the number seven represents the physical world that we can touch and smell and feel. The number eight, on the other hand, transcends the natural world. That's why the miraculous days of Chanukah are eight. Though eight emanates from beyond our senses, your soul can still reach out and be touched by its force.

- On a deeper level, the days of Chanukah are eight days of transcendence. Days of opportunity to look both within ourselves and beyond, to sense that there is far more to our existence than the world of nature could ever contain.

Is gift giving really a part of Chanukah?

Presents are wonderful – to give and to receive. Traditionally, Jewish children are given daily gifts throughout the holiday. By making it into a fun-filled occasion, many parents hope that their children will not feel that they are missing out on Christmas trees and gifts brought by Santa. But Chanukah is primarily not a season of giving but a season of growing. It is the opportunity to discover so much more – to acquire fresh insights into Jewish life and a bold new inspiration for living. It's just that gifts don't have any particular significance on Chanukah. In fact, if no one gives or receives even one present on Chanukah, they have not omitted anything central to the holiday.

When is Chanukah celebrated?

The first night of Chanukah is celebrated on the 25th of Kislev. Because of vagaries of the Jewish lunar calendar, Chanukah can begin anywhere between the end of November and the end of December.

Why does Chanukah fall on the 25th of Kislev?

Some commentators play on the Hebrew word by dividing it in half: chanu-kah – that is, they rested (*chanu*) on the 25th day (the numerical value of the letters of k and h equal 25). The Maccabees ceased fighting on the 25th of Kislev, and thus Chanukah marks their victory over the Syrians.

What is the difference between a Menorah and a Chanukiah?

A Menorah is a candelabrum that usually holds a total of seven candles, whereas a Chanukiah has room for nine candles: eight candles and a Shamash (a helper candle) that is usually at a different height then the other eight candles.

Vocabulary

Chanukiah: this is the correct name for the Chanukah Menorah.

Gelt: Yiddish for money. Sometimes money is given as a gift to the children at Chanukah time.

Latkes: potato pancakes fried in oil to remind us of the oil lasting 8 days in the holy Temple.

Maccabee: means hammer. Our hero Judah was called the Maccabee.

Shamash: the helper candle, or servant, that is always lit first, and then lights the other candles.

Sufganiah (singular) or **Sufganiot (plural):** Jelly donuts traditionally eaten at Chanukah, because they are made in oil.

Sevivon: Hebrew for dreidel, a four-sided spinning top with a different Hebrew letter on each side.

What is the ninth candle called and what is its special use?

The ninth candle is called the Shamash. It is used to light the other eight since the Chanukiah lights may not be used for practical purposes (one should not use its light for reading, moving about a room, etc.).

Do we place the Chanukiah in a special place?

To best publicize the miracle, the Chanukiah is ideally lit outside the doorway of your house, on the left side when entering. If this is not practical, then the Chanukiah should be lit in a window facing the public thoroughfare. Someone who lives on an upper floor should light it in a window. If for some reason the Chanukiah cannot be lit in a window, it may be lit inside the house on a table; this at least fulfills the *mitzvah* (commandment) of publicizing the miracle for the members of the household. Since the *mitzvah* occurs at the actual moment of lighting, the Chanukiah must be lit in a proper place. Moving the Chanukiah to a proper place after lighting does not fulfill the *mitzvah*.

What is the correct way to put in the candles and to light them?

Candles are put in from right to left, but they are kindled from left to right to pay honor to the newer object first. This also gives equal importance to the left and right showing that God's presence is everywhere. On the first night, one would place a candle on the far right, and light it with the Shamash. On the second night, one would place two candles on the far right, but light the newest one first, and work backwards.

What do I do if the Shamash goes out?

Relight it, but not from the flame of one of the Chanukiah candles. Use a match.

When does one light the Chanukiah?

The Chanukiah should preferably be lit immediately at nightfall. It is best to wait, however, until all the members of the household are present. This adds to the family atmosphere and also maximizes the *mitzvah* of publicizing the miracle. However, the Chanukiah can be lit (and the blessings said) late into the night, as long as people are still awake.

On Friday evening, the Chanukiah should be lit first, then Shabbat candles (because when Shabbat candles are lit, the lighting symbolizes the end of the work week, and lighting candles is considered work). On Saturday evening, the Chanukiah is lit after Shabbat is over.

Recipes

Latkes

Recipe courtesy of the URJ Jewish Parent Page (http://urj.org/educate/parent/archive.shtml)

Blend:
4 large grated potatoes (you may use a food processor)
1 medium onion, also grated
3 Tbsp. matzah meal or flour
3 eggs
1 tsp. salt
1/4 tsp. white pepper

Heat a frying pan or skillet, 1/8-1/4 full of cooking oil. Drop spoonfuls of the potato mixture in the heated oil, browning on both sides. Serve with sour cream and/or applesauce.

The latkes can be made in advance and frozen. Prepare as directed and freeze on cookie sheets. When frozen, pack in plastic bags. To serve, place frozen latkes in one layer on a cookie sheet and reheat at 375 degrees for 10-15 minutes until heated through.

Baked Latkes
(for those who choose not to eat fried foods)

Recipe courtesy Barbara Mark Dreyfuss

In a food processor, grate:
4 medium potatoes
1 large onion
1 clove garlic
1 egg
salt and pepper to taste

Place in greased Teflon muffin tins. Only put in enough to cover the bottom. Bake at 400 degrees until brown (about 1/2 hour). Let cool for 15 minutes.

Remove from muffin tins, carefully loosening the edges first. Serve immediately, refrigerate, or freeze and reheat at 350 degrees on a cookie sheet until heated through.

Makes 2-3 dozen.

Why is the word Chanukah spelled so many different ways.

Channukah, Chanukah, Hanukkah, and Chanuka – these are all variations in transliteration spelling of the Hebrew word. There are different systems of transliteration, and there are those who prefer one over another.

What is a dreidel?

A dreidel is a four-sided top with a different Hebrew letter on each side. It is used to play a popular children's game. The Hebrew word *sevivon* is derived from the Hebrew root meaning to turn. In Yiddish, such a top is called a dreidel.

According to an old legend, the Chanukah top, dreidel, was invented during the time of the Maccabees. Antiochus forbade the study of Torah. Nevertheless, people gathered in small groups and studied the Torah secretly and by heart. If soldiers approached, the group scattered. Another means they used to escape detection was the dreidel game. The dreidel lay on the table. At the lookouts warning, the students spun the top. When the enemy arrived, all they could see was Jews playing an innocent game. Thus, according to tradition, the dreidel saved many lives.

What are the letters on a dreidel?

Today's dreidel bears the letters *Nun* (נ), *Gimel* (ג), *Hay* (ה), *Shin* (ש). They stand for *Nes Gadol Hayah Sham*, a great miracle happened there.

What makes a dreidel used in Israel different from those used outside Israel?

The letters are different. Outside of Israel the letters refer to *a great miracle happened there*. However, in the land of Israel they stand for *a great miracle happened here!*

What are the rules for playing dreidel?

Bets are taken on what letter will be showing when the dreidel stops spinning. You may bet with Chanukah gelt, pennies, M&M's, or paper clips. It's the fun that counts.

For each spin, if it stops on the *nun*, no one wins and the next player spins; on the *gimel*, the spinner takes the pot; on the *hay*, the spinner takes half the pot; and on the *shin*, one is put into the pot.

How long should the candles burn?

The candle should contain sufficient oil (or wax) at the time of lighting to burn until at least 30 minutes after the stars come out. In the event that the light is extinguished before the prescribed time, it is proper to relight (without a new blessing). However, one is not obligated to relight; one has fulfilled the *mitzvah* with the original lighting.

Can we use an electric Chanukiah?

According to nearly all authorities, an electrified Chanukiah may not be used to fulfill the *mitzvah* of kindling the Chanukah lights. While electric bulbs undoubtedly give off light, the filaments are not considered a flame. Moreover, a requisite amount of fuel must be available when the lights are kindled. An electric Chanukiah depends on continuous generation of power to remain lit. Thus, the act of kindling in itself is insufficient to cause the lamp to burn for the prescribed period of time. Since the *Halachic* (law) principle governing the Chanukiah is that kindling constitutes the performance of the *mitzvah*, turning on an electric light would not fulfill the commandment.

What is the difference between using the lights on Shabbat and Chanukah?

The lights for Shabbat can be used for practical purposes, such as lighting a room. The candles for Chanukah can only be decorative. Therefore, one should not turn the lights of a room off when lighting the Chanukiah, making it possible for the lights to be used for practical purpose.

Why are there three blessings said on the first night of Chanukah?

The first two blessings recited over the candles on the first night of Chanukah refer specifically to the kindling of the lights and the miracle of Chanukah. The third blessing, called *Shehecheyanu*, is recited on the first night of all holidays. It expresses our gratitude for being alive and well and having reached this season of rededication.

What are the candle blessings?

Every night during Chanukah, when the candles are lit, these are the prayers that are recited – light the Shamash, say the first two prayers, then light the other candles with the Shamash.

Ba-**ruch** ata A-do-**nai** E-lo-**hei**-nu, **me**-lech ha-o-**lam**, a-**sher** ki-de-**sha**-nu be-mits-vo-**tav**, ve-tsi-**va**-nu le-had-**lik** neir shel **Chan**-nu-kah.

Blessed are you Adonai our God, Ruler of the universe, who has made us holy through the commandments and who has commanded us regarding the lighting of the Chanukah candles.

Ba-**ruch** ata A-do-**nai** E-lo-**hei**-nu, **me**-lech ha-o-**lam**, she-**a-sa** ni-**sim** la-vo-**tei**-nu ba-ya-**mim** ha-**heim** baz-**man** ha-**zeh**.

Blessed are you Adonai our God, Ruler of the universe, who made miracles for our ancestors in those days.

After the candles are lit, on the first night of Chanukah, this prayer is also recited:

Ba-**ruch** ata A-do-**nai** E-lo-**hei**-nu, **me**-lech ha-o-**lam**, she-he-che-**ya**-nu ve-ki-ya-**ma**-nu ve-hi-gi-**ya**-nu laz-**man** ha-**zeh**.

Blessed are you Adonai our God, Ruler of the universe, who created us, sustains us, and who has brought us to this season.

(Bold denotes syllabic emphasis.)

What are some different ways that you can enhance the experience of the lighting of the candles?

Dedicate each of the nights to someone in your family who is no longer living. You can reminisce about this person

Each of the eight nights a friend or family member could share a past Chanukah experience

Each of the eight nights a friend or family member could discuss how they can rededicate themselves to a cause or some important change in their life.

You could discuss a different Jewish value and how each member of the family demonstrates these values:

1. *Bal Tashchit*: not being wasteful
2. *Tza'ar Ba'alei Chayim*: being kind to animals
3. *Hachnasat Orchim*: welcoming strangers or guest to your home
4. *Kibud Av Va'em*: honoring father and mother
5. *Kibud Z'kaynim*: honoring the elderly
6. *Tzedakah*: doing righteous acts, or showing kindness to others
7. *Talmud/Torah*: Jewish learning
8. *Nedarim*: keeping one's word

Is Chanukah an important holiday?

Technically, no! Chanukah is one of the minor holidays in the Jewish calender. There are many people for whom Chanukah is the most celebrated time of the year. Perhaps this is because of Chanukah's proximity to other non-Jewish holidays. Here is a story from the *Sefat Emet* (Rabbi Yehudah Aryeh Leib Alter of Ger of Warsaw, Poland, 1847-1905, Chassidic leader and Talmudist) that helps us to understand another reason why Chanukah has gained such importance in our era.

Wicks and oils that are not fit for burning as Shabbat candles, because they don't burn well, are nevertheless usable on Chanukah. Each letter of the Hebrew word for soul, *nefesh*, stands for a component of the candle: *ner* (flame), *p'tilah* (wick), and *shemen* (oil). Those Jewish souls that don't burn so well – that are not aligned well with their Jewish identity – all during the year on Shabbat, are, due to the special power of the lights, able to burn brightly on Chanukah. For on Chanukah, perhaps more than any other time of year, one is able to get in touch with his/her Jewish identity.

Why do Jews eat fried foods at Chanukah?

Because the Chanukah miracle concerned oil, all the preferred holiday foods are fried in oil. Among American Jews, the *latke*, a pancake made of potatoes and onions fried in oil, is the food most associated with Chanukah. In Israel, the most popular Chanukah delicacy is the *sufganiah*, a fried jelly doughnut.

TEMPLE CHAI

Shavuot

May 26 & 27, 2004

6 & 7 Sivan 5764 • סיון ו' & ז' התשס"ד

Questions and Answers to help you more fully experience and enjoy this holiday

brought to you by the Outreach Committee

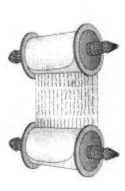

What Is Outreach?

Outreach is an effort by the Reform Jewish community to welcome and include those seeking a stronger connection to Judaism, as Jews-by-Choice, interfaith couples and families, parents of interfaith married children, or anyone interested in knowing more about Judaism.

Outreach does not seek to convert non-Jewish partners. Rather, it enables them to explore, study, and come to understand Judaism, thereby providing an atmosphere of support in which a comfortable relationship with Judaism can be fostered.

Outreach encourages people to make Jewish choices in their lives through community support and adult education, and by making Jewish resources at Temple Chai readily available.

Outreach educates and sensitizes the Jewish community to be receptive to Jews-by-Choice and intermarried couples.

Outreach enables children and young people to clarify issues, to strengthen their Jewish identity, and to examine the implications of interdating and interfaith marriage.

This brochure is brought to you by the
Temple Chai Outreach Committee
with thanks to:

Celebrationsguide.org
various web sites
and numerous resource books,
and Marcy Burgis for brochure layout and design.

All Outreach programs are open to the community.

If you have any suggestions or additions for next year, would like to get information about our Outreach programs, or would like to join our committee, please contact our Outreach committee members.

Toni Smeltzer, Chair, 480-502-4370
Rabbi Lisa Tzur
Michele and Steven Bernstein
Brad Gibson
Ginny Keller
Brenda Levin
Gloria and David Rickerd
Stephanie Schlossmacher
Doug and Francine Sumner
Debbie Popiel White

What does the word Shavuot mean?

Shavuot means weeks. Sometimes Shavuot is called the Festival of Weeks because we count each of the days from the second day of Passover to the day before Shavuot, 49 days or 7 full weeks.

What does Shavuot commemorate?

The Talmud teaches that God gave the Jews the Ten Commandments on the morning of the 6th of Sivan, the first day of Shavuot. This is the reason that we have chosen to welcome our new Torah scroll on erev Shavuot.

The holiday is also linked to the harvesting of wheat and the ripening of the first fruit in the land of Israel.

When does Shavuot take place?

Shavuot takes place on the 6th and 7th days of the Hebrew month of Sivan, beginning the evening before with an all night Torah study, or *tikkun*.

Why is Shavuot considered one of the "Three Pilgrimage Festivals?"

On Passover, Shavuot, and Sukkot, ancient Israelites journeyed on foot to Jerusalem to offer sacrifices at the Temple. Because these journeys were long and difficult for most Jews, they took on the character of pilgrimage.

Why is the Book of Ruth read on Shavuot?

Ruth, a Moabite woman who wished to join the Jewish people, describes the essence of what it means to be a Jew. She accepted Judaism with the simple statement, "Your people shall be my people and your God my God…" Her devotion is considered a model for a Jew's loyalty to the Torah. There are two other literary connections: 1. Her story of faith and devotion took place during the harvest season, and 2. Our tradition teaches us that King David, a descendant of Ruth, was born on Shavuot, and that he died on Shavuot.

What do you do on Shavuot?

In celebration, many Jews assemble the whole night in the synagogue to study Torah, other biblical books, sections of the Talmud, and additional sacred writings. This annual all-night gathering is called a *tikkun*. At daybreak, the participants break from study and recite the morning prayer service.

It is also customary to eat a dairy meal at least once during Shavuot. One reason is that it is a reminder of the promise regarding the land of Israel, a land flowing with "milk and honey." Another thought is that it is because our ancestors had just received the Torah (and the dietary laws therein), and did not have both meat and dairy dishes available.

Cheese Blintzes
from www.celebrationsguide.org

Batter:
4 eggs
2 cups water (or 1 cup milk and 1 cup water)
1-2 tsp. salt
2 cup flour

Filling:
1 pound cottage cheese, strained
1 egg yolk
1/3 cup sugar
touch of vanilla

Combine eggs, milk, salt and flour in that order.

Heat a small amount of oil in a 6-inch or 7- inch frying pan.

Pour in just enough batter to make a very thin crepe. Quickly tilt pan from side to side to spread batter evenly across pan. When crepe pulls away from the side of the pan, flip and fry for just a few seconds on the second side.

Remove crepe from pan, and stack on a plate. Continue to make crepes with the batter until no batter remains.

Blend cheese, egg yolk, and sugar.

Put a spoonful of filling toward one end of the crepe and roll the crepe. Bake 10 minutes in a 400 degree oven.

Why do Reform synagogues often have Confirmation linked to Shavuot?

Because Shavuot represents the time when Israel confirmed its faith and its commitment to Judaism by accepting the Torah and forging a covenant with God. Confirmation is a group ceremony that takes place at the end of the 10th grade which allows our students an opportunity after becoming Bar or Bat Mitzvah to "confirm" their faith and commitment to Judaism.

Why does our tradition teach that Shavuot is the most pleasant of all Jewish holidays?

Passover freed us physically from bondage, but the giving of the Torah on Shavuot redeemed us spiritually from our bondage to idolatry and immorality.

A final note...

Shavuot is a time of the giving of the Torah, rather than the time of the receiving of the torah. The sages point out that we are constantly in the process of receiving of Torah, and that we receive it every day, but it was first given at this time. Thus it is the giving, not the receiving, that makes this holiday significant.

TEMPLE CHAI
Outreach Program
2003-2004
5764

Serving the Needs of:

Interfaith Couples

Couples Considering Interfaith Marriage

Jews By Choice

Unaffiliated Individuals Interested in Judaism

Relatives of Interfaith Couples

...Anyone Concerned About Jewish Values and Traditions

Rabbi William C. Berk • Rabbi Peter S. Levi
Rabbi Lisa Tzur • Rabbi Mari Chernow
Cantor Sharona Feller

4645 E Marilyn Road • Phoenix, AZ 85032
Phone: 602-971-1234 • Fax: 602-971-5909
Email: templechai@templechai.com
www.templechai.com

What Is Outreach?

Outreach is an effort by the Reform Jewish community to welcome and include those seeking a stronger connection to Judaism, as Jews-by-Choice, interfaith couples and families, parents of interfaith married children, or anyone interested in knowing more about Judaism.

Outreach does not seek to convert non-Jewish partners. Rather, it enables them to explore, study, and come to understand Judaism, thereby providing an atmosphere of support in which a comfortable relationship with Judaism can be fostered.

Outreach encourages people to make Jewish choices in their lives through community support and adult education, and by making Jewish resources at Temple Chai readily available.

Outreach educates and sensitizes the Jewish community to be receptive to Jews-by-Choice and intermarried couples.

Outreach enables children and young people to clarify issues, to strengthen their Jewish identity, and to examine the implications of interdating and interfaith marriage.

Outreach Committee

Toni Smeltzer, Chair, 480-502-4370
Rabbi Lisa Tzur
Helaine Adler
Michelle & Steven Bernstein
Brad Gibson
Ginny Keller
Brenda Levin
Gloria & David Rickerd
Stephanie Schlossmacher

Connect With Outreach

Complete this form and return it to the temple office so we may notify you of upcoming programs. If you would like to receive a personal phone call from the Outreach Committee, let us know that too. We would be happy to talk with you.

☐ Put me on the mailing list.
☐ Please have someone call me.

Name _____

Address _____

City, State, Zip _____

Telephone # _____

Email _____

Please check all that apply:

☐ Jew By Choice
☐ Interfaith
☐ Parents of Intermarried Children
☐ Interested in Judaism

Return this form to:
Temple Chai
Attn: Outreach Committee
4645 E. Marilyn Road
Phoenix, AZ 85032

Outreach

In every generation, there have been non-Jews who ventured forth to place their lot with Jewish people. The generation of the Exodus, for example, was strengthened by the participation of many non-Israelites who joined them in the world's first major slave revolt. In Roman times, it is estimated that at least 10% of the educated Roman elites joined the Jewish people. There were many years where ghetto walls made it difficult for Jews and non-Jews to meet – though historians tell us that even in those tense times peoples managed to meet and exchange ideas, to influence one another.

In our own day, with unprecedented freedom, many Jews marry non-Jews. The Reform Movement was the first voice in the Jewish world to come forth clearly to say, "We welcome all those who come close. We honor your choice to be in our lives." We started the Outreach Movement, which is designed to make non-Jews comfortable with the Jewish community, Jewish culture, and Jewish religion. Our goal is not to convert. Our goal is to educate, to embrace, and hopefully to inspire. We especially want intermarried couples to be comfortable with Temple Chai. We want you to make friends. We hope the synagogue can be for you, as for all others, a place of intellectual, moral, emotional, and spiritual growth. We hope you can find a niche. We pray you might be willing, at times, to make this place an address for your commitments, your idealism, your love.

So welcome, welcome, welcome. Come and enjoy. Through social events, classes, services, friendships, meetings, retreats, and much more – may you be uplifted by the depth of Jewish life. The Talmud tells us, "Welcome everyone with joy." In our generation, more than ever, this is one teaching we are trying very hard to live. The traumas of Jewish life have sometimes made this difficult, but we are doing our best. So with hearts full of joy, we say yet again, welcome.

Sincerely,

Rabbi William C. Berk

Programs

Writing a New Torah
September 21, 11:30 am Temple Chai, Main Sanctuary
So you thought there were only 10 Commandments! The 613th Commandment says, "And you shall write a Torah." Artist and scribe Ruth Levi will teach us the meaning of, purpose of, reason for, and what goes into writing a Torah scroll. Then join the whole congregation at noon for the writing of the first six letters.

Basic Judaism 101
September 21, 11:00 am-12:00 pm, Temple Chai
Instructor: Ginny Keller, RN, MC, CPC
This course is the educational component of Family School. The whole congregation is invited to this 14-week course. Call the temple for the additional dates.

UAHC Introduction to Judaism
October 8, 7:00-9:00 pm, Temple Chai
Instructor: Rabbi Mari Chernow
An 18-week course of instruction in the basic principles and practices of Judaism. Come join us for an intellectual and emotional approach to the spiritual traditions of the Jewish people. For tuition fees and registration, call the temple. This course is recommended for those considering conversion.

Sukkot at Rabbi Tzur's
October 12 at 5:00 pm, Rabbi Lisa & Eran Tzur's home
Come with your family and celebrate Sukkot under the stars. Socialize with your Temple Chai family and learn the meaning and symbols of Sukkot. Potluck dairy dinner! Call the temple for directions and to RSVP.

Mitzvah Day
November 16
Participate with your Temple Chai community in bringing the *mitzvot* (commandments) of the Torah to life as we engage in community action.

Interfaith Thanksgiving Celebration
November 24, 7:00 pm, Temple Chai
The interfaith service will feature the clergy and the combined adult and children's choirs of the PV United Methodist Church and Temple Chai.

Chanukah Party
December 7, 4-6:00 pm, Richard & Julie Cross' home
Rabbi Lisa Tzur will teach about the origins of Chanukah and why the story is not included in the Bible. Come to socialize and enjoy latkes. Children will make their own *chanukiah* (many people also call this a *menorah*) while adults have an opportunity for study and discussion. Call the temple for directions and to RSVP.

Dreidel Bells
December 17, 7:00-8:30 pm
Valley of the Sun Jewish Community Center
December can be a joyous, festive, and very complex month. In this program, interfaith issues surrounding the holidays will be addressed. Sponsored by the VOSJCC. To register, call 480-483-7121 ext. 1205.

Chai Paradise Symposium
January 13, 7:30-9:00 pm Temple Chai
Rabbi William Berk, Temple Chai
Pastor Kelly Bender, PV United Methodist Church
The symposium *Join the Conversation, Different Voices, Different Texts, Same God* will be conducted as a round-table discussion of shared Biblical texts and distinctive post-Biblical texts from each of our traditions.

Kabbalat Shabbat Workshop
Thursday, February 12, 7:00-9:00 pm Temple Chai
Friday, February 13, 6:15 pm Kabbalat Shabbat Services and 7:15 Shabbat Dinner Temple Chai
Instructor: Rabbi Mari Chernow
Thursday come learn about the Kabbalat Shabbat service and take a hands on tour of the bimah.

Friday attend Kabbalat Shabbat services with your family and then share a Shabbat meal, where you will learn the prayers and rituals. Cost for the dinner is $10 for Temple Chai members and $6 for children under 12; $12 for non-members and $8 for children under 12. RSVP to the temple.

Passover Workshop
March 11, 6:30 pm Temple Chai
Instructor: Rabbi Lisa Tzur
This will be an adult interactive workshop and mock seder to help you understand Passover and teach you how to lead a seder. Learn the special melodies, bake your own matzo, and learn new and exiting ways of engaging both children and adults in the celebration of freedom.

What you always wanted to know about Interfaith issues but were afraid to ask.
April 29, 7:00 pm, Temple Chai
Instructor: Rabbi William Berk
How do I handle my child dating or marrying someone not Jewish? My parents have trouble accepting my conversion, what can I do? These and many others will be answered.

All programs open to the community.

TEMPLE CHAI

Outreach Program
2004-2005
5765

Serving the Needs of:

Interfaith Couples

Couples Considering Interfaith Marriage

Jews By Choice

Unaffiliated Individuals Interested in Judaism

Relatives of Interfaith Couples

...Anyone Concerned About Jewish Values and Traditions

Rabbi William C. Berk • Rabbi Lisa Tzur
Rabbi Peter S. Levi • Rabbi Mari Chernow
Cantor Sharona Feller

4645 E Marilyn Road • Phoenix, AZ 85032
Phone: 602-971-1234 • Fax: 602-971-5909
Email: templechai@templechai.com
www.templechai.com

What Is Outreach?

Outreach is an effort by the Reform Jewish community to welcome and include those seeking a stronger connection to Judaism, as Jews-by-Choice, interfaith couples and families, parents of interfaith married children, or anyone interested in knowing more about Judaism.

Outreach does not seek to convert non-Jewish partners. Rather, it enables them to explore, study, and come to understand Judaism, thereby providing an atmosphere of support in which a comfortable relationship with Judaism can be fostered.

Outreach encourages people to make Jewish choices in their lives through community support and adult education, and by making Jewish resources at Temple Chai readily available.

Outreach educates and sensitizes the Jewish community to be receptive to Jews-by-Choice and intermarried couples.

Outreach enables children and young people to clarify issues, to strengthen their Jewish identity, and to examine the implications of interdating and interfaith marriage.

Outreach Committee

Toni Smeltzer, Chair, 480-502-4370
Rabbi Lisa Tzur

Helaine Adler
Michelle Bernstein
Steven Bernstein
Julie Blades
Brad Gibson
Penny Goodman
Mickey Greenberg
Marc Hudson
Ginny Keller
Brenda Levin
Gloria Rickerd
David Rickerd
Cynthia Salk
Stephanie Schlossmacher
Doug Sumner
Francine Sumner
Debbie Popiel White

Connect With Outreach

Complete this form and return it to the temple office so we may notify you of upcoming programs. If you would like to receive a personal phone call from the Outreach Committee, let us know that too. We would be happy to talk with you.

❏ Put me on the mailing list.
❏ Please have someone call me.

Name _____
Address _____
City, State, Zip _____
Telephone # _____
Email _____

Please check all that apply:

❏ Jew By Choice
❏ Interfaith
❏ Parents of Intermarried Children
❏ Interested in Judaism

Return this form to:
Temple Chai
Attn: Outreach Committee
4645 E. Marilyn Road
Phoenix, AZ 85032

Outreach

In every generation, there have been non-Jews who ventured forth to place their lot with Jewish people. The generation of the Exodus, for example, was strengthened by the participation of many non-Israelites who joined them in the world's first major slave revolt. In Roman times, it is estimated that at least 10% of the educated Roman elites joined the Jewish people. There were many years where ghetto walls made it difficult for Jews and non-Jews to meet – though historians tell us that even in those tense times peoples managed to meet and exchange ideas, to influence one another.

In our own day, with unprecedented freedom, many Jews marry non-Jews. The Reform Movement was the first voice in the Jewish world to come forth clearly to say, "We welcome all those who come close. We honor your choice to be in our lives." We started the Outreach Movement, which is designed to make non-Jews comfortable with the Jewish community, Jewish culture, and Jewish religion. Our goal is not to convert. Our goal is to educate, to embrace, and hopefully to inspire. We especially want intermarried couples to be comfortable with Temple Chai. We want you to make friends. We hope the synagogue can be for you, as for all others, a place of intellectual, moral, emotional, and spiritual growth. We hope you can find a niche. We pray you might be willing, at times, to make this place an address for your commitments, your idealism, your love.

So welcome, welcome, welcome. Come and enjoy. Through social events, classes, services, friendships, meetings, retreats, and much more – may you be uplifted by the depth of Jewish life. The Talmud tells us, "Welcome everyone with joy." In our generation, more than ever, this is one teaching we are trying very hard to live. The traumas of Jewish life have sometimes made this difficult, but we are doing our best. So with hearts full of joy, we say yet again, welcome.

Sincerely,

William C. Berk

Rabbi William C. Berk

Programs

URJ Introduction to Judaism
At Temple Beth Israel
September 9, 7:00 pm
Instructors: Rabbi Mari Chernow, Rabbi Jordan Goldson, and Rabbi Jill Zimmerman

An 18-week course of instruction in the basic principles and practices of Judaism. Come join us for an intellectual and emotional approach to the spiritual traditions of the Jewish people. For tuition fees and registration, call Rabbi Chernow at the temple. This course is recommended for those considering conversion.

Sukkot at Rabbi Tzur's
October 2, 6:00 pm, Rabbi Lisa & Eran Tzur's home.

Come with your family and celebrate Sukkot under the stars. Please join us for an evening of socializing, good food and fun as we celebrate the Sukkot holiday. Learn with your Temple Chai community the meaning and symbols of Sukkot. Potluck dairy dinner! Call the temple for directions and to RSVP.

December Dialogue of Interfaith Families
November 10, 7:30 pm, Temple Chai
Facilitator: Rabbi Peter Levi

December can bring on the most perplexing dilemmas in an interfaith marriage. Rabbi Peter Levi will conduct a discussion session encouraging interfaith couples to communicate their concerns about the December Dilemma. We will also explore options of how to help children deal with this difficult time of the year, and how to deal with the in-laws and their reactions to a family's decisions. Come hear what other families have done or share your experience and concerns.

Chanukah Party
December 5, location to be determined

Rabbi Lisa Tzur will teach about the origins of Chanukah, why this holiday is not included in the Bible, what are the symbols of Chanukah and what do they mean. We will furnish the latkes and applesauce, songs, activities for children, games and more. You bring a dessert. Call the temple to RSVP and for directions.

Will My Grandchildren Be Jewish?
January 27, 7:30 pm, Temple Chai
Facilitator: Arlene Chernow, Union for Reform Judaism Southwest Regional Director of Outreach and Synagogue Community

This discussion for Jewish grandparents and those who expect to be grandparents in the future will give all participants a chance to reflect on issues surrounding of Jewish identity as it relates; to themselves personally, adult married children, and grandchildren. Arlene will lead a warm supportive discussion of the questions that arise when a child marries someone who is not Jewish. Participants will have a chance to ask questions and share concerns about the identity of their grandchildren

Your Guide to Shabbat
March 4, 5:45 at Temple Chai
Facilitator: Rabbi Mari Chernow

Start with a nosh, attend Kabbalat Shabbat services with your family, and then share a festive Shabbat meal. Participate in wonderful and stimulating table discussions followed by singing and Israeli dancing. Cost for this program will be announced. RSVP to the temple by February 28.

Passover Workshop
April 7, 7:00 pm, Temple Chai
Facilitator: Rabbi Lisa Tzur

This will be an adult interactive workshop and mock Seder to help you understand Passover and teach you how to lead a Seder. Learn the special melodies, bake your own matzo, and learn new and exiting ways of engaging both children and adults in the celebration of freedom.

The Chai Paradise Project has programs throughout the year which may be of interest to our Outreach community. This is an inter-faith exchange program initiated by members of Temple Chai and Paradise Valley United Methodist Church. The Project encourages and enables congregants to come together for educational and informational programs in order to explore and learn about the teachings and observances of our respective faiths. The Project's goals are to establish better understanding among our members, to celebrate the similarities as well as the diversity we share within our community, and to stand together against hate and intolerance. Contact Sharona Silverman at the Shalom Center for more information.

Resources

www.templechai.com
www.urj.org/outreach
www.interfaithfamily.com
www.celebrationsguide.org
www.jewishfamily.com
www.jewishnet.net
www.askmoses.com

All programs open to the community.

SCHEDULE OF SERVICES

Friday, October 3
6:15 pm – Kabbalat Shabbat

Saturday, October 4
8:45 am – Shacharit Service
8:45 am – Bat Mitzvah Ariel Salk
10:30 am – B'nai Mitzvah
Emily Miller and Nicholas Ansel
11:00 am – Torah for Tots
Ha'azinu

Sunday, October 5
Kol Nidre – see services schedule p. 4

Monday, October 6
Yom Kippur – see services schedule p. 4

Friday, October 10
6:15 pm – Kabbalat Shabbat

Saturday, October 11
8:45 am – Shacharit/Sukkot Services
8:45 am – Family Congregation
10:30 am – B'not Mitzvah
Jordana Barness and Sarah Lustiger
4:00 pm – CCC Sukkot Celebration
Sukkot First Day

Friday, October 17
6:15 pm – Kabbalat Shabbat

Saturday, October 18
8:45 am – Shacharit/Yizkor Services
10:30 am – B'not Mitzvah
Jessica Lebowitz and Rebecca Harris
5:00 pm – CCC Simchat Torah
6:15 pm – Simchat Torah
Shemini Atzeret

Friday, October 24
6:15 pm – Kabbalat Shabbat

Saturday, October 25
8:45 am – Shacharit Service
8:45 am – Family Congregation
8:45 am – Bar Mitzvah Daniel Cadoff
10:30 am – B'nai Mitzvah
Jay and Renee Roth
Bereshit

Friday, October 31
6:15 pm – Kabbalat Shabbat

Saturday, November 1
8:45 am – Shacharit Service
8:45 am – Bar Mitzvah Jeremy Goldberg
10:30 am – B'nai Mitzvah
Ariel, Asher, and Eliza Molk
11:00 am – Torah for Tots
Noach

Join us every Friday at 5:45 pm before Kabbalat Shabbat services for a Shabbos Nosh. Come nosh and schmooze, then light the Shabbat candles as a community.

Babysitting is available for Friday evening Kabbalat Shabbat services.

Candle Lighting Times

October 3	5:53 pm
October 10	5:44 pm
October 17	5:35 pm
October 24	5:27 pm
October 31	5:20 pm

Vol. 27 No. 2   Tishri / Cheshvan 5764   October 2003

Temple Chai Renews Committment to Outreach

OUTREACH…our commitment to making everyone feel a part of the temple community. Our Outreach Program serves the needs of interfaith couples, couples considering interfaith marriage, Jews by choice, relatives of interfaith couples…anyone concerned about Jewish values and traditions.

We invite our Outreach community to celebrate Sukkot at Rabbi Lisa and Eran Tzur's home on Sunday, October 12 at 5:00 pm. This will be a dairy potluck dinner where you will have the opportunity to socialize and learn the meaning and symbols of Sukkot. Children are invited. For directions and to RSVP, please contact the temple office at 602-971-1234.

The UAHC "Introduction to Judaism" is a course of instruction in the basic principles and practices of Judaism. It is an intellectual and emotional approach to the spiritual traditions of the Jewish people. Rabbi Mari Chernow will teach the class beginning October 8 at 7:00 pm. Call Rabbi Chernow at 602-971-1234 for more information.

Every month, we will be bringing you a story by a congregant who is part of our Outreach family. I think you will be very touched by their stories. If you would like to write your story and/or be put on our mailing list for future Outreach Programs, or if you have any questions, please contact me.

Toni Smeltzer, Outreach Chair, 480-502-4370, toni@mindspring.com

My Experience as a "Jewish Father" and a "Christian Man"
By Doug Sumner

For 10 years, I have been the Christian spouse in an interfaith marriage and a member of Temple Chai. I was raised in a traditional and devout Norwegian-American Lutheran family and church in Northern Minnesota. My wife, perhaps my cultural opposite, was raised in a mostly liberal and secular Jewish family in Westchester County, New York. Although our discoveries about each other and our backgrounds were initially about humorous ethnic differences, as we became more serious about each other, the magnitude of the life-changing decisions and challenges that were ahead of us became much more evident and real.

My extended Lutheran family includes four uncles and four first cousins who are Lutheran ministers, and a grandmother and mother who were strong spiritual matriarchs and leaders. As traditional as

continued on page 13

"Happenings of the Month!"

Arts:	"Entartete Musik," November 9, 5:30 pm (page 18)
Community:	Blood Drive, October 26, 8:30 am (page 10)
Education:	"Introduction to Judaism," October 8, 7:00 pm (page 6)
Family:	Simchat Torah, October 18 (page 5) Sefer Safari at the Zoo, November 2, 12:30 pm (page 11)
Healing:	Service of Hope and Comfort Under the Sukkah, October 14, 7:00 pm (page 5 & 8)
Religious:	Yom Kippur, October 5 & 6 (page 4)
Social:	"Bowling for Chai," November 1, 7:00 pm (page 12 & insert)

OUTREACH

PROGRAMS

Outreach, continued from page 1

they were, they were always very supportive of Israel and of the important role Jews had played historically and today. However, when it came to the real possibility that my parents would have Jewish grandchildren, their tolerance was tested at a very personal level. How would their son reconcile and retain his own strong Christian faith and how would they relate to and have the assurance of the spiritual well-being of their grandchildren? Of course, my parents' concerns were also part of the internal dialogues I had while deciding to marry Francine, raise our children Jewish, and integrate into a synagogue and culture that was literally foreign to me.

Once these life-changing spiritual decisions were made, and they were part of our marriage covenant, I committed to becoming an active member of the temple with my wife and strongly supporting our children's Jewish education and upbringing. Initially, I was very concerned and uncertain of how this transition would happen, what my role would be, and what impact it would have on my own Christian beliefs. What I did have, though, was a strong personal faith, based on experience, which consoled me that Francine was the woman I was meant to marry, that Judaism was the foundation of Christianity, and as a result, God would support and nurture our growth as a family.

After years of raising three children and participating with my wife at Temple Chai, I feel very comfortable in my role as an active "Jewish father" and a committed "Christian man." However, I continue to strive for more growth, both in Judaism and Christianity. As a Jewish father, I am committed to learning Hebrew and to be a part of my children's education. I am in the Advanced Judaic studies program, and I attend services and religious school events. However, the one area that has helped me personally the most, as a Christian involved in Judaism, is relating the history and rituals of Judaism to Christianity.

For example, relating the Jewish liturgy to the Christian liturgy provides me with a feeling that worship service that I attended as a child is very similar to the worship service I am sharing with my children. Similarly, learning more about the growth of Christianity in the early centuries and how it grew in many ways out of Judaism provides comfort that the two religions are related and that my involvement in both religions is not contradictory.

Although I am comfortable being an integral part of our Jewish family life, I know there are other Christian spouses that are not as comfortable and have not become as involved as I have. Making a lifelong commitment to marry a spouse who has a religious and cultural background significantly different from yours, dropping, to some degree, your involvement in your own religion, and acting as a role model for your children's religious education in a different faith is, to say the least, difficult and a growth experience. Interfaith marriage is not a simple designation. It is lifelong personal experiences and ongoing internal dialogues, which makes it impossible to prescribe a road map or process for getting through it. From my experience though, it is about doing what you think is right, taking risks, having faith, and nurturing the spiritual growth of your spouse, your children, and yourself.

B'Yachad

Our mission is to build community at Temple Chai by bringing people together. We do this by providing events, opportunities for service and funding for Temple activities.

Judaica Shop News

Official ISRAELI ARMY BADGES now available at the Judaica Shop. Collect them all!

Holocaust Tickets

If you are going to be in Washington, D.C. the night of Thursday, October 16, 2003, and would like to visit the U.S. Holocaust Memorial Museum during it's special evening hours from 6:30 to 9:00 pm, please contact Barbara at 602-971-1234 x 212. Up to six passes are available.

Go to the Theater!!

On Saturday, October 25, 2003, come to Broadway Palms Dinner Theatre for "Westside Story." Bus service will be provided from the temple and back, and the cost will be $40.00 per person. We will meet at the temple at 5:30 pm.

All Temple Chai members are invited. Please mail checks made out to B'Yachad to Barbara Lewis, 18222 N. 24th Place, Phoenix 85032 or to Frank Rader, 4825 E. Nisbet Road, Scottsdale 85254. Reservations MUST be in by October 10 and your check is your receipt.

Also plan for "Cats" on May 29, 2004. Any questions, please call Barbara Lewis at 602-493-7287.

OUTREACH

Connect with Outreach

At our last Outreach committee meeting we made a very significant decision that our programs would be open to the community. After reading all the information that has come out about interfaith relationships and how many are unaffiliated, we decided that it was of the utmost importance that the Outreach community have an opportunity to participate, learn, and get connected through programming that deals with their specific issues and concerns. So please pass this information on to any of your friends, family, or co-workers that you think would benefit from our Outreach Programs. Remember, Outreach serves the needs of interfaith couples, couples considering interfaith marriage, Jews by choice, unaffiliated individuals interested in Judaism, relatives of interfaith couples, and anyone concerned about Jewish values and traditions. If you have any questions or concerns that you would like to see addressed, please give me a call.

Two upcoming programs are:

Mitzvah Day, November 16th. This is an opportunity to participate with your Temple Chai community in bringing the *mitzvot* (commandments) of the Torah to life as we engage ourselves in community action. Contact either Morrie Baker at 480-922-9617 or Jennifer Cohen 602-787-2633 to participate.

Dreidel Bells, December 17th, 7:00-8:30 pm. December can be a joyous, festive, and very complex month. In this program interfaith issues surrounding the holidays will be discussed. This is sponsored by the Valley of the Sun Jewish Community Center at no charge and will be held at the VOSJCC on Scottsdale and Sweetwater. Call 480-483-7121 ext.1205 to register.

Toni Smeltzer-Chair
480-502-4370

My Story

by Stephanie Schlossmacher

In 1998 I began reading about Judaism as a way to enrich my spiritual practice. A friend encouraged me to try services at Temple Chai. I was surprised to find that they were in Hebrew! I felt everyone there must have known I was an imposter as I tried to follow along. After a year and a half of classes and monthly meetings with Rabbi Tzur, I decided to convert. I was nervous about the day. Could I convert without a Jewish spouse? Would I pass the "test"? Well, there was no test, and the day of my conversion was wonderful and meaningful. Even though my husband, Ted, is not Jewish, he supported me through the entire process.

My in-laws, however, were not so happy. They are missionaries for an evangelical Christian denomination. I feel like they blame me for the spiritual demise of their son and grandchildren – especially now that Ted is considering conversion. My family members are evangelical Christians and are also concerned. Leaving the church for Judaism has put a strain on my relationship with both sides of the family. The tension has decreased over the past few years, but may yet remain for many more.

When I first converted, I didn't feel any different. I started to observe the holidays, but it felt forced. It is difficult to have no Jewish relatives – especially around the annual holidays. (I could really have used a bubbe my first Chanukah as I struggled to cook the latkes.) Things started to change when we moved closer to temple and began to get involved. We met dear friends who became our Jewish family. Being able to celebrate with them has made the holidays seem more festive – like they are truly my holidays.

More than any other practice, Shabbat has strengthened my Jewish identity. Every week that I light the candles and say the blessings, I reaffirm that my household is Jewish. At first it was difficult to slow down and observe Shabbat. It took a few years, but now it would be unnatural to not celebrate the holiday that has brought us so much joy. My two-year-old daughter loves to help prepare for the evening meal. Ted and I enjoy going to Kabbalat Shabbat services. We cherish the time spent together as a family.

In some ways, being Jewish is still very alien to me, but as time passes, my practice feels more and more authentic. I am doing this Jewish thing in my own way. I have found deep meaning and joy in belonging to the Jewish community, celebrating Shabbat, and gathering with dear friends for the Holidays.

Save the Date

Saturday,

March 20, 2004

Celebration of

Rabbi William

& Susan Berk

Connect with Outreach

December – a month filled with celebrations, decisions, and many times, frustrations. What to observe? What not to! How do I do it? What do I tell my children about the Christmas tree at Grandma's? And, is the correct spelling Chanukah or is it Hanukah? These are some of the questions that challenge many Outreach families this time of the year. Come have your questions answered and have fun at our

Chanukah Party
Sunday, December 7, 4:00-6:00 pm
At the home of Richard and Julie Cross
Children invited

Your children will have the opportunity to make their own Chanukiah (a special Menorah with nine branches), and Rabbi Tzur will do a teaching about Chanukah as well as answer your questions. There will be plenty of time to socialize and enjoy eating latkes. Please join us for this fun get together. RSVP to the temple at 602-971-1234.

There is also a wonderful program at the Valley of the Sun Jewish Community Center, **Dreidel Bells**, on December 17 from 7:00-8:30 pm that talks about the interfaith issues surrounding the holidays. Call 480-483-7121 ext. 1205 to register.

Upcoming Events

January 13: **Chai Paradise symposium** at Temple Chai led by Rabbi William Berk and Pastor Kelly Bender of the Paradise Valley United Methodist Church. See page 16 for more information.

February 12 and 13: a **Kabbalat Shabbat workshop** with Rabbi Mari Chernow. On Thursday, February 12, we will learn all about the prayers and how to prepare a Shabbat dinner. Then we will celebrate Shabbat together at services and at dinner afterward.

Please check out our updated Outreach program brochure for additional information and programs.

Looking forward to seeing all of you at our Chanukah party, Toni Smeltzer, Chair, 480-502-4370

My Story
by David Rickerd III

My path to Judaism was rather circuitous. I was born and raised Roman Catholic. My mother was very active in the church at that time. My father was an atheist. In retrospect, that may have opened the door to questioning my faith. At age 20, I began to contemplate and express serious doubts about my role in the church and explore other religions.

I delved into other religious choices, but I never found the "home" that I was looking for. I often felt valued only for my wallet rather than my soul. I grew tired of having others look down their noses at me because I was an outsider. I yearned for a spiritual home.

I finally found that home when I married Gloria. We had agreed prior to marriage that any children that we had would be raised Jewish. We also agreed that I would not convert, as I had absolutely no intention of becoming a Jew. This arrangement worked well for awhile, but after Nicole's birth, Gloria felt a growing need to be affiliated with a synagogue. Eventually, I started attending with her to watch Nicole. After a period of about six months, I asked Gloria to make an appointment for me with the rabbi to discuss conversion. After I picked her up off the floor, we began the journey that brings me to today.

Along the way, there were multiple challenges, most notably my mother. She was not at all pleased about my decision to convert to Judaism, and many harsh words were exchanged. I also had to deal with the prejudice in my workplace, which was sufficient that I did not feel comfortable revealing my choices/religion. I also had to explain my desire to become Jewish to my other children. At the time, David was 19, Jessica was 18, Michael was 10, and Brandon was 8. None of the children voiced any strong objections or even much of an opinion. Michael and Brandon, however, were elated that they could have eight days of Chanukah instead of one day at Christmas.

Other challenges arose in celebrating holidays with my family. This occurred despite the fact that I was the only one of five siblings who practiced any religion. There were many offensive comments made which my brothers and sister dismissed as kidding around. Eventually these were replaced by apathy, if not true acceptance. Even my mother has quietly come to terms (three plus years later) and now says that I have a shoe-in to heaven with all the religions that I have tried. Clearly, she still does not fully understand or accept the depth of my commitment and faith, but she is trying. We no longer yell at each other.

Moving to Arizona 2½ years ago was a fresh start for me. I could finally be fully Jewish. I am open and proud of my religion. I am quite verbal about being a Jew. I have no need or desire to hide who I am.

This past July, Gloria and I took full custody of Michael and Brandon. I am now raising my non-Jewish 12- and 14-year-old children in our Jewish home. They had attended services with us back east, but this was now 24/7 into a much more observant home. There was also the issue of our youngest child, Nicole, who knew nothing but Judaism. She had attended synagogue-based nursery school and now attends Religious school. On a regular basis, she brings more and more Judaism into the household, including reciting *Hamotzi* on a nightly basis. After much anguish and discussion, we have decided to allow the boys to choose their own religion. They attend all synagogue events and services with us, but sometimes remain in the courtyard or lobby. I am saddened by the fact that they were not born Jewish, but my hope is that they will discover, as I have, the beauty and wonder in Judaism as I continue to expose them to it. I am encouraged by the fact that Brandon expresses some interest and enjoys learning Hebrew at the Looking Glass School. I feel blessed that there is no conflict among my children about religion.

I attribute much of my current, peaceful state of mind to the "family" and support that I have found at Temple Chai. Becoming Jewish brought a unity to my family and strengthened my relationship with Gloria in ways that I never envisioned. My children are growing up in a happy, stable home of which Judaism is the core. I continue to grow, becoming a better husband, father, and person. My journey continues, but I now know where I am going.

OUTREACH

Connect with Outreach

Diversity is one of the elements that makes Temple Chai so special. We have created a culture of inclusion. Jews by choice, interfaith families, and interracial families are all welcomed and invited to be part of our family. Our Outreach programming is geared to making our diverse temple community more knowledgable and therefore more comfortable with Jewish holidays, services, and cultural ways. We hope you have enjoyed our holiday brochures and our programs to date. We welcome any suggestions and ideas you might have to make our Outreach programming useful to you.

Chai Paradise Symposium

January 13, 7:30-9:00 pm at Temple Chai, Rabbi William Berk and Pastor Kelly Bender of the Paradise Valley United Methodist Church will lead a round-table discussion. Join the conversation, *Different Voices, Different Texts, Same God*. See page 16 for more information.

Kabbalat Shabbat

Thursday, February 12, 7:00-9:00 pm at Temple Chai. Rabbi Mari Chernow will take you on a hands-on tour of the bimah as well as walking you through the prayers of the Kabbalat Shabbat service. Babysitting will be provided.

Friday, February 13, 6:15 pm. Join us at Kabbalat Shabbat services, and then join Rabbi Chernow at Shabbat dinner afterwards, where you will learn the blessings for lighting the Shabbat candles, wine, bread, and the blessing for your children.

Loviks Catering will be providing dinner for members at $10 per adult and $6 per child under 12. For non-members, the dinner will be $12 for adults and $8 for children under 12.

Reservations are required for this program. Please call the temple to reserve your place.

Toni Smeltzer, Chair, 480-502-4370

Interfaith Families
A daughter and mother's journey
by Ariel and Cynthia Salk

My mom is Christian, my dad is Jewish. In my house, we celebrate Chanukah, Christmas, Easter, and Passover. My dad loves Christmas not because of the religious part but because he likes all of the family activities. My mom loves getting together with our friends and making a Seder at Passover. But, we never really attended temple or church. When I was in preschool we attended a Unitarian Congregation for a few years, then we slowly stopped going.

In the 5th grade, I decided I wanted to expand my understanding from just celebrating holidays to learning about my Jewish heritage. We talked to Rabbi Tzur to see what we were getting into. She explained that if I started going to temple, I could no longer call myself Christian. She also explained that some temples wouldn't consider me as Jewish because my mom wasn't Jewish. Rabbi Tzur made me feel very welcomed at Temple Chai so I began studying for my bat mitzvah.

At first, it was confusing…I didn't even know what a Torah was. I couldn't start with my grade level and it was embarrassing. Then I caught up with my class and made new friends. In my classes I learned how to read Hebrew, about the Holocaust, and what it means to be Jewish. My Hebrew tutor helped me keep on track. She didn't just help me learn the prayers, but to understand what they meant. Now that my bat mitzvah is over, I still enjoy the 8th grade religion class and being with my temple friends.

My parents have been very supportive of my choice. Instead of trying to talk me out of my decision, my mom supported me. Instead of having a small part in my bat mitzvah, she listened to my classes, she made me study, signed me up for activities, arranged for a tutor, and planned an awesome party.

I think it's cool my mom didn't change her religion just for her marriage. I'm proud that she sticks with what she believes in and doesn't change who she is to make it easier for her family.

If my mom had been Jewish, I would have started Hebrew school sooner. It's kind of good that she wasn't because, this way, I chose my religion, which to me is a lot stronger than if it had been chosen for me. It's not what you are born into… it's what you believe in… that's your religion.

When I got married, the fact that my husband and I were raised in different faiths didn't seem much of an issue. Though I consider myself a spiritual person, attending church or temple was not a priority for either of us. When my girls were young, we began attending a Unitarian service, and thought it might be a "fit" for our family. My husband wasn't comfortable, and we drifted away and dealt with our conflict by not addressing it. We continued to honor and celebrate each other's holidays and tried to raise our girls in a loving and spiritual way.

When my daughter, Ariel, decided she wanted to "become Jewish," I was stunned. I wanted to be respectful of her choice and of my husband's (and her) heritage, but I felt left out. I felt my husband and children were entering a land where I didn't belong. Nevertheless I was determined to support my daughter and decided our younger daughter should join her sister in Hebrew school.

As Ariel's bat mitzvah approached, I became anxious. Years ago, when I worked for a caterer, I had witnessed b'nai mitzvah parties. I could not understand how people could lavish such amounts on parties for children. It seemed indulgent and very, very far from religion or God. I wanted no part of this for my child. I was also anxious because for the first time, I lacked the knowledge to prepare my daughter for what lay ahead. I knew I needed help.

I asked around and found a tutor who not only guided my daughter but guided me in finding God in the bat mitzvah. When I sat with the two of them and listened to my daughter sing her prayers, the beauty of it melted my heart. I was able to celebrate my daughter and her choice in a very meaningful way. Yes…the party cost more money than I planned, but when I stood on the bimah and looked out at the sea of love and support for my daughter by Jews and Christians alike, it was thrilling. My Christian family and friends remarked again and again how Rabbi Tzur had respected and welcomed them. They were also deeply touched by the experience. At the party, I realized that celebrating this rite of passage was not about indulgence but an attempt to carry on a centuries-old tradition in today's manner.

There are many paths to God. I am not alone. I simply have found a larger community who will also embrace and guide my children into the future.

Opening Doors to Shabbat

Congregation:	Beth Tikvah Congregation
Address:	300 Hillcrest Blvd.
	Hoffman Estates, IL 60195-3168
Phone Number:	(847) 885-4545
Contact's Name and E-mail:	Stu Gallup, outreachbtc@comcast.net
Number of Member Units:	320
URJ Region:	Great Lakes Council
Rabbi:	Max Weiss
Outreach chairperson:	Stu Gallup

Brief Description: Using a presentation format we projected our entire Shabbat service on a screen for all to follow. All prayers were transliterated along with explanations. Instead of a traditional sermon the rabbi had a question and answer session.

Program Goal: Bring people into the synagogue to learn about the Shabbat service and Judaism in general. Using the presentation format as opposed to the prayerbook presented an easy-to-follow format for people who don't normally attend services.

Target Population: New members, interfaith families, community members, those interested in learning about Judaism.

Number of Participants: Sixty-five at each session, 195 total.

Number and Length of Sessions: Three sessions, one hour each.

Staffing Required: Normal Friday night service staffing.

Total Cost of Program: $650.

Source of Funding: $300 grant for the ad, $50 donated printing, $300 general Outreach budget.

Fee for Attendees: Free.

Logistics: Computer, LCD projector, screen.

Instructions to Facilitator: Make sure you use a bright enough projector and have the screen high enough for all to read the bottom lines.

Evaluation of Program: All three sessions were well received. The ads drew nonmembers from the community as well as local church groups. Doing it three times during the year was the right amount. One of the services was a Torah service where we held up the Torah rolled to the portion we were reading and all were able to see as the cantor chanted.

Follow-up: The presentation format can be used at other services as well. The format works well to help people follow along. It also allows the services to be posted on the temple Web site for members to download and refer to on their own.

"OPENING DOORS TO SHABBAT"

at Beth Tikvah Congregation
Hoffman Estates

Friday November 5th, 2004 7:30pm
Friday January 7th, 2004 7:30pm
Friday March 11th, 2004 7:30pm

An **educational Jewish Shabbat** service open to the community.

Interested in learning about **Judaism**?
Haven't been to the **synagogue** in a while?
Are you in an **Interfaith** marriage or relationship?

Come spend a **Friday Night Service** learning about the symbols, prayers and customs associated with Shabbat.
In place of a Sermon the Rabbi will answer questions from the group.

OPEN TO ALL
Non-Jews, Non-Members and Interfaith Families are encouraged to attend.

For more information please contact

Beth Tikvah Congregation
www.beth-tikvah.org
outreachbtc@comcast.net
847-885-4545

300 Hillcrest Blvd.
Hoffman Estates, IL 60195

WHAT IS OUTREACH ?

God loves the stranger, providing food and clothing for each one. You too must love the stranger, for you were strangers in the land of Egypt.
Deuteronomy 10:19

Let your house be open wide.
Pirke Avot 1:5

As a Reform Congregation we are committed to actively welcoming all and building a vibrant, inclusive congregational community. Outreach is one of the ways we do this. Outreach activities center on the mitzvah of *ahavat ger*, loving the stranger - anyone who feels distanced from Judaism, God, Torah and Israel. Outreach is focused on welcoming to our community a diversity of Jews and their families, interfaith and inter-racial couples, new Jews and those interested in Judaism, Jews of color, gay and lesbian individuals and families, single adults and blended families, rich and poor, young and old and in between, women and men.

If your life has been touched by an interfaith relationship or if you are exploring Judaism, Beth Tikvah is here to offer guidance and support. We offer opportunities to share your experiences and learn from others in a non-threatening, friendly environment.

The goal of Outreach is to offer supportive programming with the help of our Rabbi, Cantor, educators and facilitators. If there are any interfaith issues in your family, please feel free to contact Beth Tikvah Outreach to ask any questions. We strive to reflect the views and orientations of all members and the community.

Outreach is focused on:

- Welcoming new Jews-by-choice and educating those investigating Judaism.
- Welcoming interfaith families to take part in synagogue life, to learn more about Judaism, and to raise their children as Jews.
- Assisting young adults in strengthening their Jewish connection and identity.
- Inspiring Jews to engage more fully in the synagogue community, especially those who feel disconnected or distant.
- Educating and sensitizing the congregational community to be accepting of all that seek a place in our congregation.
- Educating the entire community on Jewish customs and practices.
- Opening up Inter-religious dialogue with other congregations in the community.

Even though Beth Tikvah operates from a Jewish perspective, we do not proselytize or pressure anyone to convert. In fact, Judaism regards any coerced conversion as invalid. However, anyone who wants to learn more about Judaism or conversion to Judaism should discuss their feelings and concerns with Rabbi Weiss.

Throughout the year Outreach will be sponsoring various activities. All of these are designed for the entire congregation to attend. These are not just intended for "outreach families". Some of the programs we will be planning are:

- **Opening Doors to Shabbat and other Holidays and Festivals**
  See other Side
- **Holiday Cooking and Baking**
  Interfaith and Non-Interfaith families sharing different Holiday time family recipes and stories.
- **Thirty Something get-togethers**
- **Discussions on the close "Proximity" holidays**
  Open discussions on how different interfaith families handle "proximity" holidays (Hanukkah/Christmas, Passover/Easter).
- **Inter-religious topic discussions**
  Meeting with other religious congregations to discuss various topics of interest and current events.

If you have any outreach questions please contact Stu Gallup outreachbtc@comcast.net *or 847-779-2437 (Daytime) / 847-742-9280 (Evening)*

OUTREACH

UPCOMING OUTREACH EVENTS
Services and Programs are for all in the community to attend.

Opening Doors to Rosh Hashanah and Yom Kippur – An educational overview of the symbols, traditions and prayers that you will see and hear during the High Holy Days. An opportunity to ask questions about the holidays to the Rabbi and Cantor.

Wednesday 9/8/04
7:30pm – 9:00pm

Opening Doors to Shabbat – For this educational Shabbat Service a unique Shabbat prayer book filled with explanations will be used. Many prayers in Hebrew and English will be projected on a screen for all to follow along. This service is designed for all to attend; there is always something new to learn.

Friday 11/5/04   7:30pm – 9:00pm
Friday 1/7/05   7:30pm – 9:00pm
Friday 3/11/05   7:30pm – 9:00 pm

Beth Tikvah Congregation
300 Hillcrest Blvd.
Hoffman Estates, IL 60195
www.beth-tikvah.org

For more information or to join the Outreach committee please contact Stu Gallup (outreachbtc@comcast.net)
847-742-9280 Evening / 847-779-2437 Daytime

Opening Doors to Shabbat

An Educational Learning Service Sponsored by Beth Tikvah Outreach

---

The Day of Rest   שַׁבָּת

- The Heaven and the earth were finished, and all their array. On the 7th day God finished the work that He had been doing, and He ceased on the 7th day from all the work that He had done. And God blessed the 7th day and declared it holy, because on it God ceased from all the work of creation that He had done.
  (Gen 2:1-3)

- God called the light Day, and the darkness He called night. And there was evening and there was morning, a first day.
  (Gen 1:5)

Kabbalat Shabbat is the name of the Friday night service.

This part of our Shabbat service was not added to our liturgy until the sixteenth century.

Early Jews imagined Shabbat as a queen and would go into the fields to sing and greet Shabbat as the sun set in the west.

How do you mark special occasions? When do you feel closest to God? Why do you think Shabbat was pictured as a queen?

Chapter Four Outreach Programming All Year for All **263**

Hinei Mah Tov הִנֵּה מַה טוֹב

הִנֵּה מַה טוֹב וּמַה נָּעִים שֶׁבֶת אַחִים גַּם יָחַד.

*Hi-nei mah tov u-mah na-im
she-vet a-chim gam ya-chad*

Behold how good and how pleasant for people to dwell together in unity.

Hinei Mah Tov is part of Psalm 133

Candlelighting שֶׁל שַׁבָּת

בָּרוּךְ אַתָּה יְיָ אֱלֹהֵינוּ מֶלֶךְ הָעוֹלָם,
אֲשֶׁר קִדְּשָׁנוּ בְּמִצְוֹתָיו,
וְצִוָּנוּ לְהַדְלִיק נֵר שֶׁל שַׁבָּת.

*Ba-ruch A-tah, A-do-nai,
E-lo-hei-nu,
Me-lech ha-o-lam,
A-sher ki-d'-sha-nu b'-mitz-vo-tav,
v'tzi-va-nu, l'-had-lik ner shel Shab-bat.*

Blessed are You, Source of Light, who hallows us with mitzvot, and inspires us to kindle Shabbat lights.

May God bless us with Shabbat joy.

May God bless us with Shabbat holiness.

May God bless us with Shabbat peace. Amen.

Lecha Dodi   לְכָה דוֹדִי

לְכָה דוֹדִי לִקְרַאת כַּלָּה. פְּנֵי שַׁבָּת נְקַבְּלָה:
שַׁבָּת שָׁלוֹם שַׁבָּת שָׁלוֹם שַׁבָּת שָׁלוֹם וּמְבוֹרָךְ

L'chah do-di lik-rat kal-lah,
p'nei Shab-bat n'kab-lah.
Sha-bat sha-lom sha-bat sha-lom
Sha-bat sha-lom u-m'vo-rach

Come Beloved, let us welcome the bride, the coming of Shabbat.

Barchu   בָּרְכוּ

We Stand Together Before God

בָּרְכוּ אֶת יְיָ הַמְבֹרָךְ:
Bar-chu et Adonai ha-m'vo-rach!
Praised is God who is to be praised!

בָּרוּךְ יְיָ הַמְבֹרָךְ לְעוֹלָם וָעֶד:
Ba-ruch Adonai ha-m'vorach l'olam va-ed!
Praised is God who is to be praised forever!

Ma'ariv Aravim   מַעֲרִיב עֲרָבִים

בָּרוּךְ אַתָּה יְיָ, אֱלֹהֵינוּ מֶלֶךְ הָעוֹלָם,
אֲשֶׁר בִּדְבָרוֹ מַעֲרִיב עֲרָבִים

Ba-ruch A-tah A-do-nai, E-lo-he-nu Me-lech ha-o-lam a-sher bid-va-ro ma-a-riv a-ra-vim

Thank You God for the world and all that is in it.

Ma'ariv Aravim   מַעֲרִיב עֲרָבִים

Thank You for clouds and rain that make plants grow.
Thank You for rivers and streams and lakes and seas.
Thank You for beaches of sand and banks of snow.
Thank You for leaves that blow on tall trees.

Thank You for the cool earth and the green grass.
Thank You for the bright sun and the moon's light.
Thank You for the stars and planets on their nightly path.
We thank You God for day and night.

Ahavat Olam אַהֲבַת עוֹלָם

אַהֲבַת עוֹלָם בֵּית יִשְׂרָאֵל עַמְּךָ אָהָבְתָּ

God, thank You for the gift of Torah, for the gift of education. Thank You for allowing us to uncover the secrets of Your universe.

We pray that you will always be kind to us, allowing us to draw close to you in prayer and study. May our lives always follow your paths and our minds always pursue your truths. We are your people and you are our God.

בָּרוּךְ אַתָּה יְיָ, אוֹהֵב עַמּוֹ יִשְׂרָאֵל.

Shema שְׁמַע

The Shema is part of Deut 6:4

שְׁמַע יִשְׂרָאֵל, יְיָ אֱלֹהֵינוּ, יְיָ אֶחָד:

Sh'ma Yis-ra-eil, A-do-nai E-lo-hei-nu A-do-nai e-chad!

בָּרוּךְ שֵׁם כְּבוֹד מַלְכוּתוֹ לְעוֹלָם וָעֶד.

Ba-ruch sheim k'vod mal-chu-to l'o-lam va-ed!

Listen, Israel, Adonai is our God, Adonai is one!
Blessed is God forever and ever!

V'ahavta ואהבת

וְאָהַבְתָּ אֵת יְיָ אֱלֹהֶיךָ, בְּכָל־לְבָבְךָ,
וּבְכָל־נַפְשְׁךָ, וּבְכָל־מְאֹדֶךָ.

V'-a-hav-ta eit A-do-nai E-lo-he-cha
b'-chol l'-vav-cha u-v'-chol
naf-sh'-cha u-v'chol m'-o-de-cha.

The prayer we call V'ahavta is actually composed of quotes from three different sections of the Torah.

Deut 6:5-9, Deut 11:13-21, Num 15:37-41

V'ahavta ואהבת

You shall love the Eternal your God with all your mind, with all your strength, with all your being.

Set these words, which I command you this day, upon your heart. Teach them faithfully to your children; speak of them in your home and on your way, when you lie down and when you rise up. Bind them as a sign upon your hand; let them be a symbol before your eyes; inscribe them, on the doorposts of your house, and on your gates.

Be mindful of all My Mitzvot, and do them; so shall you consecrate yourselves to your God. I, the Eternal, am your God who led you out of Egypt to be your God; I, the Eternal, am your God.

Redemption   גְּאֻלָּה

When will redemption come?

When we master the violence that fills our world.

When we treat other people as we would like to be treated.

When we grant every person the rights we claim for ourselves.

When we sing Mi Chamocha we are celebrating our freedom and praying for all people to be free and safe.

Mi Chamocha   מִי כָמֹכָה

מִי כָמֹכָה בָּאֵלִים יְיָ, מִי כָּמֹכָה נֶאְדָּר בַּקֹּדֶשׁ,
נוֹרָא תְהִלֹּת, עֹשֵׂה פֶלֶא: מַלְכוּתְךָ רָאוּ
בָנֶיךָ, בּוֹקֵעַ יָם לִפְנֵי מֹשֶׁה: זֶה אֵלִי! עָנוּ וְאָמְרוּ:
יְיָ יִמְלֹךְ לְעֹלָם וָעֶד: בָּרוּךְ אַתָּה יְיָ גָּאַל יִשְׂרָאֵל:

Mi cha-mo-cha ba-ei-lim A-do-nai, mi ka-mo-cha ne-dar ba-kodesh. No-rah t'-hi-lot o-sei fe-leh: Mal-chu-t'cha ra-u va-ne-cha, bok-kay-a yam lifnei Moshe: Zeh Eili! anu v'am-ru:

A-do-nai yim-loch l'-olam va'ed. Ba-ruch A-tah A-do-nai, Ga-al Yis-ra-eil.

Who is like You, O Eternal, among the mighty; who is like You, awesome in praise, doing wonders?

Your children saw Your might at the shore of the sea. "This is my God!" they proclaimed. "The Eternal shall reign forever!"

We praise You, God, Protector of Israel.

Mi Chamocha is part of Ex. 15:11

Evening Prayer — הַשְׁכִּיבֵנוּ

הַשְׁכִּיבֵנוּ יְיָ אֱלֹהֵינוּ לְשָׁלוֹם,וְהַעֲמִידֵנוּ מַלְכֵּנוּ לְחַיִּים. וּפְרוֹשׂ עָלֵינוּ סֻכַּת שְׁלוֹמֶךָ.

May we have peace while we sleep, God, and when we awake, may we find a world changed and calm, a world filled with love. Spread over us the shelter of Your peace; give us wisdom; and be our source of help.

Protect us from hatred and plague; from war, famine and anguish. Help us be better people. We praise You, O God, whose sukkah of peace is spread over us, over all Your people Israel, and over Jerusalem.

בָּרוּךְ אַתָּה יְיָ, הַפּוֹרֵשׂ סֻכַּת שָׁלוֹם עָלֵינוּ וְעַל כָּל עַמּוֹ יִשְׂרָאֵל וְעַל יְרוּשָׁלָיִם.

For Shabbat — וְשָׁמְרוּ

וְשָׁמְרוּ בְנֵי יִשְׂרָאֵל אֶת הַשַׁבָּת, לַעֲשׂוֹת אֶת הַשַׁבָּת לְדֹרֹתָם בְּרִית עוֹלָם: בֵּינִי וּבֵין בְּנֵי יִשְׂרָאֵל אוֹת הִיא לְעוֹלָם, כִּי שֵׁשֶׁת יָמִים עָשָׂה יְיָ אֶת הַשָׁמַיִם וְאֶת הָאָרֶץ, וּבַיּוֹם הַשְׁבִיעִי שָׁבַת וַיִּנָּפַשׁ.

*V'sham-ru v'nei Yis-ra-eil et ha-Shab-bat,
la-a-sot et ha-Shab-bat l'do-ro-tam b'rit o-lam.
bei-ni u-vein b'nei Yis-ra-eil, ot hee l'o-lam,
ki shei-sheit ya-mim a-sah A-do-nai et
ha-sha-ma-yim v'et ha-ar-etz, u-va-yom
hash-vi-ee, sha-vat va-yi-na-fash.*

The Children of Israel shall keep the Shabbat, observing the Shabbat in every generation as an eternal covenant.

It is a sign for ever between Me and the Children of Israel, for in six days the Eternal God made heaven and earth, and on the seventh day He rested and was refreshed.

Tefillah תְּפִילָה

This prayer is called "Tefillah" which means "prayer". This reflects the importance of this section to the service.

(We Stand)

אֲדֹנָי שְׂפָתַי תִּפְתָּח וּפִי יַגִּיד תְּהִלָּתֶךָ׃

A-do-nai s'fa-tai tif-tach
u-fi ya-gid t'hi-la-te-cha.

Eternal God, open my lips, that my mouth may declare Your glory.

Our Ancestors אָבוֹת וְאִמָּהוֹת

We praise You, our God and God of Abraham and Sarah, God of Isaac and Rebecca, God of Jacob, Leah and Rachel, the great, mighty and awesome God, God most high. You are the source of loving kindness, creator of all, You remember the faith of ancestors and bring redemption to their descendants out of love alone. You are Sovereign, helper, savior and shield. Praised are You, the Eternal, Shield of Abraham and help of Sarah.

Our Ancestors   אָבוֹת וְאִמָּהוֹת

Ba-ruch A-tah A-do-nai E-lo heinu vei-lo-hei a-vo-tei-nu v'imo-tei-nu: E-lo-hei Av-ra-ham, E-lo-hei Yitzchak, vei-lo-hei Ya-a-kov. E-lo-hei Sa-ra, E-lo-hei Riv-ka, E-lo-hei Lei-ah, vei-lo-hei Ra-chel.

בָּרוּךְ אַתָּה יְיָ אֱלֹהֵינוּ וֵאלֹהֵי אֲבוֹתֵינוּ וְאִמּוֹתֵינוּ, אֱלֹהֵי אַבְרָהָם, אֱלֹהֵי יִצְחָק וֵאלֹהֵי יַעֲקֹב. אֱלֹהֵי שָׂרָה אֱלֹהֵי רִבְקָה, אֱלֹהֵי לֵאָה וֵאלֹהֵי רָחֵל.

Our Ancestors   אָבוֹת וְאִמָּהוֹת

Ha-eil ha-ga-dol ha-gi-bor v'ha-no-rah Eil el-yon gomeil cha-sa-dim to-vim v'-ko-nei ha-kol v'-zo-cheir chas-dei avot v'-i-ma-hot u-mei-vi g'-u-lah liv-nei v'-nei-hem l'-ma-an sh'mo b'-a-ha-vah. Me-lech o-zeir u mo-shi-a u-ma-gein. Ba-ruch Atah A-do-nai, ma-gein Av-ra-ham v'ez-rat Sa-rah.

הָאֵל הַגָּדוֹל הַגִּבּוֹר וְהַנּוֹרָא, אֵל עֶלְיוֹן, גּוֹמֵל חֲסָדִים טוֹבִים, וְקוֹנֵה הַכֹּל, וְזוֹכֵר חַסְדֵי אָבוֹת וְאִמָּהוֹת, וּמֵבִיא גְאֻלָּה לִבְנֵי בְנֵיהֶם לְמַעַן שְׁמוֹ בְּאַהֲבָה: מֶלֶךְ עוֹזֵר וּמוֹשִׁיעַ וּמָגֵן: בָּרוּךְ אַתָּה יְיָ, מָגֵן אַבְרָהָם וְעֶזְרַת שָׂרָה

God's Power גְּבוּרוֹת

Great is the power of Your love. You have made us in Your image And raised us high above all creatures. You have exalted us to struggle against evil, to strive for holiness, to plant seeds of love in all our dwellings. And You, the Eternal One, help us to face death with the trust that what is good and lovely shall not perish.

Almighty Creator, joyfully we embrace Your call to life. Help us to Live with courage, that we may hallow our lives as we sanctify Your name.

Holiness קְדוּשָׁה

אַתָּה קָדוֹשׁ וְשִׁמְךָ קָדוֹשׁ וּקְדוֹשִׁים בְּכָל יוֹם יְהַלְלוּךָ, סֶּלָה. בָּרוּךְ אַתָּה יְיָ, הָאֵל הַקָּדוֹשׁ

A-tah ka-dosh v'-shem-cha ka-dosh uk-do-shim b'-chol yom y'-hal-l'lu-cha se-lah. Ba-ruch A-tah A-do-nai, ha-El ha-Ka-dosh.

You are holy, Your name is holy, and all who strive to be holy daily sing your praise. Praised are You, the holy God.

(Be seated)

Prayer for Peace — שָׁלוֹם רָב

שָׁלוֹם רָב עַל יִשְׂרָאֵל עַמְּךָ תָּשִׂים לְעוֹלָם, כִּי אַתָּה הוּא מֶלֶךְ אָדוֹן לְכָל הַשָּׁלוֹם. וְטוֹב בְּעֵינֶיךָ לְבָרֵךְ אֶת עַמְּךָ יִשְׂרָאֵל בְּכָל עֵת וּבְכָל שָׁעָה בִּשְׁלוֹמֶךָ. בָּרוּךְ אַתָּה יְיָ, הַמְבָרֵךְ אֶת עַמּוֹ יִשְׂרָאֵל בַּשָּׁלוֹם

Sha-lom rav, al Yis-ra-el am-cha, ta-sim le-olam, ki at-ah hu me-lekh a-don le-chol ha-sha-lom. V-tov be-ain-ne-cha le-va-rech et am-cha Yis-rael, be-chol eit, u-ve-chol sha-ah bi-shlo-me-cha. Ba-ruch A-tah A-do-nai ha-m'va-raich et a-mo Yis-ra-eil ba-sha-lom

Bless us and all people with peace. A peace that starts with me and spreads to all people around the world. A peace that lasts forever so that no person is ever hungry, ever thirsty. May peace descend like rain upon us watering our hearts, our minds our souls and making us whole.

Bless us and all people with peace.

A peace that starts with me and spreads to all people around the world.

A peace that lasts forever so that no person is ever hungry, ever thirsty.

May peace descend like rain upon us watering our hearts, our minds our souls and making us whole.

Personal Prayer — עֹשֶׂה שָׁלוֹם

עֹשֶׂה שָׁלוֹם בִּמְרוֹמָיו הוּא יַעֲשֶׂה שָׁלוֹם עָלֵינוּ וְעַל כָּל יִשְׂרָאֵל, וְאִמְרוּ אָמֵן:

O-seh sha-lom bim-ro-mav, Hu ya-a-seh sha-lom a-lei-nu v'-al kol Yis-raeil v'-im-ru a-mein.

Adonai, You are the God of peace. Please give us, our families and all the world lives of peace.

Mi Shebeirach – Prayer for Healing
מִי שֶׁבֵּרַךְ

Mi shebeirach avoteinu
Avraham, Yitzchak, v'Yaakov
Mi shebeirach imoteinu
Sara, Rivkah, Leah, v'Rachel.

May the One who blessed our mothers
May the One who blessed our fathers
Hear our prayer, hear our prayer,
Hear our prayer, hear our prayer,
and bless us as well.

Bless us with the power of Your healing
Bless us with the power of Your hope
May the pain and loneliness we're feeling
Be diminished by the power of Your love.

Bless us with the
vision fo rtomorrow.
Help us to reach out
to those in pain.
May the warmth of friendship
ease our sorrow.
Give us courage, give us faith,
show us the way.

Mi shebeirach avoteinu
Mi shebeirach imoteinu

Hear our prayer, hear our prayer,
Hear our prayer, hear our prayer,
and bless us as well.

Aleinu
עָלֵינוּ

עָלֵינוּ לְשַׁבֵּחַ לַאֲדוֹן הַכֹּל, לָתֵת גְּדֻלָּה
לְיוֹצֵר בְּרֵאשִׁית, שֶׁלֹּא עָשָׂנוּ כְּגוֹיֵי
הָאֲרָצוֹת, וְלֹא שָׂמָנוּ כְּמִשְׁפְּחוֹת הָאֲדָמָה, שֶׁלֹּא שָׂם חֶלְקֵנוּ כָּהֶם,
וְגֹרָלֵנוּ כְּכָל הֲמוֹנָם וַאֲנַחְנוּ כּוֹרְעִים וּמִשְׁתַּחֲוִים וּמוֹדִים,
לִפְנֵי מֶלֶךְ, מַלְכֵי הַמְּלָכִים, הַקָּדוֹשׁ בָּרוּךְ הוּא

A-lei-nu l'sha-bei-ach la-a-don ha-kol, la-teit g'-du-la l'-yo-tzeir b'-rei-sheet,
she-lo a-sa-nu k'-go-yei ha-a-ra-tzot, v'-lo sa-ma-nu k'-mish-p'-chot ha-a-da-
mah, she-lo sam chel-kei-nu ka-hem v'-go-ra-lei-nu k'-chol ha-mo-nam.

Va-a-nach-nu kor-im u-mish-ta-cha-vim u-mo-dim, lif-nee Me-lech, Mal-chei
Ha-m'lachim, Ha-ka-dosh Ba-ruch Hu.

בַּיּוֹם הַהוּא יִהְיֶה יְיָ אֶחָד, וּשְׁמוֹ אֶחָד:
Ba-yom ha-hu y'-hi-yeh A-do-nai e-chad, u-sh'mo e-chad
On that day God will be one and God's name will be one.

We must praise the God of all, to ascribe greatness to the molder of creation.

Who has set us apart from the other families of the earth, giving us a destiny unique among the nations.

We therefore bend our knees and bow in awe and thanksgiving before the One who is sovereign over all, the Holy One, The Blessed One.

Mourner's Kaddish   קַדִּישׁ יָתוֹם

יִתְגַּדַּל וְיִתְקַדַּשׁ שְׁמֵהּ רַבָּא בְּעָלְמָא דִּי בְרָא כִרְעוּתֵהּ, וְיַמְלִיךְ מַלְכוּתֵהּ בְּחַיֵּיכוֹן
וּבְיוֹמֵיכוֹן וּבְחַיֵּי דְכָל בֵּית יִשְׂרָאֵל, בַּעֲגָלָא וּבִזְמַן קָרִיב וְאִמְרוּ אָמֵן:
יְהֵא שְׁמֵהּ רַבָּא מְבָרַךְ לְעָלַם וּלְעָלְמֵי עָלְמַיָּא:

Yit-ga-dal ve-yit-ka-dash she-mei ra-ba be be-al-ma di-ve-ra chi-re-u-tei,
ve-yam-lich mal-chu-tei b'-cha-yeichon u-ve-yo-mei-chon
u-ve-chayei de-chol beit Yis-ra-eil, ba-a-ga-la u-vi-ze-man ka-riv, ve-i-me-ru:
A-mein. Ye-he she-mei ra-ba me-va-rach le-a-lam u-le-al-mei al-ma-ya.

Mourner's Kaddish   קַדִּישׁ יָתוֹם

יִתְבָּרַךְ וְיִשְׁתַּבַּח, וְיִתְפָּאַר וְיִתְרוֹמַם וְיִתְנַשֵּׂא וְיִתְהַדָּר וְיִתְעַלֶּה וְיִתְהַלָּל
שְׁמֵהּ דְּקֻדְשָׁא בְּרִיךְ הוּא לְעֵלָּא מִן כָּל בִּרְכָתָא
יְהֵא שְׁלָמָא רַבָּא מִן שׁוּשִׁירָתָא, תֻּשְׁבְּחָתָא וְנֶחֱמָתָא, דַּאֲמִירָן בְּעָלְמָא, וְאִמְרוּ אָמֵן.
יְהֵא שְׁלָמָא רַבָּא מִן שְׁמַיָּא וְחַיִּים עָלֵינוּ וְעַל כָּל יִשְׂרָאֵל,
וְאִמְרוּ אָמֵן: עֹשֶׂה שָׁלוֹם בִּמְרוֹמָיו
הוּא יַעֲשֶׂה שָׁלוֹם עָלֵינוּ וְעַל כָּל יִשְׂרָאֵל, וְאִמְרוּ אָמֵן:

Yit-ba-rach ve-yish-ta-bach, ve-yit-pa-ar ve-yit-ro-mam ve-yit-na-sei,
ve-yit-ha-dar ve-yit-a-leh ve-yit-ha-lal she-mei de-ku-de-sha, be-rich hu,
le-eila min kol bi-re-cha-ta ve-shi-ra-ta, tush-be-cha-ta ve-ne-che-ma-ta,
da-a-mi-ran be-al-ma, ve-i-me-ru: a-mein. Ye-hei she-la-ma ra-ba min she-maya
ve-cha-yim a-lei-nu ve-al kol Yis-ra-eil, ve-i-me-ru: a-mein.
O-sheh sha-lom bi-me-ro-mav, hu ya-a-seh sha-lom a-lei-nu ve-al kol Yis-ra-eil,
ve-i-me-ru: a-mein.

Kiddush

בָּרוּךְ אַתָּה יְיָ אֱלֹהֵינוּ
מֶלֶךְ הָעוֹלָם, בּוֹרֵא פְּרִי הַגָּפֶן

*Ba-ruch A-tah A-do-nei, E-lo-hei-nu
Me-lech ha-o-lam, bo-reh p'ri ha-ga-fen*

Blessed O Lord or God Ruler of the Universe
who created the fruit of the vine

Kiddush

בָּרוּךְ אַתָּה יְיָ אֱלֹהֵינוּ מֶלֶךְ הָעוֹלָם, אֲשֶׁר קִדְּשָׁנוּ בְּמִצְוֹתָיו וְרָצָה בָנוּ,
בְּאַהֲבָה וּבְרָצוֹן הִנְחִילָנוּ זִכָּרוֹן לְמַעֲשֵׂה בְרֵאשִׁית, כִּי הוּא יוֹם תְּחִלָּה
וְשַׁבַּת קָדְשׁוֹ
זֵכֶר לִיצִיאַת מִצְרָיִם, כִּי בָנוּ בָחַרְתָּ וְאוֹתָנוּ קִדַּשְׁתָּ מִכָּל הָעַמִּים,
לְמִקְרָאֵי קֹדֶשׁ,
וְשַׁבַּת קָדְשְׁךָ בְּאַהֲבָה וּבְרָצוֹן הִנְחַלְתָּנוּ. בָּרוּךְ אַתָּה יְיָ, מְקַדֵּשׁ הַשַּׁבָּת.

*Ba-ruch A-tah A-do-nei, Elo-hei-nu, Me-lech ha-olam,
a-sher ki-d'sha-nu b'mitz-vo-tav, v'ra-tzah va-nu,
v'Shab-bat kod-sho b'a-ha-vah uv'ra-tzon hin-chi-la-nu,
zi-ka-ron l'ma-a-seh v'rei-shit. Ki hu yom t'chi-lah, l'mik-ra-ei ko-desh,
zei-cher li-tsi-at Mitz-rai-yim. Ki va-nu va-char-ta,
v'ota-nu ki-dash-ta mi-kol ha-a-mim, v'Shab-bat kod-sh'cha
b'a-ha-vah uv'ra-tzon hin-chal-ta-nu.
Ba-ruch A-tah, A-don-ai m'ka-deish ha-Shab-bat.*

Adon Olam

אֲדוֹן עוֹלָם אֲשֶׁר מָלַךְ, / בְּטֶרֶם כָּל יְצִיר נִבְרָא.
לְעֵת נַעֲשָׂה בְחֶפְצוֹ כֹּל, / אֲזַי מֶלֶךְ שְׁמוֹ נִקְרָא.
וְאַחֲרֵי כִּכְלוֹת הַכֹּל, / לְבַדּוֹ יִמְלוֹךְ נוֹרָא.
וְהוּא הָיָה, וְהוּא הֹוֶה, / וְהוּא יִהְיֶה, בְּתִפְאָרָה.
בְּלִי רֵאשִׁית בְּלִי תַכְלִית, / וְלוֹ הָעֹז וְהַמִּשְׂרָה.
וְהוּא אֵלִי וְחַי גּוֹאֲלִי, / וְצוּר חֶבְלִי בְּעֵת צָרָה.
וְהוּא נִסִּי וּמָנוֹס לִי, / מְנָת כּוֹסִי בְּיוֹם אֶקְרָא.
בְּיָדוֹ אַפְקִיד רוּחִי, / בְּעֵת אִישַׁן וְאָעִירָה.
וְעִם רוּחִי גְּוִיָּתִי, / יְיָ לִי וְלֹא אִירָא.

A-don o-lam, a-sher ma-lakh / b'-te-rem kol yi-tzeir niv-ra.
L'eit na'-a-sah v'-chef-tzo kol / a-zai me-lekh sh'-mo nik-ra.
V'-a-cha-rei kich-lot ha-kol / l'-va-do yim-lokh no-ra.
V'hu ha-ya, v'-hu ho-veh / v'-hu yi-he-yeh b'-ti-fa-ra.
V'-hu E-chad, v'-ein shei-ni / l'-ham-shil lo, l'-hach-bi-ra.
B'-li rei-shit, b'-li takh-lit / v'-lo ha-oz v'-ha-mis-ra.
V'-hu ei-li, v'-chai go-a-li / v'-tzur chev-li b'-eit tza-ra.
v'-hu ni-si, u-ma-nos li / m'-nat ko-si b'yom ek-ra.
B'-ya-do af-kid ru-chi/ b'-eit ish-an v'-a-e-ra.
V'-im ru-chi g'-vi-ya-ti/ A-do-nai li, v'-lo i-ra.

Lord of the Universe, He reigned alone, while yet the universe was naught. When by His will all things were wrought, then first his sovereign name was known. And when the all shall cease to be, in dread lone splendor He shall reign.

He was, He is, He will remain in glorious eternity. For He is One, no second shares his nature or his loneliness. Unending and unbeginning all strength is His, all sway He bears. He is the Living God to save, my Rock while sorrow's toils endure. My Banner and my Stronghold sure, the Cup of Life whene'er I crave. I place my soul within His palm before I sleep as when I wake. And though my body I forsake, rest in the Lord in fearless calm (Medieval Poem).

The Synagogue

- The term Synagogue:
  - Greek term given to the Jewish house of prayer and study means "coming together"
  - In Hebrew the term would be Beth Kenesset or House of Meeting
  - Another term Shool from the Yiddish school, if the Synagogue was also used as a Bet Hamidrash or place of study
  - In the last 100 years Reform and Conservative movements have adopted the term Temple

Elements of the Synagogue and Services

- Sanctuary: Area of the Synagogue used for prayer.
- Bimah: Hebrew for platform, place where the Rabbi and Cantor stand and lead the service and where the Torah is read.
- Mizrakh: Hebrew word for east. Synagogues are built facing east in the direction of Jerusalem.
- Ner Tamid: Eternal light placed in the center area of the Bimah.
- Sefer Torah: The five books of Moses: Genesis (Bereshit), Exodus (Shemoth), Leviticus (Vayikra), Numbers (Demidbar), Deuteronomy (Devarim)
- Aron Kodesh: Holy Ark in Hebrew is located at the eastern wall of the Sanctuary, in the central location. It is where the Torah scrolls are kept.

Elements of the Synagogue and Services

- Rabbi: From the Hebrew Rabi meaning my teacher
- Chazzan: Hebrew for Cantor. Leads the chanting of the service.
- Gabbai: Person responsible for everything else in the service.
- Ba'al Koh-Rey: In Hebrew "master of reading" reads the Torah during Torah serrvices.
- Trope: Notes used to chant the Torah.
- Siddur: Prayerbook in Hebrew. Used to document the liturgy.

Chapter Five

From Generation to Generation

Building community is about providing support and fellowship for people at different times in their lives. Identifying how you can provide programs for your various target audiences will enable your congregation to connect with members of all generations. This chapter provides three programs that reach out to those who want to feel connected to and supported by the congregation.

Synaplex™ at B'nai Israel is a flexible format of cultural, educational, spiritual, and social events that offer expanded opportunities to learn, gather, pray, and enjoy Shabbat together. The program offers a variety of Shabbat experiences for a diverse community of congregants of different ages and different interests. Programs range from "Tot Shabbat" to "Healing Services" to "Torah Yoga." There really can be something for everyone!

Considering ways to engage your teenagers? Looking for ways to better meet the needs of your older members? **The Challah Wagon** is intended to serve new members, teens, interfaith families, and homebound members by enabling teens to use their new driver's licenses to deliver challah and flowers with instructions for blessings for a Shabbat dinner, and a weekly Torah commentary from the rabbi. This "gift" can be given to new members or can be part of the work of your youth group, caring community, or confirmation class.

Babies and Bagels Club is a monthly group for families with preschool-age children and older siblings. Offering programs for the entire family can create a feeling of community and friendship among families with children of similar ages. A program of this kind can deepen the Jewish knowledge of both children and parents and is a fun way to attract newcomers and engage young families.

Synaplex™ at B'nai Israel

Congregation:	Congregation B'nai Israel
Address:	2710 Park Avenue Bridgeport, CT 06604
Phone Number:	(203) 336-1858
Contact's Name and E-mail:	Rabbi Greene, fgreene@congregationbnaiisrael.org
Number of Member Units:	850
URJ Region:	Northeast Council
Rabbis:	James Prosnit, Fred Greene
Outreach Chairperson:	Dana Fingleton

Brief Description: Synaplex™ is a flexible format of cultural, educational, spiritual, and social events offering expanded opportunities to learn, gather, pray, and enjoy Shabbat together. Like a multi-screen theater, Synaplex™ offers a variety of Shabbat experiences for our diverse Jewish community. This is the first year that we have implemented Synaplex and it is still being developed. All of the enclosed materials and worksheets are still works-in-progress.

The typical format of Synaplex Shabbat is fairly consistent on Friday nights: *Oneg, Kabbalat Shabbat* service, community dinner, and a special program. Saturdays are more flexible. Our regular opportunities remain the same (8 A.M. service, breakfast, Torah study, 11 A.M. service) as on every Saturday; there are additional offerings scattered throughout the day.

NOTE: While the model of Synaplex™ was conceived by STAR (Synagogues: Transformation and Renewal), the programs and events B'nai Israel has offered have been designed, implemented, and marketed exclusively by B'nai Israel. The relationship between STAR and B'nai Israel is one where STAR provides occasional technical support by training participating congregations in marketing, assessment, planning, and volunteer recruitment.

Program Goals:
(Desired) Initial Outcomes
- Greater involvement in congregation among members
- Stronger connection between congregants
- Enthusiasm within community for dynamic Jewish experiences
- Increased awareness among unaffiliated/underinvolved Jews (and their families) about B'nai Israel through secular media and word-of-mouth
- Increased attendance at synagogue activities, including and beyond Synaplex events

(Desired) Sustained Outcomes
- Increased involvement in synagogue and broader Jewish community
- Increased *tzedakah* in synagogue and broader Jewish community
- Increased volunteerism within congregation
- Increased attendance at worship experiences and learning opportunities
- Increased efforts by congregational leadership to reach out and be more inclusive of members on the fringes of community, the underinvolved, and the unaffiliated

Target Population: Within B'nai Israel—youth group (BIFTY), families with preschoolers, parents with elementary school-age children, seniors, empty nesters, spiritual seekers. Also seeking former members and young adults, but the greatest emphasis is the underinvolved who are already connected to B'nai Israel.

Some of the programs/opportunities had specific groups in mind (e.g., Tot Shabbat). The approach thus far has been to provide a variety of choices linking people to opportunities for community, spiritual growth, and learning. Naturally, some of the experiences had shared themes (e.g., Tot Shabbat will include young families looking for community).

We are responding to people's needs more effectively by offering a wide variety of community, study, and spiritual growth experiences. Such activities include:

- Panel discussion on mental health
- Healing services
- Learners' services
- Art with Avi (Avi Zuckerman, an Israeli artist, bringing together families to make their own *chanukiot*)
- Art & Soul Workshop—an experience that intertwined art, movement, breathing, and contemplation to unlock spiritual power
- Panel discussion on America at war, two congregants who were experts in Just War theory and ethics of war presented
- Scholar in Residence programs
- Tot Shabbat
- Rosh Chodesh: It's A Girl Thing (sixth-grade girls)
- Seniors talking about the "The Merchant of Venice" when the movie came out with professor of medieval literature
- Torah Yoga
- Meditation experiences

Number of Participants: Hundreds. Every week, we track the number of people who attend our regular Shabbat worship service on Fridays at 6:15 P.M. and Saturdays at 8:00 A.M. Typically we have 110 people on Friday nights for services. On Synaplex Shabbat, the average increase is 125 percent. On Saturday mornings, our 8:00 A.M. service attendance averages 55 people each week. It remains the same, but our additional programs generally have 10 to 30 people each. Thus, typically, we have approximately 175 people join us for *Kabbalat Shabbat*, Torah study, and our 8 A.M. minyan Shabbat morning. (This does not include an 11 A.M. Shabbat service, usually attended by friends and family of our b'nei mitzvah.) On a Synaplex Shabbat, that number can easily double and has even quadrupled because of the variety of opportunities to connect.

Number and Length of Sessions: Every program varies.

Staffing Required: Our associate rabbi is the lead staff person. A Synaplex team has been created to plan programs, implement, market, and assess the initiative and its monthly programs. Our outreach and membership chairperson has been apprised of the initiative and collaborates with people identified to us as new or in need of connection.

Total Cost of Program: $30,000 estimate (this is our first year, program is not complete).

Source of Funding: Various synagogue funds, including restricted funds to bring in special guests (speakers, artists, etc.), general budget (communications), Associate Rabbi's Discretionary Fund, and

$5,000 grant from STAR (Synagogues: Transformation and Renewal) that can be used for marketing and assessment.

Fee for Attendees: All programs are free except community dinners.

Plan of Action: See attached flow chart for implementing Synaplex Shabbat program.

Instructions to Facilitator: *Must* have buy-in from staff, co-workers, and board of trustees.

Evaluation of Program: There are two objectives that need to be assessed. The first is the quality of the program and all of the experiences that are being offered associated with the program. The second is the leadership development component that will determine its implementation.

Regarding the programming component, Synaplex has been terrific. We have more people having Shabbat experiences whenever we offer Synaplex versus non-Shabbat experiences.

Part of Synaplex's success is the volunteer recruitment component. We are not only engaging people to help with marketing materials and press releases, but we also use "member experts" in different fields of study or members with special interests who are "guest speakers" or facilitators of activities.

In our evaluations, we see that most people learn about the events through our newsletter and separate Synaplex invitations (see enclosed). Individuals not already connected with B'nai Israel are learning about Synaplex and our congregation largely through press releases in the secular press and on our Web site.

We are also funneling people from other adult learning opportunities and outreach initiatives (Intro class, Taste of Judaism, interfaith couples' seminars, etc.) to our Synaplex programs to help create connections and open more doors to Jewish living.

We are finding that people who have been engaged are strengthening their connections. A few look at Synaplex as a retreat experience, moving from one program to the next. Most participants will come to the program that they find most attractive.

Overall, participants enjoy and appreciate the offerings. Naturally, there are times when some of our guests are better presenters than others.

Other findings from anecdotal and written assessments:

- It has helped to link people to other members (both new and veteran).
- It has engaged a number of new volunteers in a serious way.
- More and more people are looking for what Synaplex will offer.
- We are increasing awareness of our "brand"—Congregation B'nai Israel as an innovative, welcoming congregation that is making great efforts to meet people where they are.
- It is perceived that people who are checking in at Synaplex events are getting more connected with the community.

Challenges:
Synaplex is very labor intensive to promote, implement, and manage volunteers. All our programs have been successful. However, many of the underinvolved who are members still do not participate often. We are hoping that our template for monthly brochures being designed for next year will interest people enough to read (one of our greatest challenges) so that they will learn about the offerings. (One congregant has a marketing agency, CircleOne Marketing. He had three graphic designers provide

proposals for marketing materials. After focus groups, we are in the second round of determining our template for next year's promotional materials.)

We also plan to increase opportunities and provide some spiritual growth experiences to run concurrently with our main service.

Follow-up:
We are tracking attendance and compiling a database of e-mail addresses to continue to invite people back again. We are also linking Synaplex to other opportunities for learning and spiritual growth, promoting Synaplex activities at our regular worship services, in adult education classes, Introduction to Judaism classes, Taste of Judaism, etc.

Brit Synaplex: Outline for a Synaplex Team Member

At Congregation B'nai Israel, we value the time that volunteers give to the synagogue. We want to make your experience both meaningful and enjoyable. To help make that happen, we've created a Volunteer Covenant/Pact (or *b'rit* in Hebrew). This *b'rit* spells out what we hope you will give to our STAR Synaplex initiative and what we hope you will gain through your volunteer commitment.

What we hope you will give:
- Encouragement to peers, friends, and others you think may be interested in participating in one of the Shabbat experiences offered through our Synaplex initiative and to volunteer in an area of their interest. (Just think how much more vibrant our congregation would be if each volunteer involved five new people in B'nai Israel's Synaplex programs!)
- To share your enthusiasm with others about using Synaplex Shabbatot as gateways to stronger Jewish experiences for the members of our diverse B'nai Israel community.
- To participate in *occasional* phone conferences and online training information provided by STAR to learn how to implement our programming and assessment efforts more thoughtfully and effectively.
- To take part in Synaplex communications and discussions, primarily via e-mail and telephone, as well as group meetings approximately every six to eight weeks on Thursday nights. (Schedule to be determined; good food guaranteed!)
- Qualities that are necessary for this team include, but are not limited to, a love for being Jewish and a desire to make that feeling contagious; an open mind; an ability to think out of the box with regard to synagogue programming and Shabbat experiences; an interest in communicating with others (marketing); being responsive to "meet people where they are"; recruiting people to participate (actively engaging individuals and encouraging them to connect); publicizing events through announcements and other media.

What we hope you will receive:
- Enhanced love for being Jewish.
- Excitement and meaning in getting new people involved.
- Satisfaction for opening new doors to Jewish experiences to longtime members of our community.
- Enjoyment from working with a group of like-minded, creative peers, who are committed to the ongoing process of making our synagogue a welcoming place that meets the Jewish needs of its members.

<u>Estimated time commitment</u>: One hour per week. Not necessarily consistently, nor does it need to be all at once. Rabbi Greene will be coordinating the efforts of this team. For more information, please contact him at 336-1858 or fgreene@congregationbnaiisraeol.org.

B'nai Israel Synaplex Task List

Line up Speakers or Entertainers (Programming Subcommittee)

_____ Clear date (have alternatives available) with rabbi(s), Synaplex coordinators, and office staff.
_____ Find out if there's an honorarium or fee and get approval from Synaplex chair or rabbi.
_____ When date is finalized, MAKE SURE IT GETS INCLUDED IN THE SYNAGOGUE CALENDAR.
_____ Where suitable, get a signed contract.

Publicity (Publicity/Marketing Subcommittee)

_____ Collect weekend information for flyer.
_____ E-mail to participants and event chairs.
_____ Text (bios, program description, date/time, reservation requirements, costs, childcare, etc.).
_____ Contact guest for description of program, bio, photo as early as possible (Programming Committee).
_____ Touch base with event chair to coordinate external and internal publicity.
_____ Gather info and create flyers and postings for events.
_____ E-mail flyer to Kinkos (we have an account with the Post Road store, which delivers).
_____ Determine quantity.
_____ Think of other venues for publicity, depending on the audience to be served (e.g., Hillel, JCC).

Publicity Includes

_____ Bulletin
_____ Press releases for the Jewish and secular press (some may have early deadlines)
_____ Mailings to congregants
_____ E-mails to congregants
_____ Flyers posted in the community and for distribution to cohort groups (i.e., religious school, nursery school, Brotherhood, seniors, etc.)
_____ Postcards

Publicity DEADLINES:
By the 1st of previous month to Pat Marchetti for synagogue bulletin (e.g., March 1st for April bulletin)

Two Weeks Prior to an Event

_____ Mail postcards
_____ E-mail to congregants

For the Event

_____ Following month Synaplex flyer ready for distribution at scheduled Synaplex event (e.g., April flyer for March event)
_____ Signs with activities and location

Room Set-up

_____ Determine if any equipment needs to be rented or borrowed.
_____ Get room set up form from Amy—needs to be submitted one week prior to the event.
_____ Work out floor plan (furniture needed and timing with designated person).
_____ Determine time for set up/Friday AM or PM.
_____ Determine who will do the actual set up.
_____ Determine how you will get in the building that day if beyond regular synagogue hours.
_____ Determine who will be in charge of signage for the event.

Event and Volunteer tasks

_____ Determine event chair for each Synaplex activity.
_____ Recruit and direct volunteers as needed.
_____ Team of 3 to 5 people to greet for service (welcome and wear Synaplex/BI button).
_____ Arrange word-of-mouth and other recruitment efforts to invite people to dinner, lunch, and other Synaplex events the week prior to events.
_____ Event chair reach out to publicity committee.
_____ Announcements at services.
_____ Calls to cohort groups.
_____ Sign in at each event with name and e-mail.

If Synaplex Dinner or Luncheon, Need the Following as Appropriate

_____ Set up Friday AM or PM (or Saturday AM if lunch).
_____ Recruit 2 to 4 people (takes less than one hour to set up).
_____ Ask Amy to print out registration list for those who signed up, showing who has/has not paid.
_____ Ask office to supply pre-addressed envelopes for those who haven't paid.
_____ 5 people to register.
_____ Check-in for registered participants (2 people).
_____ Determine paid and unpaid.
_____ Collect payment from unpaid participants or provide B'nai Israel addressed envelope (use billing as a last resort—be sure to collect name, address, and phone number).
_____ Mark as paid on list.
_____ Register and collect payment from unregistered participants (2 people).

_____ SIGN IN with e-mail and name (1 person).
_____ Have cash box with petty cash available.
_____ See Rabbi Greene about petty cash request.
_____ Display and distribute flyers for this month's and next month's Synaplex activities.

Refreshments/Food

_____ Offer choice for vegetarian meals.
_____ Order dinner, arrange desserts, beverages.
_____ Amy arranges food with Fred Kaskowitz from Woods End Deli three weeks prior to date.
_____ Check with Amy re: food arrangements.
_____ Amy will call Monday then again Thursday to confirm final counts.
_____ If an event is on Friday evening, contact Amy to talk about possible increase in *Oneg Shabbat* food and beverages.

Other Details

_____ Determine if there will be child care.
_____ If so, where, when, who, RSVP deadline?
_____ If the event coincides with Shabbat/ holiday ritual, determine who will lead blessings (i.e., staff, clergy, or lay people) and have a handout of blessings (Hebrew, English, transliteration) for program participants as well as other materials needed (e.g., candles, wine, challah, matches).
_____ Be sure to clarify any costs involved and how they will be handled.

288 The Outreach and Membership Idea Book

Synaplex Flow Chart

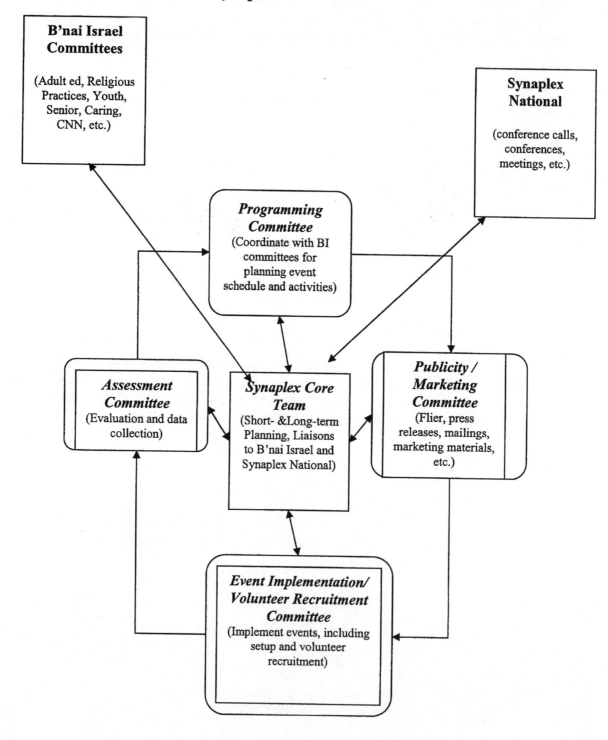

Synaplex at Congregation B'nai Israel, Bridgeport, CT[1]

Thank you for joining us for our **Chanukah Storytelling** program this evening. This program is part of our new Synaplex initiative in innovative Shabbat programming. Please help us plan for future events by completing this short survey form.

On a scale of 1 to 6, with 6 being the highest positive score, please rate the **Chanukah Storytelling** program on the following dimensions:

	Extremely Dissatisfied					**Extremely Satisfied**
Overall experience	1	2	3	4	5	6
Feeling welcomed	1	2	3	4	5	6
The quality of the program	1	2	3	4	5	6
The Shabbat experience	1	2	3	4	5	6
	Strongly Disagree					**Strongly Agree**
I found the program to be meaningful.	1	2	3	4	5	6
I learned something new from this program.	1	2	3	4	5	6
I would recommend this program to my friends.	1	2	3	4	5	6

Are you a member of Congregation B'nai Israel? _____ Yes _____ No

Would you describe your synagogue attendance as: major holidays _____ occasional _____ monthly _____ regular _____ not at all _____

How did you hear about this program? Bulletin _____ Happenings e-mail _____ flyer _____ from a friend _____ previous Synaplex experience _____ other _____

Do you plan to attend any other Shabbat program this weekend? _____ Yes _____ No
If yes, which program (s)_____

What subjects would you like to explore in the future? _____
_____
_____

Additional Comments and Suggestions _____
_____
_____

Thank you and Shabbat Shalom!!

---

[1] We are planning to design an easier questionnaire and utilize either zoomerang.com or surveymonkey.com to continue our assessment process.

CONNECTICUT POST RELIGION

RELIGION EDITOR
SEV RINALDI, 330-6309
srinaldi@ctpost.com

SATURDAY, OCTOBER 30, 2004

'Synaplex' brings variety to worship in synagogue

By AMANDA CUDA
acuda@ctpost.com

As an authority on such topics as war and politics, Peter Temes has spoken all over the country.

But there's one place where Temes, president of Antioch New England Graduate School in New Hampshire, and author of "The Just War: An American Reflection on the Morality of War in Our Time" (Ivan R. Dee, $25), hasn't spoken. It's his synagogue, Congregation B'nai Israel in Bridgeport.

"I've been giving talks all this last year about these issues everywhere, but never in the synagogue," said Temes, who lives in Fairfield. "And this is the most important place of all to talk about this."

Temes broke that streak Friday, when he, along with fellow congregant and Fairfield resident Joel Rosenthal, spoke on the war and politics at the synagogue. The talk was part of a new program at B'nai Israel, called Synaplex.

Synaplex, which will be offered at the synagogue occasionally on Shabbat, or the Sabbath, is akin to a movie multiplex, in that it offers congregants a number of ways to worship. In addition to the typical prayer service, programs can include speakers, like Rosenthal and Temes, dinners, text studies and any number of activities.

"The basic idea is to provide a range of different experiences so that people can experience the Jewish community in a variety of ways," said Rabbi Fred Greene, who is coordinating the Synaplex project at B'nai Israel.

▶ Please see B'NAI on B2

Andrea A. Dixon/Connecticut Post
Firm shake: Congregation B'nai Israel Rabbi James Prosnit shakes hands with Joe Temes, 6, before an evening service. Looking on is Peter Temes, left, and Joel Rosenthal, who were the guest speakers at the service.

B'nai Israel Synaplex reaches out to community

Continued from B1

For instance, he said, those who might not turn out for the prayer service might stop by for dinner, or to hear a speaker.

"We realize that people have different needs and different interests," Greene said. "We're trying to reach the needs of a diverse population."

It also utilizes the services of community members like Temes and Rosenthal, who have expertise in certain areas, which they can pass on to members.

The program is funded through a grant from the Minneapolis-based group Synagogues: Transformation and Renewal, a philanthropic organization that fosters innovation among synagogues in reaching out to congregation members.

STAR started the Synaplex initiative last September, in hopes of drawing more people to synagogue on Shabbat. B'nai Israel is one of 17 synagogues nationwide to offer Synaplex, and one of only two in Connecticut. Beth El Temple in West Hartford implemented it last year.

"I feel like, in some way, we're not doing anything new, but taking the existing framework and reinventing it," said STAR Executive Director Rabbi Hayim Herring.

Like Greene, he said that many people appreciate a wide range of options in their worship. "There is no magic bullet, no one size fits all approach to reinvigorating synagogue life," Herring said. "This is really responding to the diverse needs of the community. Prayer just doesn't cut it for a lot of people anymore. It's a tough entry point [into a synagogue]."

Herring said that offering a range of programs has done wonders for attendance at many of these synagogues. He said that, on average, attendance for synagogues that have implemented Synaplex increases 78 percent for Friday night services and 51 percent for Saturday morning services.

Already, the program has benefited B'nai Israel. Greene said that about 160 people came to Friday night's service, nearly double the turnout the synagogue normally sees, and 70 people came to the dinner following the service (other dinners have drawn about 30 people, Greene said). About 90 turned out for the guest speakers.

Greene said, as B'nai Israel's program moves forward, a number of unique opportunities, such as a program called "It's a Girl Thing," aimed at building self-esteem in pre-teen girls are planned. Other programs in the works include meditation, storytelling and more guest speakers.

"Some of our programs will be learning focused, some will be focused on worship and some of it will be social," he said.

Those attending Friday night's service said they were excited about the possibilities of Synaplex. Bari Dworken of Monroe has belonged to B'nai Israel since childhood, and said the idea has a lot of potential.

"I think it's very exciting that we'll have some new options and educational programs here," she said. "We are quite a diverse congregation and there is a diverse Jewish population in this area that is unaffiliated. The more we reach out, the greater the possibility of touching people's lives."

Those interested in learning more about B'nai Israel's Synaplex program can call the synagogue 336-1858.

Synagogue Launches SYNAPLEX™
B'nai Israel Receives Grant for Innovative Shabbat Experiences

Congregation B'nai Israel received a two-year $10,000 grant from Minneapolis-based STAR (Synagogues: Transformation & Renewal) to strengthen its ability to connect in meaningful ways with the 900 households affiliated with B'nai Israel.

The Synaplex Initiative seeks to enable Jewish individuals and families to celebrate Jewish life through a menu of innovative options in the realms of prayer, study and social and cultural programs during Shabbat in the synagogue.

If Shabbat is the Jewish "prime time," then we are going to begin to offer a wider variety of opportunities to connect to Shabbat and others in our diverse, thoughtful Jewish community. Each month, B'nai Israel will launch a Synaplex Shabbat, opening a wide variety of "gateways" for people to connect prayer, learning and community building.

Its next Synaplex Shabbat is December 10-11, featuring a Chanukah Celebration with renowned Storyteller, Peninnah Schram. Schram is an internationally known storyteller, teacher, author, and recording artist. Recipient of the National Storytellers Network Lifetime Achievement Award "for sustained and exemplary contributions to storytelling in America," Peninnah will help us publicize the miracle of Chanukah and celebrate our season of joy!

On Friday night, December 10, a time for refreshments and gathering will begin at 5:45 p.m. (Oneg Shabbat). The worship service begins at 6:15 p.m. There is a community dinner (RSVP and payment required for dinner) at 7:20 p.m. and a special presentation by Peninnah Schram will be at 8:30 p.m.

Saturnday morning, December 11, there is a Shabbat morning worship service at 8:00 a.m., community breakfast at 9:15 a.m. A Text study on the Book of Job at 9:30 a.m.

Saturday also includes:

- **Tot Shabbat** at 10:00 a.m. - a festive Shabbat experience for toddlers, nursery school children and their parents (& grandparents, too!), with crafts, singing and stories.
- **Healing Service** at 10:45 a.m. - an innovative worship experience, finding ways of opening up our prayers to the needs of Jews who are ill and those who care for them.
- **Art with Avi** - Israeli artist Avi Zuckerman will lead people of all ages make their own copper Chanukiyah for the holiday! This program is appropriate for all ages. RSVP is necessary. Cost $10 per person (or per chanukiyah; children under 4th grade will need parents' assistance). Followed by Havdallah and lighting our new Chanukiyot!

All gatherings will be held at Congregation B'nai Israel, 2710 Park Avenue, Bridgeport.

Our participation in Synaplex is supported by STAR (Synagogues: Transformation and Renewal). STAR is committed to renewing Jewish life through congregational innovation and leadership development, and is a philanthropic partnership of the Charles and Lynn Schusterman Family Foundation, Jewish Life Network/Steinhardt Foundation, and The Samuel Bronfman Foundation. Learn more at www.starsynagogue.org.

Congregation B'nai Israel embraces all who seek connections with Judaism and a Jewish community. Our congregation thrives through diversity, melding respect for traditions with openness to new ways of experiencing Judaism. You are warmly invited to come experience the expression of these values with us, through our array of spiritual, educational, community service and social opportunities. Our community includes those from Fairfield, Trumbull, Easton, Bridgeport, Monroe and other surrounding towns.

For further information, contact Rabbi Fred Greene at fgreene@congregationbnaiisrael.org or 203-336-1858 x135.

 @ b'nai israel

America at War:
A Discussion of Ethics, War & Peace
with B'nai Israel members

Peter Temes, Ph.D., President of Antioch Graduate School, New Hampshire and author of *The Just War: An American Reflection on the Morality of War in Our Time* (2004)

Joel Rosenthal, Ph.D., President, Carnegie Council on International Affairs and Peace and Adjunct Professor of Politics at New York University

Friday, October 22
- 5:45 *Oneg* & Refreshments
- 6:15 *Kabbalat Shabbat Service*
- 7:15 Community Dinner
  RSVP required
- 8:15 Discussion with Drs. Temes and Rosenthal

Saturday, October 23
- 8:00 Shabbat morning service
- 9:00 Brotherhood Breakfast (all are welcome)
- 9:30 Text Study: Jewish Texts and Armed Conflict
- 10:00 Tot Shabbat—A festive Shabbat experience for toddlers, nursery school children and their parents (and grandparents, too!)

Congregation B'nai Israel
2710 Park Avenue, Bridgeport
203.336.1858

For more information, to RSVP for dinner, call 336-1858 or go to www.congregationbnaiisrael.org/synaplex.htm

Congregation B'nai Israel is thrilled to be part of the national Synaplex Initiative, a program of STAR (Synagogues: Transformation and Renewal). As part of our participation in the program, you will be seeing announcements and information about exciting new programs all centered around Shabbat celebration in the synagogue. STAR is an initiative of the Charles and Lynn Schusterman Family Foundation, Jewish Life Network/Steinhardt Foundation, and the Samuel Bronfman Foundation.

Please make your reservation for dinner by **Tuesday, October 19.** Number of adults____
The Cost is $15 for each adult, $10 per child (ages 5-13), Under 5 is free. Number of children____

Name _____
Address _____
Phone _____
Email _____
Names of Guests/Family _____

Synaplex at Congregation B'nai Israel, Bridgeport, CT
Session Evaluation: America at War Joel Rosenthal & Peter Temes
October 22, 2004/ 8 Heshvan 5765

Each item was rated on a scale of 1 to 5 with 1 as "strongly agree" and 5 as "strongly disagree". Means (averages) have been calculated. (42 Evaluations)

The Instructors/Facilitator:	1	2	3	4	5	Mean
• Presented the theme clearly	27	11	4	0	0	1.45
• Seemed well prepared	37	3	2	0	0	1.17
• Was enjoyable	32	7	3	0	0	1.31
• Engaged the participants	31	8	3	0	0	1.33
• Exceeded my expectations	20	15	5	1	0	1.59

- I would make time to learn with this Instructor/Facilitator again   32 YES 0 NO

The Program:	1	2	3	4	5	Mean
• I learned something new	28	8	2	1	0	1.38
• I would pursue this topic further	23	10	4	3	0	1.68
• Made me think	31	5	4	1	0	1.39
• Exceeded my expectations	15	13	10	0	0	1.87
• The scheduled time was good	24	9	3	5	0	1.73
• The facility/room was comfortable	18	10	10	1	1	1.88

- Were you here for Shabbat dinner?   33 YES 6 NO
- Were you here for our Shabbat service? 35   4 NO
- Will you consider attending another Synaplex Program?   39 YES 0 NO

1. What was one thing you particularly liked about the presentation?

Highly qualified, intelligent and knowledgeable speakers 10
Interaction with audience and each other, informal, questions and answers 5
Topic was meaningful, thought provocative and current 6
Speakers leading the discussion were congregants
Intelligence and warmth of the speakers
Presentations appropriately short
History behind a Just War
Philosophical and ethical grounding for action
The second speaker was very vibrant!
In the dining room

2. What might have made this program more meaningful and interesting to you?

Speakers and participants often could not be heard, better acoustics, microphones   10
Clear, concise and relevant questions (write out?)   5
Hold in a smaller area set up better for discussion   2
More time 3
More from the presenters   2
Might be interesting to have a more controversial topic to stir debate
Earlier time, too tired to participate
More concrete examples, a little too abstract

3. How did you hear about the program?

Bulletin   17
Flyers   5
Email   3
Friends   5
Rabbi   2
Announcement at Services   3

4. What subjects would you like to explore in the future?

Anti Semitism
Peace for Israel
Animal Rights
Environmental Issues
Ethics in Medicine
End of Life Issues
Immigration
No Child Left Behind
Abortion
Ethics
Reflections on the Presidential Election
Stem Cell Research
Gay Marriage
Current Events – Foreign and Domestic
Morality   2
Jewish values and how they are impacted by or have impact on major issues such as poverty, health, etc.

# @ b'nai israel

BROTHERHOOD SCHOLAR-IN-RESIDENCE

Peter Pitzele
Playing With Fire: New Ways Of Encountering Torah

Peter Pitzele has been a professor of Literature at Harvard University and the Director of Psychodrama Services at Four Winds Hospital. He has blended his knowledge of literature with the improvisational methods of psychodrama to develop Bibliodrama, a new way of looking at biblical stories. He is the author of two books *Our Fathers' Wells: A Personal Encounter with the Myths of Genesis* and *Scripture Window: Towards a Practice of Bibliodrama*.

Feel free to engage Synaplex in any or all of the following opportunities

Friday, November 5

- 5:45 *Oneg* & Refreshments
- 6:15 *Kabbalat Shabbat Service*
- 7:15 Community Dinner
  RSVP required
- 8:15 What Is Bibliodrama? Midrash And Mischief In The Garden Of Eden

**For more information, to RSVP for dinner, call 336-1858
or go to
www.congregationbnaiisrael.org/synaplex.htm**

Congregation B'nai Israel
2710 Park Avenue, Bridgeport

Saturday, November 6

- 8:00 Shabbat morning service
- 9:00 Brotherhood Breakfast
- 9:30 Torah Study with Peter Pitzele
- 10:00 Tot Shabbat—A festive Shabbat experience for toddlers, nursery school children and their parents (& grandparents, too!)
- 10:45 *The Still, Small Voice Within: Guided imagery, meditation and creative introspection.* Enjoy Jewish meditation through simple, pleasant experiences to deepen awareness and quiet the mind with Allison Spitzer London. No previous meditation experience of any kind required.
- 4:00 The Voices Of Sarah: A Retrospective, followed by Havdallah

Congregation B'nai Israel is thrilled to be part of the national Synaplex Initiative, a program of STAR (Synagogues: Transformation and Renewal). As part of our participation in the program, you will be seeing announcements and information about exciting new programs all centered around Shabbat celebration in the synagogue. STAR is an initiative of the Charles and Lynn Schusterman Family Foundation, Jewish Life Network/Steinhardt Foundation, and the Samuel Bronfman Foundation.

Please make your reservation for dinner by <u>Monday, November 1.</u>   Number of adults____
The Cost is $15 for each adult, $10 per child (ages 5-13), Under 5 is free.   Number of children____

Name _____
Address _____
Phone _____
Email _____

A Chanukah Celebration with Peninnah Schram

Peninnah Schram is an internationally known storyteller, teacher, author, and recording artist. Recipient of the National Storytellers Network Lifetime Achievement Award "for sustained and exemplary contributions to storytelling in America," Peninnah will help us publicize the miracle of Chanukah and celebrate our season of joy!

A special presentation for our youngest friends & their families,
Preschool through third grade
Friday, December 10 at 5:30 p.m.

You are invited to join the rest of the congregation for Shabbat services at 6:15 p.m. (babysitting is available with RSVP to Gail) and dinner at 7:15 p.m.
For more info, go to www.congregationbnaiisrael.org/Synaplex.htm

---

Tot Shabbat

Saturday, December 11 @ 10-11am
Meet us in the Youth Lounge (downstairs)

Tot Shabbat is a fun-filled Shabbat experience for families with infants, tots, and preschoolers — the very youngest friends of Congregation B'nai Israel.

Shabbat Stories ✡ Lots of singing! ✡ Blessings for candles, juice, and challah! ✡ Arts & Craft Projects ✡ Noisy, restless children welcome! ✡ Great for grandparents!

Join Rabbi Greene & Elaine Chetrit, Director of Family Education, for a fun way to connect to Judaism with warmth and creativity!

Congregation B'nai Israel is thrilled to be part of the national Synaplex™ Initiative, a program of STAR (Synagogues: Transformation and Renewal). As part of our participation in the program, you will be seeing announcements and information about exciting new programs all centered around Shabbat celebration in the synagogue. Watch your mailbox for news! To learn more about the program, go to www.congregationbnaiisrael.org/Synaplex.htm

Chapter Five   From Generation to Generation   297

B'nai Israel Invites You to a...

Chanukah Celebration

SATURDAY, DECEMBER 11
4:00-6:00 P.M.

Art With Avi

Join Avi Zuckerman, Israeli artist extraordinaire, to make your own CHANUKAH MENORAH! A perfect way to celebrate—appropriate for all ages! Afterwards, we will celebrate Havdalah and light our new Chanukiot!

RSVP IS <u>REQUIRED</u> BY DEC. 7: CALL 336.1858 OR AMY@CONGREGATIONBNAIISRAEL.ORG.
COST: $10 PER MENORAH. CHILDREN IN GRADES K-3 NEED AN ADULT'S ASSISTANCE. ALL CHILDREN NEED TO BE ACCOMPANIED BY AN ADULT.

Congregation B'nai Israel is thrilled to be part of the national Synaplex Initiative, a program of STAR (Synagogues: Transformation and Renewal). As part of our participation in the program, you will be seeing announcements and information about exciting new programs all centered around Shabbat celebration in the synagogue. STAR is an initiative of the Charles and Lynn Schusterman Family Foundation, Jewish Life Network/Steinhardt Foundation, and the Samuel Bronfman Foundation.

Torah Yoga

Date: March 5, 2005
Time: 4:00 p.m.
FREE
Space is Limited

RSVP to Amy: 203.336.1858 | amy@congregationbnaiisrael.org

Join Andrea Rudolph and certified yoga instructor Joy Abrams to experiment with a new approach to yoga and Torah by combining the classic yoga postures with the wisdom of Jewish mystics. Wear loose, comfortable clothing & bring a yoga mat or beach towel. No experience necessary. *Space is limited. Reservations required.*

Community...Study...Spiritual Growth...
What are you seeking? You can find it at a Synaplex Shabbat. B'nai Israel is exploring ways to strengthen community and celebrate the "Jewish primetime" in meaningful ways. B'nai Israel participates in Synaplex through a grant from Synagogues: Transformation and Renewal (STAR). STAR is an initiative of the Charles and Lynn Schusterman Family Foundation, Jewish Life Network/Steinhardt Foundation, and the Samuel Bronfman Foundation.

Art with Susan
Make Your Own
Elijah's Cup or Miriam's Cup
For Passover

Community...Study...Spiritual Growth...
What are you seeking? You can find it at a Synaplex Shabbat. B'nai Israel is exploring ways to strengthen community and celebrate the "Jewish primetime" in meaningful ways. B'nai Israel participates in Synaplex through a grant from Synagogues: Transformation and Renewal (STAR). STAR is an initiative of the Charles and Lynn Schusterman Family Foundation, Jewish Life Network/Steinhardt Foundation, and the Samuel Bronfman Foundation.

Date: Saturday, March 5, 2005
Time: 4:00 p.m.

Congregation B'nai Israel
2710 Park Ave., Bridgeport
www.congregationbnaiisrael.org

Join Susan Walden and make your own Elijah's Cup or Miriam's Cup for Passover. This project is for the whole temple family, ages 10-120! Followed by Havdalah.
Reservations required.
Cost: $10 per cup.
RSVP: 336-1858 or welcome@congregationbnaiisrael.org

בני ישראל

Tot Shabbat

Saturday May 14
Meet us in our Chapel
10:00 a.m. to 11:00 a.m.

Tot Shabbat is a fun-filled Shabbat experience for families with infants, tots, and preschoolers...
the *very youngest friends* of Congregation B'nai Israel

- Shabbat Stories
- Lots of singing
- Blessings for candles, juice, and challah
- Arts & Craft Projects
- Noisy, restless children welcome
- Great for grandparents
- Building a Community of Children & Parents

OPEN TO THE WHOLE COMMUNITY

Join Rabbi Greene & Elaine Chetrit, Director of Family Education, for a fun way to connect to Judaism with warmth and creativity!

Tot Shabbat celebrates the joy and magic of the Sabbath
Come, learn alongside your child!

Community...Study...Spiritual Growth...
What are you seeking? You can find it at a Synaplex Shabbat. B'nai Israel is exploring new ways to strengthen community and celebrate the "Jewish primetime" in meaningful ways. Our congregation is grateful to STAR (Synagogues: Transformation and Renewal) for its grant to participate in this Synaplex initiative. STAR is an initiative of the Charles and Lynn Schusterman Family Foundation, Jewish Life Network/Steinhardt Foundation, and the Samuel Bronfman Foundation. To learn more about Synaplex, go to www.congregationbnaiisrael.org/Synaplex.htm.

CONGREGATION B'NAI ISRAEL
PARK AVENUE TEMPLE
2710 PARK AVENUE • BRIDGEPORT, CONN. 06604 • TELEPHONE 336-1858

FOR IMMEDIATE RELEASE
Event date: April 8-9, 2005

For additional information:
Rabbi Fred Greene
fgreene@congregationbnaiisrael.org
203.336.1858 x135

Art & Soul Exploration, Healing Weekend at B'nai Israel

(Bridgeport, CT) Congregation B'nai Israel is sponsoring a variety of exciting events as part of its Synaplex™ weekend on April 8 and 9. Congregation members and interested area residents of all ages are invited to tap into their spirituality in a variety of ways throughout the weekend.

Synaplex is an innovative initiative that seeks to help people experience Shabbat- the "Jewish Primetime" that takes place from sundown on Fridays through sundown on Saturdays-in new and meaningful ways.

The April 8-9 Synaplex weekend will embark on Friday evening with a community dinner followed by an Art & Soul experience with Artist-in-Residence Harriet Carew, who holds a Masters of Divinity from Hartford Seminary. Participants will explore creativity and spirituality through movement, music, painting and reflection. Artists and non-artists alike will discover the freedom in creating "soul art."

The Synaplex weekend continues on Saturday, April 9 at 9:30 am, expanding on the Art & Soul experience with a three-hour workshop. There will also be a Shabbat Meditation Walk through Lake Mohegan in Fairfield, beginning at 9:30 a.m. and a Healing Service at B'nai Israel at 11:00 a.m. for those seeking hope and wholeness in response to loss, struggle, illness and life's every day challenges. For families with toddlers and preschoolers, there is a Tot Shabbat experience at 10:00 a.m. to introduce the spirit of the Sabbath and Judaism to young children and meet other families in the community.

Friday night dinner reservations are required ($15 per adult, $10 per child ages 5-13). Cost of Saturday morning workshop is $25. Loose, comfortable clothing recommended. For more information call Congregation B'nai Israel at 203-336-1858 or check the temple's website at www.congregationbnaiisrael.org.

Congregation B'nai Israel is one of 29 congregations in the country to participate in Synaplex™, sponsored by STAR (Synagogues: Transformation and Renewal). Synaplex™ seeks to enable

Jewish individuals and families to celebrate Jewish life through a menu of innovative options in the realms of prayer, study and social and cultural programs during the Sabbath in the synagogue.

Our participation in Synaplex™ is supported by STAR (Synagogues: Transformation and Renewal). STAR is committed to renewing Jewish life through congregational innovation and leadership development, and is a philanthropic partnership of the Charles and Lynn Schusterman Family Foundation, Jewish Life Network/Steinhardt Foundation, and The Samuel Bronfman Foundation. Learn more at www.starsynagogue.org.

Congregation B'nai Israel embraces all who seek connections with Judaism and a Jewish community. Our congregation thrives through diversity, melding respect for traditions with openness to new ways of experiencing Judaism. You are warmly invited to come experience the expression of these values with us, through our array of spiritual, educational, community service and social opportunities. Our community includes those from Fairfield, Trumbull, Easton, Bridgeport, Stratford, Shelton, and other surrounding towns.

More information is available at www.congregationbnaiisrael.org.

*****

Shabbat Meditation Walk

Join B'nai Israel's own
Mark Schiff
at Lake Mohegan Recreation Area, Fairfield**
Morehouse Highway, Eastfield Circle

DATE: Saturday, April 9
TIME: 9:30 a.m. at B'nai Israel
RSVP: Amy at 336-1858 or amy@congregationbnaiisrael.org. *Space is limited.* Reservations are required.
INFO: Need good walking/hiking shoes for uneven terrain. Walk will be 1-1.5 hours long. Bring Your Own Water Bottle.
WHERE: We will gather at B'nai Israel and leave promptly to go to Lake Mohegan. Friends who want to meet us there directly at the reserve can meet us in the parking lot at 9:40 a.m.

**The venue has been changed from Devil's Den to Lake Mohegan. We promise to return to Devil's Den for a future gathering!

Community...Study...Spiritual Growth...
What are you seeking? You can find it at a Synaplex Shabbat. B'nai Israel is exploring ways to strengthen community and celebrate the "Jewish primetime" in meaningful ways. B'nai Israel participates in Synaplex through a grant from Synagogues: Transformation and Renewal (STAR). STAR is an initiative of the Charles and Lynn Schusterman Family Foundation, Jewish Life Network/Steinhardt Foundation, and the Samuel Bronfman Foundation.

Congregation B'nai Israel | 2710 Park Avenue, Bridgeport
203.336.1858 | www.congregationbnaiisrael.org

A Jewish Healing Service

Saturday, April 9
11:00 a.m. to 12noon

Jewish healing offers the creative use of Jewish resources, combined with psychological insights and community to those seeking wholeness, comfort and connection in challenging times.

When illness, loss and significant life challenges confront us we may discover that our ability to cope is disrupted, our habitual way of viewing life is challenged and we may be in need of greater and perhaps new types of support. This experience is for those who face these challenges and feel a sense of isolation, of brokenness, yet desire to search for ways to heal the spirit by find meaning, comfort and community in the midst of their challenges.

Join Rabbi Fred Greene in a creative worship experience that offers healing and a path towards wholeness by looking into Jewish tradition and exploring it with a new eye.

Community...Study...Spiritual Growth...
What are you seeking? You can find it at a Synaplex Shabbat. B'nai Israel is exploring new ways to strengthen community and celebrate the "Jewish primetime" in meaningful ways. Our congregation is grateful to STAR (Synagogues: Transformation and Renewal) for its grant to participate in this Synaplex initiative. STAR is an initiative of the Charles and Lynn Schusterman Family Foundation, Jewish Life Network/Steinhardt Foundation, and the Samuel Bronfman Foundation.

The Challah Wagon

Congregation:	Congregation Emeth
Address:	PO Box 1430 Gilroy, CA 95021
Phone Number:	(408) 847-4111
Contact's Name and E-mail:	Rabbi Miller, Rabbi@emeth.net
Number of Member Units:	61
URJ Region:	Pacific Central West Council
Rabbi:	Yitzhak J. Miller
Outreach Chairpersons:	Debbie Zajac, Denise Weyl-Flynn

Brief Description: The Challah Wagon is intended to serve new members, teens, interfaith families, homebound members, and the general community by enabling teens to use their newly acquired driver's licenses to deliver challah and flowers, together with instructions for blessings for a Shabbat dinner, and weekly Torah commentary from the rabbi. Deliveries are made to subscribing families every Friday. Challah and flowers are given for free to new members for the first month of their membership as a welcome to the congregation. Subscriptions also underwrite the cost of complimentary challah and flowers to homebound or nursing-home-bound members. The program currently operates at a profit.

Target Population: New members, interfaith families, homebound members, teens.

Number of Participants: 25 percent of the congregation!

Number and Length of Sessions: Ongoing program.

Staff Required: One hour/week administrative, one hour/week of rabbi's time to prepare commentary, two hours/week for teens to make deliveries.

Total Cost of Program: $3.75 for challah and flowers (provided by local businesses at cost), $18 per week per teen driver. Project currently runs at a 20 percent per family profit to the congregation.

Sources of Funding and Fees: $36 per month subscription per household. Also, this year, we received a small federation grant to kick off the project.

Logistics: Need a good ongoing relationship with a challah-baker (we trained our local bakery) and a florist. E-mail reminders to recipients on Wednesdays proved helpful, asking that if they are not going to require delivery that week, they simply reply to the e-mail (proceeds from that week are donated to charity). Many people who didn't want the subscription themselves wanted to sponsor it for someone else, including gift subscriptions. Once the program is up and running, it runs pretty smoothly.

Evaluation: Highly successful program—easy to run! Not only has the program had all of the outreach benefits we hoped for (including teens, reaching out to homebound members, welcoming new members, etc.), but also the program has had many unforeseen benefits, such as members sponsoring homebound members and giving subscriptions as gifts. In fact, the real estate agent in the congregation has given a six-month subscription to other people in the congregation whom she helped buy a house as a "welcome to your new home" gift.

The program has also:
- Encouraged Shabbat dinner time for families;
- Helped educate interfaith and other families how to "do Shabbat dinner";
- Provided a "marketing" opportunity for the congregation to help members understand the goals of the congregation.

Chapter Five From Generation to Generation **307**

The Challah Wagon
Is coming to your neighborhood

Your subscription of $36 per month provides:

- ❏ Challah & fresh flowers to your door every Friday
- ❏ Shabbat Torah information and discussion material
- ❏ Complimentary Challah & fresh flowers for Shabbat to Jews in local nursing homes
- ❏ Service begins December 3rd
- ❏ Members in Good Standing may bill their congregation accounts

| Flowers provided at a discount by:
SAFEWAY ON TENNANT
MORGAN HILL | Please Support our Sponsors | Challah provided at a discount by:
MORGAN HILL BAKERY
VINEYARD TOWN CENTER |

The "Challah Wagon" will be driven by teens in the congregation, helping keep them involved with their Jewish Community!!!

This sounds great!! Sign me up!!

Name_____   Email_____

Address_____   Phone_____

❏ 1 month   ❏   ~~6~~ 7 months   ❏   ~~12~~ 13 months
                       get 1 month free!!   get 1 month free!!
                                                          PLUS
                                                 A free book of
                                                 Shabbat Blessings

308 The Outreach and Membership Idea Book

SHABBAT SHALOM!
From Congregation Emeth
Your South Valley Jewish Community

THE CHALLAH WAGON
is generously supported by the following merchants who provide their products at substantially reduced cost.
PLEASE SUPPORT THEM!!!

**MORGAN HILL BAKERY
VINEYARD TOWN CENTER**

**SAFEWAY ON TENNANT
MORGAN HILL**

SHABBAT BLESSINGS

O God, You are the light by which we see the ones we love. As we kindle these lights, we begin a holy time. May we and all Israel find in it refreshment of body and spirit, and the sense that You are near to us at all times.

WE LIGHT THE CANDLES AND SAY:

Ba-ruch a-ta Adonai, Eh-lo-hei-nu בָּרוּךְ אַתָּה יי אֱלֹהֵינוּ
meh-lech ha-o-lam a-sher מֶלֶךְ הָעוֹלָם, אֲשֶׁר
ki-d'sha-nu b'mitz-vo-tav v'tzi-va-nu קִדְּשָׁנוּ בְּמִצְוֹתָיו וְצִוָּנוּ
l'had-lik ner shel Shabbat. לְהַדְלִיק נֵר שֶׁל שַׁבָּת.

We praise You, Eternal God, Sovereign of the universe: You hallow us with Mitzvot, and command us to kindle the lights of Shabbat.

WE HOLD THE CUP AND SAY:

Ba-ruch a-ta Adonai, Eh-lo-hei-nu בָּרוּךְ אַתָּה יי אֱלֹהֵינוּ
meh-lech ha-o-lam, bo-rei מֶלֶךְ הָעוֹלָם, בּוֹרֵא
p'ri ha-ga-fen. פְּרִי הַגָּפֶן.

Ba-ruch a-ta A-do-nai, Eh-lo-hei-nu בָּרוּךְ אַתָּה יי אֱלֹהֵינוּ
meh-lech ha-o-lam, a-sher ki-d'sha-nu מֶלֶךְ הָעוֹלָם, אֲשֶׁר קִדְּשָׁנוּ
b'mitz-vo-tav v'ra-tza va-nu, v'shabbat בְּמִצְוֹתָיו וְרָצָה בָנוּ, וְשַׁבָּת
ko-d'sho b'a-ha-va u-v'ra-tzon קָדְשׁוֹ בְּאַהֲבָה וּבְרָצוֹן
hin-chi-la-ta-nu, zi-ka-ron l'ma-a-sei הִנְחִילָנוּ, זִכָּרוֹן לְמַעֲשֵׂה
v'rei-sheet. Ki hu yom t'chi-la בְרֵאשִׁית. כִּי הוּא יוֹם תְּחִלָּה
l'mik-ra-ei ko-desh, zei-cher לְמִקְרָאֵי קֹדֶשׁ, זֵכֶר
li-tzi-at Mitz-ra-yim. Ki va-nu לִיצִיאַת מִצְרָיִם. כִּי־בָנוּ
va-char-ta v'o-ta-nu ki-dash-ta mi-kol בָחַרְתָּ וְאוֹתָנוּ קִדַּשְׁתָּ מִכָּל־
ha-a-mim, v'sha-bat kod-sh'cha הָעַמִּים, וְשַׁבַּת קָדְשְׁךָ
b'a-ha-va u-v'ra-tzon hin-chal-ta-nu. בְּאַהֲבָה וּבְרָצוֹן הִנְחַלְתָּנוּ.
Ba-ruch a-ta Adonai, m'ka-deish בָּרוּךְ אַתָּה יי מְקַדֵּשׁ
ha-shabbat. הַשַּׁבָּת.

We praise You, Eternal God, Sovereign of the universe, Creator of the fruit of the vine.

We praise You, Eternal God, Sovereign of the universe: You call us to holiness with the Mitzvah of Shabbat: the sign of Your love, a reminder of Your creative work, and of our liberation from Egyptian bondage: our day of days. On Shabbat especially, we hearken to Your call to serve You as a holy people. We praise You, O God, for the holiness of Shabbat.

WE BLESS THE MEAL:

Ba-ruch a-ta Adonai, Eh-lo-hei-nu בָּרוּךְ אַתָּה יי אֱלֹהֵינוּ
meh-lech ha-o-lam, ha-mo-tzi מֶלֶךְ הָעוֹלָם, הַמּוֹצִיא
leh-chem min ha-a-retz. לֶחֶם מִן הָאָרֶץ.

We praise You, Eternal God, Sovereign of the universe, for You cause bread to come forth from the earth.

March 4-5, 2005   Shabbat Vayakhel   24 Adar I, 5765
Torah Portion: Exodus 35:1-38:20

In this week's Torah Portion

Building the Tabernacle:

Following Moses' instructions from a few Torah portions ago, the Israelites begin to build the tabernacle (the portable sanctuary in the wilderness). In addition to the detailed description of the construction, there are two particularly interesting episodes in this Torah portion.

First, Moses is told that G-d has given special artistic talents to a certain person named Bezalel, and therefore he is to supervise the crafting of the tabernacle (an interesting footnote is that the most renowned art school in Israel is named for this Biblical figure, and is called the Bezalel Academy of Art).

Second, the Israelites respond to Moses' request for gifts from which to create the tabernacle en masse. In fact, the Torah portion tells that Moses had to request that the people stop bringing gifts because there were too many for the artists to use!

1) Most of us were brought up with the claim "You can do anything if you set your mind to it". Judaism does not necessarily claim that this is true. This Torah portion reinforces the Jewish perspective that each person has specific individual gifts, and it is the individual's responsibility to determine those gifts and use them to serve humanity and G-d.

   a) Do you agree with Judaism's claim that each person has different natural gifts?
   b) If so, what personal work have you done to determine your own gifts?
   c) What do you think your natural gifts are?
   d) How do you put your natural gifts to work in the world?

2) In a capitalist culture that places finances as the highest value, it is hard to conceptualize people donating more to a project than was needed. But in the culture of ancient Egypt, serving G-d was likely viewed as much more important than personal possessions.

   a) What are your highest values?

Golden Calves

The "sin of the golden calf" (in this week's Torah portion) is taken by Jewish tradition as the worst sin the Israelites have ever committed. It becomes the archetypal symbol for anytime the nation of Israel or any Jew is drawn to any form of idolatry.

Today, much discussion revolves in Jewish circles about our modern American "golden calf", materialism. How ironic that today our most distracting and harmful form of idolatry also focuses on something made of physically expensive materials.

Judaism does not, however, expect us to lead a life of poverty and asceticism. In fact, the Talmud teaches that it is a SIN not to enjoy the "produce of our labors".

1. How can we "enjoy the produce of our labors"

CONGREGATION EMETH

CLOSE TO HOME
The Jewish Community in Your Community

WARM & FRIENDLY
The Personal Attention You Deserve From Your Synagogue

INCLUSIVE AND WELCOMING
Judaism for Your Life

Make Torah a way of life
and welcome Every Person as a Friend

Thank you to our Challah Wagon Driver:
AARON PALM

The Challah Wagon is partially funded by a grant from
Jewish Federation of Greater San Jose

Commentary & discussion provided by:
Rabbi Yitzhak Miller

April 1-2, 2005　　　Shabbat Sh'mini　　　22 Adar II, 5765
Torah Portion: Leviticus 9:1-11:47

Euthanasia

Babylonian Talmud - Tractate Kethuboth 104a (500CE)
The following is the most oft-quoted Jewish teaching undergirding the laws of euthanasia:

On the day when Rabbi [Judah haNasi] (the author of the Mishna) died the Rabbis decreed a public fast and offered prayers for heavenly mercy.
Rabbi's nursemaid ascended the roof and prayed: 'The immortals desire Rabbi [to join them] and the mortals desire Rabbi [to remain with them]; may it be the will [of God] that the mortals may overpower the immortals. But, when she saw how often he resorted to the privy, painfully taking off his *tefillin* and putting them on again (for they are not allowed in the bathroom), she changed her mind and instead prayed: 'May it be the will [of the Almighty] that the immortals may overpower the mortals'. As the Rabbis incessantly continued their prayers for [heavenly] mercy (which according to Jewish tradition prevents the angel of death from entering) she took up a jar and threw it down from the roof to the ground. [For just a moment] they ceased praying, the angel of death entered, and the soul of Rabbi departed to its eternal rest.

Shulchan Aruch, Tractate Yoreh Deah 339:1 (1550CE)
Even if a patient has agonized for a long time, and he and his family are in great distress, it is forbidden to hasten his death by, for instance: closing his eyes, or removing a pillow from under his head, or placing an object such as feathers or the synagogue key under his head.

Commentary to Shulchan Aruch, Yoreh Deah 339:1 (1600CE)
However, if there is an obstacle that prevents the departure of the soul, such as noise outside or salt present on the dying person's tongue, we may stop the noise or remove the salt so as not to hinder death.

Discussion Questions:
1. What do you glean about the Jewish views of euthanasia from the above texts?
2. How do they compare to your pre-existing views?
3. In what ways do these texts influence your views?

Judaism and Terry Schiavo

Judaism has two fundamental maxims which periodically come into conflict in medical decisions.

First and foremost is Judaism's affirmation that the sanctity of life trumps all other values and laws. Even the toast we make over a glass of wine: *"l'chayim"* means "to life!".

In addition, Judaism requires us to do our part to help people medically. "Leave it to G-d" is not a Jewish view of medicine. In fact, the Talmud prohibits a Jew from living in a town where there is no doctor.

But what are we to do with medical technology that can now "keep people alive" beyond what Judaism defines as death? What limits are there when our medical acumen can breathe for people, eat for people, and circulate blood for people? The texts to

CONGREGATION EMETH

CLOSE TO HOME
The Jewish Community in Your Community

WARM & FRIENDLY
The Personal Attention
You Deserve From Your Synagogue

INCLUSIVE AND WELCOMING
Judaism for Your Life

Make Torah a way of life
and welcome Every Person as a Friend

Thank you to our Challah Wagon Driver:
AARON PALM

The Challah Wagon is partially funded by a grant from
Jewish Federation of Greater San Jose

Commentary & discussion provided by:
Rabbi Yitzhak Miller

E-mail prior to first delivery

Dear Challah Wagon Subscriber:

Thank you for signing up to receive fresh Challah and Flowers on Friday afternoons before 6:00 p.m. Your current subscription will begin on _____, and will end on _____. Your subscription also includes a wonderful Shabbat Blessing and weekly Torah Commentary and discussion topics.

Add the following sentence if signed up for one year:
We hope you enjoy the complementary Shabbat Table Handbook and Shabbat for Starters CD for signing up for one full year.

Please remember to contact us at (admin@emeth.net) if you plan to be out of town on a particular Friday and would prefer not to receive your delivery that week.

As you know, your subscription not only provides you a wonderful Shabbat table, but also helps keeps teens involved at Emeth, provides funding for Emeth's programs, and supports Jews in nursing homes or care facilities. Thank you for supporting Jewish life in the South Valley!

Lisa Lewis
Congregation Administrator

Weekly reminder e-mail

Dear Challah Wagon Subscriber:

Just a friendly reminder that your fresh Challah and Flowers will be delivered this Friday afternoon. Please let me know if you will be out of town and would prefer not to receive your delivery this week.

Otherwise, enjoy and have a beautiful Shabbat table!

Lisa Lewis
Congregation Administrator

Gift Subscription for new members or other gift subscriptions

(New Members): [Let us add yet another welcome to Congregation Emeth! As part of your welcome, we would like to give you a free one-month subscription to the Challah Wagon,] OR (Gift subscription): [_____ has signed you up for a gift subscription to the Challah Wagon,] which delivers fresh Challah and Flowers on Friday afternoons directly to your home before 6:00 p.m. All you need to do to accept is hit "reply" and say "Yes!" Your current subscription will begin on _____, and will end on _____. Your subscription also includes a wonderful Shabbat Blessing and weekly Torah Commentary and discussion topics.

(Continue as per new subscriber e-mail)

Babies and Bagels Club

Congregation:	Temple Emanu-El
Address:	225 N. Country Club Road Tucson, AZ 85716
Phone Number:	(520) 327-4501
Contact's Name and E-mail:	Mila Anderson, temple@templeemanueltucson.org
Number of Member Units:	800
URJ Region:	Pacific Southwest
Rabbis:	Samuel M. Cohon, David Freelund
Membership Director:	Barbara Zaslofsky
Program Coordinator:	Mila Anderson

Brief Description: The Babies and Bagels Club is a monthly group for families with preschool-age children and older siblings. This year we've had a variety of programs that involved the entire family. At the temple, we had Family Night at the Movies (Jewish children's movie and pizza dinner at the temple), Pre-Passover Cookie Baking Party, and joined the rest of the congregation at the Greatest Hanukkah on Earth and the Purim Extravaganza. Outside of temple programs include a trip to the planetarium for Rosh HaShanah (Reach for the Stars in the New Year), a zoo walk and animal encounter (Help Noah Find the Animals), and a Babes in Bowling Shoes family bowling night. We've also had two parenting discussions (Raising a Moral Child, Practicing Values Every Day) that are grounded in Torah and Jewish teaching. While parents engaged in a discussion led by the rabbis, the kids had activities in the temple preschool with preschool teachers. Parents receive handouts on Jewish holidays and practical suggestions on incorporating more Judaism in their lives.

The Babies and Bagels Club is designed to create a feeling of community and friendship among families with preschool-age children who are associated with Temple Emanu-El. This program attracts families who are at the Temple Emanu-El preschool, temple member families from other preschools, and friends of each of the two categories. The events are advertised to the preschool community, temple-wide, and to the community in general. All events are open to all, members and nonmembers. The events are all free to participants.

This program is designed to be a way for families to get together to deepen their Jewish knowledge in a nonthreatening, all-inclusive, and welcoming way. This program is particularly attractive to intermarried families who are testing their Jewish experience. It is a fun and simple way for the family to do something Jewish together.

Program Goals:
- Strengthen the connection between the Temple Emanu-El Preschool and the temple.
- Invite unaffiliated preschool families to experience Jewish activities.
- Give all parents a deeper understanding and knowledge of Jewish holidays and values (many of the events are centered around a particular Jewish holiday).
- Give preschool parents an opportunity to discuss parenting in a Jewish context.

Target Population: Temple Emanu-El Preschool families, temple families that are not part of the preschool, unaffiliated Jewish families in Tucson, and intermarried families.

Number of Participants: Varies for each event; between seven and thirty families.

Number and Length of Sessions: Twelve monthly sessions per year; each meeting is two to three hours.

Staffing Required: Administrator to oversee the program; rabbi to lead parenting discussions and family workshops.

Total Cost of Program: Administrator salary, admission and fees for events outside of temple, snacks for events, craft materials for projects, printing costs of brochures and handouts.

Source of Funding: The program is funded by a grant from the Novak Trust, Elaine Marcus, and Earl Feldman.

Fee for Attendees: Free

Logistics and Instructions to Facilitator:
The administrator needs to:
- Write up the schedule of events for the year based on the kinds of events parents express interest in and create brochure.
- Write ads and announcements.
- Make monthly flyers.
- Arrange monthly programs, activities, and food.
- Prepare materials on temple programs and activities if participants inquire about other temple options.
- Assemble a mailing list of young families to receive the yearly brochure.

The administrator needs to be aware of the sensitivities of non-Jewish parents raising Jewish children, to be open to their questions, and to know where to refer them within the temple and the Jewish community if they need additional services or support. The program needs to have a balance between being content-rich in Judaica and having fun. These are nonthreatening family outings with a group of people who can become a support network in the temple.

Evaluation of Program: Although the Babies and Bagels Club is only in its first year, the program has been very successful. Attendance at these activities has varied anywhere between seven and thirty families. One event a month seems to be a perfect balance with busy family schedules. Families engage, meet, and talk with each other; there is a fun, social atmosphere with opportunity to form friendships. The programs are welcoming to all, and several preschool families have brought their friends who were completely new to the temple.

Babies and Bagels serves as an excellent bridge between the preschool and the temple, especially for the preschool families who are not temple members. Many intermarried families fall in this category —they feel strongly enough to send their child to a Jewish preschool but are hesitant to get more involved in temple life or are not sure about how to add more Jewishness to their homes. One preschool dad had never been inside the main part of the temple and saw the sanctuary for the first time during the Family Night at the Movies; he marveled at how beautiful it was and how spiritually moved he felt.

Some of the most popular and well-received events this year have been the Raising a Moral Child parenting discussions where the parents got to talk with other adults (uninterrupted!) while the kids were playing in the preschool. The level of this text-based discussion and the resulting interest in Jewish law suggests that some of the parents might be intrigued by adult Jewish study.

Families who attend Babies and Bagels events are more involved in overall temple activities, are more informed about temple life and events, and are more comfortable getting involved in temple activities. They are attending monthly Tot Shabbat dinners and services. They have inquired about the religious school and the preschool. One family went on to Stepping Stones from this program. Two signed up for the monthly Jewish Home and Family class. Most importantly, families who otherwise would not have done so are coming to the temple and are making happy, pressure-free memories here.

Follow-up: We are constantly gathering feedback to continuously improve the program and better respond to the needs of young families at the temple, the preschool, and in the community at large. We are also working on increasing the exposure of the program in new mailing lists, the media, and family-oriented publications and organizations (such as local mom's groups).

Some of the programs we are working on for next year include a trip to the botanical gardens for Tu B'Shvat, exploration of the Desert-Sonora museum to experience Moses' trek through the wilderness, planting flowers in pots for Shavuot, a High Holy Day family workshop, making a *Havdalah* set, and making chocolate matzah for Passover. There will also be a parenting discussion on raising a Jewish child (per parental request), designed not only to inform Jewish parents, but also to address the questions of intermarried families who are trying to explore religious options in their home.

Resources made available to Babies and Bagels participants are preschool and religious school brochures, the temple calendar, Adult Education Academy brochures, all temple flyers and brochures, the monthly newsletter, and the URJ Outreach brochures "Becoming a Jew" and "Intermarried? Reform Judaism Welcomes You." They are told about the holidays, informed about upcoming events, and given temple flyers at the events.

Temple Emanu-El Young Family Programs

Preschool Shabbat

Every Friday at 10:15 am in the chapel
Join the Temple Emanu-El Preschool children and the Rabbis on the rug for a fun, causal service with songs, stories, Kiddush and challah

Tot Kabbalat Shabbat

Every first Friday of the month
Potluck dinner at 5:30 pm, a fun child-centered Shabbat service at 6:15, followed by a dessert oneg and play

Pray and Play

Every third Saturday of the month
A fast-paced children's service with Torah stories and songs, then Kiddush and a play date on the playground

Torah Tots

Sunday mornings during Religious School
Stories, Torah, holidays, songs, arts and crafts, snacks and play for children and parents

Babies and Bagels Club

Monthly Programs
Fun, educational monthly activities for families with preschool age children held at Temple Emanu-El and other locations

Temple Emanu-El
225 N. Country Club Rd.
Tucson, AZ 85716
(520) 327-4501
www.templeemanueltucson.org

Temple Emanu-El presents...

The Babies and Bagels Club

A monthly play, eat and discuss group for preschool age families

Temple Emanu-El
225 N. Country Club Road
Tucson, AZ 85716
(520) 327-4501
www.templeemanueltucson.org

Welcome to the Babies and Bagels Club, a new monthly group for families with preschool-age children. We will play, discuss parenting and ethical issues, eat, create, and have fun together. All families are welcome to join.

August 2004
Rosh Hashana Pray and Play
Temple Emanu-El
Saturday, August 21, 10:00 am
~Rosh Hashana activities and crafts

September 2004
Reach for the Stars in the New Year
Flandreau Science Center, U. of A.
Saturday, September 18, 3:30 pm
~Hands-on scientific exploration, snack picnic, Havdallah service

October 2004
Help Noah Find the Animals
Reid Park Zoo
Sunday, October 17, 10:00 am
~Zoo walk, Noah's Ark activities, snacks

November 2004
"While They Hop on One Foot" Discussion: Raising a Moral Child
Temple Emanu-El
November 14, 10:30 am
~Discussion for parents with the Rabbi, activity for kids, then nosh together

December 2004
Greatest Hanukkah on Earth!
Temple Emanu-El
Sunday, Dec. 12, 4:45 pm, dinner 6:15 pm
~Babies and Bagels Club table for dinner

January 2005
Family Night at the Movies
Temple Emanu-El
Saturday, January 8, 5:00 pm
~Popcorn, pizza, pj's, children's movie

February 2005
"While They Hop on One Foot" Discussion: Practice Values Every Day
Temple Emanu-El
February 6, 10:30 am
~Discussion for parents with the Rabbi, activity for kids, then nosh together

March 2005
Purim Extravaganza
Temple Emanu-El
Sunday, March 20, 10:00 am
~Theater, music, costumes, rides, food, merriment and obligatory silliness

April 2005
Pre-Passover Cookie Baking Party
Temple Emanu-El
Saturday, April 16, 4:00 pm
~Making, baking, eating cookies & crafts

May 2005
Babies in Bowling Shoes
Lucky Strike Bowling on Speedway
Sunday, May 15, 4:00 pm
~Rollin' family fun

Babies and Bagels events are open to all. Most events are free. Please call Mila Anderson at 327-4501 for more information and to let us know you're coming.

The Babies and Bagels Club is reaching for the stars!

Join us at Flandreau Science Center at University of Arizona

(1601 E. University Blvd., Northwest corner of University Blvd. and Cherry Ave., across from the Visitor Center)

on Saturday, September 18 at 3:30 pm

Lots of hands-on scientific experimentation and activity, followed by a snack picnic outside under the olive trees and a Havdallah service

Call Mila at 327-4501 or 881-5531 to let us know you're coming

The Babies and Bagels Club is going wild!

We're going to Reid Park Zoo to help Noah find the animals to put on the ark!

Join us there on Sunday, October 17 at 10:00 am. We'll walk through the zoo, "gather" the animals, then meet on the grass for a snack picnic and Noah's Ark activity.

 Temple Emanu-El's Babies and Bagels Club is a monthly group for families with preschool age children. All families are welcome, members and nonmembers.

Call Mila Anderson at 327-4501 for additional information and to let us know you're coming

Noah's Ark and the Flood

The earth became corrupt before God; the earth was filled with lawlessness. God said to Noah, "I have decided to put an end to all flesh; I am about to destroy them with the earth. Make yourself an ark... and of all that lives, you shall take two of each into the ark to keep alive with you; they shall be male and female. For My part, I am about to bring the Flood." Noah built the ark and brought in two of each kind of animals plus seven of each kosher animal, as well as his wife, sons and sons' wives. Rain fell on the earth forty days and forty nights, the waters rose and destroyed all living things on earth. After 150 days, God sent a wind to dry the earth. Noah sent out a dove to see whether the earth was still covered with water; the dove came back. Seven days later again he sent out the dove; this time it returned with an olive branch. Noah took his family and the animals out of the ark and offered a sacrifice to God. God established a covenant with Noah and his sons that never again shall God send a flood to destroy the earth and made a rainbow as reminder of this covenant.

As you walk through the zoo and look at the animals, think how hard Noah's job was to take care of them all!

- Which animals needed extra tall ceilings?

- Which animals didn't need to go in the ark and could be *next* to the ark?

- Which animals eat meat (carnivores); which eat fruit, grasses or leaves (herbivores)?

- Noah let the animals get exercise on the deck; which animals run the fastest? Which walk the slowest?

- Which animals would be the hardest to take care of? Which would be the least trouble for Noah and his family?

Temple Emanu-El's Babies and Bagels program for families with preschool age children visited the Reid Park Zoo last month, where they learned about kosher and non-kosher animals, talked about Noah's Ark and had hands-on encounters with a tortoise, a ferret, a hedgehog and a snake. Fourteen families participated in the event.

Rebecca Lohse, an education specialist at the zoo, displays a tortoise.

The Babies and Bagel Club presents...
The Premier "While They're Hopping on One Foot" Discussion:

Raising a Moral Child
Sunday, November 14 at 10:30 am

Parents meet for a discussion led by Rabbis Samuel M. Cohon and David Freelund, grounded in Jewish ethics, on how to instill morals and values in young children. Kids will have activities and a play date with preschool teachers. Then we will all have a potluck lunch (Temple will provide bagels).

So how often do you get to talk to other parents uninterrupted for an hour, anyway?

Temple Emanu-El's **Babies and Bagels Club** is a monthly group for families with preschool age children (older siblings are welcome). All families are invited, members and nonmembers.

Call Mila Anderson at 327-4501 for additional information and to let us know you're coming.

The Babies and Bagels club presents...

Family Night at the Movies

Saturday, January 8, 2005
at 5:00 pm
Movie: "An American Tail – Feivel Goes West"
in Sy Juster at Temple Emanu-El

Pizza, popcorn and pajamas!

 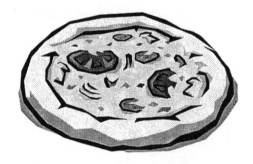

~We'll have a pizza dinner and popcorn with the movie
~We'll watch "Feivel Goes West," the second of Steven Spielberg's "An American Tail" movies with an all-star cast.
~We'll get comfy on the floor and kids can come in pajamas

Call Mila Anderson at 327-4501 to let us know you're coming so we know how much pizza to get.

The Babies and Bagel Club presents...
A Parenting Discussion:

Practicing Values Every Day
Sunday, February 6 at 10:30 am

Parents meet for a discussion led by Rabbi David Freelund, grounded in Jewish ethics, on how to instill morals and values in young children. Kids will have activities and a play date in the preschool. Then we will all have a potluck lunch (Temple will provide bagels and cream cheese).

So how often do you get to talk to other parents uninterrupted for an hour, anyway?

 Temple Emanu-El's **Babies and Bagels Club** is a monthly group for families with preschool age children (older siblings are welcome). All families are invited, members and nonmembers – bring a friend.

Call Mila Anderson at 327-4501 for additional information and to let us know you're coming.

Selected Resources and References to Use for Program Materials

American Academy of Pediatrics. (2005). *Television and the Family.* (http://www.aap.org/family/tv1.htm).

Kaufman, Ron. (1996). *How Television Images Affect Children.* (http://www.turnoffyourtv.com/healtheducation/children.html).

University of Illinois at Chicago. (2005). *Moral Development and Moral Education: An Overview.* (http://tigger.uic.edu/~lnucci/MoralEd/overviewtext.html).

 The Babies and Bagels Club presents...

Pre-Passover Cookie Baking Party

Saturday, April 9 at 4:00 pm
in Sy Juster Auditorium

Join us as we make, bake, decorate and sample our cookies and get ready for Passover

Babies and Bagels Club is a monthly play, eat and discuss group for preschool age families (and older siblings); everyone is welcome – bring a friend! No fee for this activity.

Please RSVP to Mila Anderson at 327-4501 to let us know you're coming – we don't want to run out of chocolate!

Temple Emanu-El
225 N. Country Club Road
Tucson, AZ 85716
(520) 327-4501
www.templeemanueltucson.org

For further information about Outreach and Synagogue Community programming, contact
The William and Lottie Daniel Department of Outreach and Synagogue Community at the
Union for Reform Judaism
633 Third Avenue
New York, NY 10017-6778
(212) 650-4230
outreach@urj.org
www.urj.org/outreach